Selected Work

Frank Vickery

T0163073

Frank Vickery was born in 1951 at Blaen-y-cwm in the Rhondda Valley. He left school at the age of fifteen with no qualifications. After taking part in plays for the local Boys' Club, he started writing and had his first success at the age of twenty-one when his comedy, *After I'm Gone*, won The Howard De Waldon Trophy for the Best One Act Play in Great Britain.

He co-founded The Parc and Dare Theatre Company and it was with this company that he wrote many of his earlier plays. His first professional writing commission came in 1981 when he wrote *All's Fair* for Spectacle Theatre Company. He has since written extensively for theatre, radio and television. He is the Artistic Director of Grassroots Productions which he founded and has written, directed and performed in many of his own productions. A recent success was his role of Teddy in his comedy *Granny Annie* (2007) and he has also appeared in productions as diverse as *Twelfth Night* and several pantomimes. Most of his own work has been published by Samuel French and a new play, *Barkin'* will be produced in the autumn of 2008.

Frank Vickery lives and works in the Rhondda Valley from where he draws most of his inspiration. When asked if he ever saw a time when he would leave his reply has been, "I've absolutely no doubt that I will leave the Rhondda one day... but it'll be feet first and in a box!"

Selected Work

Frank Vickery

Edited by Phil Clark

Parthian
The Old Surgery
Napier Street
Cardigan
SA43 1ED

www.parthianbooks.co.uk

First published in 2007
Selected work © Frank Vickery 2007
All Rights Reserved
More information on the work of Frank Vickery
can be found at www.frankvickery.co.uk

These plays are published with the kind permission
of Samuel French Ltd.

ISBN 978-1-902638-46-1

Cover design by Lucy Llewellyn
Inner design by books@lloydrobson.com
Printed and bound by Dinefwr Press, Llandybïe, Wales

Published with the financial support of the Welsh
Books Council

British Library Cataloguing in Publication Data – A
cataloguing record for this book is available from the
British Library

Contents

Wherever Laughter

Frank Vickery is one of the unsung heroes of Welsh theatre. He has been called 'the Welsh Alan Ayckbourn', but this is to undervalue the ascerbic, humorous, loving care with which he dissects the lives, language and behaviour of the people and area he knows so well – the Welsh Valleys. The mines may be gone, but the landscape is in his blood. It seeps through his writing, invading the speech patterns of an aspirant post-industrial community, a green carpet of optimism that heals the black scars of the past. In the tradition of every great *farceur* his plays move from a point of normality to a conclusion of black improbability, leaving a trail of exhilarating wit and wild mayhem in their wake.

Do the plays travel? But of course. The universality of Frank Vickery's situations transcends any parochial vernacular, and wherever laughter is to be heard, Frank Vickery will always have a voice.

This edition of his work, edited so admirably by Phil Clark, the director who has done most to broadcast Frank Vickery's talent, is both timely and apposite. To those who have not experienced the plays live on stage, they will bring pure joy on the page.

Michael Bogdanov, March 2007

Vickery at The Sherman

In 1990 I was appointed Artistic Director of The Sherman Theatre, Cardiff's – indeed South Wales' – only producing theatre.

When I arrived at The Sherman in January 1990, I had inherited a season of plays on the Mainstage and in the Studio Theatre that had been programmed by the previous Artistic Director. The Sherman creates its own professional work with The Sherman Theatre Company; presents visiting theatre companies' productions from throughout Britain; and is home to a number of amateur theatre companies.

As part of that spring 1990 season, an amateur company called The Parc and Dare Theatre Company, from Treorchy in the Rhondda, had been programmed to play on the Mainstage. I discovered that this company had been bringing their work to The Sherman for a number of years and had started off performing in the Studio Theatre (capacity 160). They had been so successful that Sherman management had moved the work to the Mainstage (capacity 480), and they were playing to full houses for a week. I was naturally impressed that an amateur company could play to capacity audiences on the Mainstage; but what was more phenomenal was that all their plays were new plays written by their co-director Frank Vickery.

I watched my first Frank Vickery play in Spring 1990 as part of a full auditorium of theatre-goers who fell about laughing at the comedy situations of this Rhondda-based play. The audience was ecstatic, night after night. They talked endlessly in the foyer during the interval and after the show about the theatre they had witnessed. The audience had incredible empathy with the content of the work and, as I was to discover, an undaunting loyalty to the work of the playwright. I had not witnessed such a loyalty to a playwright's work for many years. I had a certain amount of envy for what I was witnessing. I knew then that

that was what I wanted to create at the Sherman Theatre throughout the year – a type of theatre that an audience felt involved with, and expressed an ownership of the form and the content.

My first instinct was to meet the playwright, Frank Vickery. I discovered that he had only just given up his full time job as a machinist in an upholstery factory in the Rhondda to become a full-time playwright. He already had some fifteen of his plays published by Samuel French in London; and consequently his work was being produced by other amateur companies throughout Britain. But when I mentioned the work of Vickery, and how successful it had become, to other professional theatre practitioners and Arts funding organisations in South Wales, they were, on the whole, dismissive of his work and his success.

I was, to be blunt, a little foxed by this reaction. Here was a working class writer, writing about what he knew best – his community – playing to capacity audiences throughout South Wales; and getting his work published. Surely this was a success story, something that Wales and the Arts world should shout about and celebrate. But no, here was work that was largely being ignored by the professional theatre movement of Wales, and in the main being discriminated against predominantly because of its success.

My first meeting with Frank was a fairly low-key affair. We met; we chatted. I asked him what his ambitions were. He explained, quite simply to write plays and get them on stage in order to give them back to his community. He wanted to write for the professional theatre. He had worked briefly with Spectacle Theatre – the professional community theatre company in the Rhondda – and had written a little for regional television in Wales. There was no doubt that his heart lay in creating work for big stages that reflected the working class communities.

I asked him if there were any common threads to his work, or themes that constantly fascinated him. His response was simple and straightforward. He was obsessed with the 'taboos' of life. The issues that people found hard to talk about in public life but had strong opinions about in private. That, for him, was where the drama/theatre of his plays existed. He revealed to his audiences in a public arena the issues, characters and situations that were only ever discussed in private behind closed doors, not just in the Rhondda, but throughout the world.

Our meeting was simple, but exciting. I asked him if he was interested in writing for the Sherman Theatre Company. He said a definite yes. I asked if he had any thoughts on what he wanted to write. He said yes. He wanted to write a comedy set in the women's cancer ward of a Rhondda Hospital; and he wanted to write the main character for a Welsh actress he had never met but always admired – Menna Trussler. At that moment, *A Kiss on the Bottom* was commissioned and the character of Marlene was invented.

It was obvious to me that here was a writer hungry for work; fully resourced with ideas; and more than ready to create a body of work that would have its roots in the communities and people of South Wales, but also have a universal relevance. He reminded me of a group of writers of the 1930/40/50s in Wales who had written about and for their respective communities. Many of these 20th Century Welsh writers had been a part of my youth when I had been involved in community and amateur drama. Writers such as J O Francis, who had written a number of short plays reflecting rural communities which always involved such mythical characters as Twm Tinker and Dicky Bach Dwl. Francis' work, again, looked at the working class but with rural characters such as the poacher, the tinker, the gypsy and the farmer. Much of his drama was created around breaking or stretching the laws of the rural community. The work of T C Thomas in Brecon, again, predominantly centred around rural communities and the 'scams' that went on just after the war. These were often the starting points of a series of his plays about a mythical railway signalman, Davy Jones. Many of the plays were eventually recorded as a television series by BBC Wales. Vickery himself was an admirer and friend of the prolific Valley playwright Einon Evans who influenced and encouraged Frank in his early years. If you look at the work of these predominantly amateur playwrights, they too seem obsessed, like Vickery, with the taboos of life. The injustice of life. The unspoken. The naughtiness and the breaking of the social rules and codes.

Little did I know when I commissioned *A Kiss on the Bottom* that it would be the beginning of a ten-year partnership with Frank, when I would commission him to write thirteen plays for the stage, television and radio. During the ten years, many of the plays were nominated for such prestigious awards as London Weekend Television Plays in Stage Awards (*Erogenous Zones*), The Writers Guild of Great Britain Awards 1993 (*Erogenous Zones*), The Lloyds Bank Playwright of Year Award 1994 (*Loose Ends*), and BAFTA (British Association of Film and Television Awards) CYMRU nominations for *The Drag Factor* (1995) and *Green Favours* (1994).

For most of my working life, I had been part of the community theatre movement of Britain. I had been creating theatre of social or political content that had a direct relevance to its community. I believed, and still do, that theatre should hold a mirror to society and through reflection offer a means for change through observation. By observing characters, attitudes and actions, audiences can question their own beliefs and ask themselves if they need to change the way in which they view the world and therefore, possibly, influence change within their community.

Vickery's work often holds a mirror to his community and asks serious questions of its audience, but often through the use of comedy. This can often be seen through the women in his plays. They are strong, well-rounded and extremely influential characters. Vickery openly accepts that the women in his own family, and the hundreds of women he worked with in the upholstery factory, have influenced his life. His sharp ear for language and recognised speech patterns, his ability to listen to gossip and everyday language, along with his ability to create recognisable characters, are the main traits that have made him a playwright of the people and his immediate community.

In 1994, the BBC Radio 4 arts programme *Kaleidoscope* broadcast a review of Frank's work at The Sherman and reported, 'Vickery... has a relationship with his audiences that Ayckbourn, Godber, Russell, or Bleasdale might envy.' Indeed, for a while, Vickery was known as 'The Welsh Alan Ayckbourn'. This reference, I think, referred to his popularity more than to the content of the work. Ayckbourn was writing about the middle classes of Middle England, whereas Vickery was writing about and for the working-class communities of South Wales. Vickery made no apologies for this, and continues to do so today. He is honest when he says that he writes about what he knows.

Vickery has always been a great admirer of the work of Ayckbourn. Like Ayckbourn, he has been as interested in the form as in the content of the play. Ayckbourn's now famous plays *The Norman Conquests* and *Time of My Life* both experiment with time and form. In the trilogy, *The Norman Conquests*, all three plays happen simultaneously in time; using the same characters in three different locations around one household, one in the garden (*Round and Round the Garden*), another in the dining room (*Table Manners*), and the third in the sitting room (*Living Together*). In *Time of My Life*, he has one central story being told backwards, forwards, and in the present time simultaneously.

Vickery too has often experimented with time and form, and a number of the plays in this volume are examples of this practice. In *Erogenous Zones* he uses flashbacks and nightmares; whilst in *Roofs and Wings*, Acts One and Two are simultaneous in time, using the same characters. In *Pullin' the Wool*, he puts the past story on stage at the same time as the present action. These techniques all serve to engage an audience and demand that they are continuously involved with the action, placing them at the centre of the drama. Often the audience know more about the onstage situation than some of the characters; consequently creating a terrific tension between stage and audience, enhancing and sharing the drama of the moment.

He created his early work for the amateur company of Parc and Dare Theatre. There was always an input into the work by the actors; and he created characters for certain actors, knowing that his material was in safe and competent hands.

I was soon to learn that if the partnership between Frank and myself was to be successful, I would do best to involve him in the complete process, particularly casting. Throughout the Nineties, he wrote parts in his plays for specific Welsh actors, and I knew that if we cast the plays successfully, with Frank's approval, then there was a stronger possibility of success, just as there had been with the Parc and Dare Company.

Again, BBC Radio 4 commented on his work, 'A celebration rather than a social realistic reconstruction... the kind of people that we see on Frank Vickery's stage are not seen on Welsh Television, British Television, or in the theatre and I think those people who are interested in seeing British working-class life in its variety should pay attention to the kind of success that he's having.'

This book records three of the thirteen plays he has written for The Sherman: *A Kiss on the Bottom* (1991); *Erogenous Zones* (1992); and *Roots and Wings* (1995). They are all mainstage plays and all produced by The Sherman Theatre Company. All premiered at The Sherman, and many of them toured throughout the Rhondda Valleys and the rest of Wales.

There is no doubt that the ten years that I worked with Vickery took me closer to my audience. There was no way I could ignore what they thought and felt about the content of the work, and the role theatre played in their lives. His admirers wrote to me; talked to me in the bar; wrote and defended bad reviews in national newspapers, and generally stayed loyal to Vickery and the act of theatre going. Through my work with Frank, I began to have a real dialogue with the audience; something I feel is often lacking in British mainstage theatre today.

To date, Vickery has some thirty published plays. He writes for the stage, radio and television, but he is still relatively unknown outside of Wales. So why isn't he famous? It's a familiar question in Wales. What is not questionable, in my mind, is that the work of Vickery can stand proud in a portfolio of British comedy writing for the theatre in the 1990s. The problem for Wales, and not the playwright, is how to get our Welsh work into the British portfolio with status. We still have a long road to travel; but the quality of the work is way ahead of the promoters in Wales.

Here are three thoughts to ponder upon which have relevance to the debate:

'Welsh culture has to be self-confident enough to take on all comers. The idea that we can be swamped has to be rejected.'

Dafydd Elis Thomas MP, *Planet*, Sept 1988

'If you are liked by the people, it's almost impossible to be liked by the Arts Establishment.'

Sir Kyffin Williams, BBC Wales, 2003

But I'll leave the last word to Frank himself:

'Well, I think that what makes me slightly different to everyone else is that I write about working-class people for working-class people. One of the things I am really proud of is that I get people to come into the theatre who normally wouldn't be seen dead in the theatre, but they come because they like my particular brand of humour and they know they're going to have a good time.'

Frank Vickery, *Kaleidoscope*, BBC Radio 4, 1994

Phil Clark, September 2007

Phil Clark started his career in the early 1970s as an actor in Theatre in Education (TIE) and Community Theatre. In the 1980s he was director of TIE and Community Theatre at the Crucible Theatre, Sheffield. Throughout the 1990s he was Artistic Director of the Sherman Theatre in Cardiff. He now works as a freelance theatre director and writer.

Selected Work

A Kiss on the Bottom

First performed by the Sherman Theatre Company
at the Sherman Theatre, Cardiff, 17th November 1991.

Cast:

Marlene	–	Menna Trussler
Lucy	–	Shelagh Gough
Grace	–	Joanna Field
Bev	–	Donna Edwards
June	–	Kathryn Dimery

Creative Team:

Director	–	Phil Clark
Designer	–	Nick MacLiammoir
Company Stage Manager	–	Maggie Higgins

NOTE

Nurse 1 and Nurse 2 are non-speaking roles and can be
played by assistant stage-managers. The actress playing
June can double as the Domestic and Sister.

"A devilishly humorous, profoundly poignant... an
unexpected delight of a performance"

Amy Stackhouse

*For Menna, whose inspiration for me knows no bounds
and in celebration of the life and works of Joanna Field.*

Act One

Scene One

A women's ward in East Glamorgan Hospital.

There are three beds with chairs, etc, surrounding them, and each bed has a locker containing a water jug, tissues, personal belongings, 'Get Well' cards and so on. The curtains are drawn around Grace's bed, down left. Marlene's bed is centre. MARLENE is nowhere to be seen – presumably, she is down gossiping in the solarium or the sluice. June's bed is down right. There is a colour television at the foot of this bed. JUNE is fully dressed and is packing a few things into a weekend case. She is in her late twenties, with straight shoulder-length hair, which she constantly places behind at least one ear. She is quietly spoken and reserved.

MARLENE enters, carrying a magazine. She wears a nightgown and slippers. She stands half in and half out of the doorway.

MARLENE: (*Calling to someone down the corridor*) Hallo Emrys, how are you? (*She doesn't wait for a reply*) Walking better today, I see. Be going home tomorrow, I s'pect. (*She moves into the ward and throws the magazine on to her bed*) Ahh, nice to see old Emrys up and about. Mind, I still say sixty-three is too old to be circumcised. (*She has a little laugh at the thought of it, then goes to JUNE and stops her from packing her case*) All packed and ready to go, are you?

JUNE smiles rather uncomfortably and nods.

MARLENE: I wish to God I was going home.

JUNE reaches for a bottle of squash on top of her locker.

3

MARLENE: Oooh, are you taking that bottle of squash with you? 'Cos I'll have it if you're not going to bother. I do enjoy a drop of squash, I do see, but our Roy won't bring me some in, no matter how many times I ask.

JUNE hands her the bottle.

MARLENE: (*Surprised*) Ooh, thanks very much. (*She puts it on her locker*) Are you sure? Anything else you got there? Books, magazines, I don't mind what. Hey, your colour telly'd be nice.

JUNE: Oh... no... um. I'm afraid I –

MARLENE: (*Laughing*) I'm only joking you silly bugger. Still – we'll miss it though, won't we? Well, me and Grace that is. (*She nods in GRACE's direction, still giggling*) Yes, it's back to watching *Murder She Wrote* in the solarium for us. (*Calling*) What do you think, Grace? She's taken the colour telly with her. (*She stands just behind JUNE*) The woman in the bed before you left her telly here for a good couple of days. Well she didn't leave it here – her family did. We must have had a lend of it for the best part of a week. It was until well after the funeral, I know that.

Pause.

MARLENE: Like that she went. (*She snaps her fingers*) Course I'm telling you now because you're going home, but I didn't say nothing before because you looked the nervous type to me.

Pause. JUNE puts fruit from her bedside into a carrier bag.

4

MARLENE: Yes, just like that she went. (*She snaps her fingers again*) She was sharing some of her grapes with me one minute, and the next – she was gone. I don't touch 'em now. Grapes. I eat all fruit, mind. But I don't touch a grape – not now.

JUNE immediately hands MARLENE the bag of fruit.

MARLENE: Oooh, thanks very much. (*She puts the bag away in her locker*) Are you sure? Hey, I hope you didn't think I was hinting or anything?

JUNE: No. No, of course not. They'll only go to waste.

MARLENE: Doing you a favour then, am I?

JUNE nods and forces a smile.

MARLENE: (*Sitting on a chair right of June's bed*) Packed everything away now, have you? You haven't forgotten nothing? Soap? Flannel? What about your talc I fancied with that lovely smell? Have you remembered to pack that?

JUNE: Yes.

MARLENE: (*Disappointed*) There you are then.

JUNE clips the case together.

MARLENE: Shall I give you a hand? You're never going to manage that and the telly.

JUNE: Oh... no. It's all right.

MARLENE: You don't want to strain yourself, mind.

JUNE: No. Really. They're not very heavy.

MARLENE: You want to be careful. You don't want to do too much too soon. I remember I was too weak to lift a spoon after I had *my* D and C.

JUNE is highly embarrassed.

MARLENE: Sure you can manage now?

JUNE: (*Almost blurting it out*) Robert is picking me up.

MARLENE: Oooh. Robert? (*She gets up from the chair and sits on June's bed*) Who's he then?

JUNE: (*Insisting*) A friend.

MARLENE: Oh ay, that's right. (*She pauses*) I see.

JUNE: (*Trying to be assertive*) No you don't. You don't see anything. He's a very nice man with a very nice wife and they are both very kind to me and... (*She becomes upset and stops. She searches her coat for a hanky but doesn't find one.*)

MARLENE: Hang on a minute. (*She gets a box of tissues from her bed.*)

JUNE: (*Taking one and wiping her nose*) Thank you. I'm sorry.

MARLENE: (*Looking into the box*) And I am – I've run out now. (*She holds up the empty box*) Only a joke. (*She takes the box and puts it in the plastic rubbish bag on the side of June's locker*) I'll have plenty later on. I've asked Roy to bring some in. (*She pauses*) What time is he coming then? This Robert?

JUNE: (*Unzipping her case and looking for something*) Any time now.

MARLENE: He's the one who visited you last night, I suppose? (*She sits at the bottom of the bed.*)

JUNE: (*Annoyed*) Jenny was coming too. But something cropped up at the last minute.

MARLENE: (*Nodding; not completely convinced*) Well, he must have got a good job, anyway.

JUNE takes a deep breath – MARLENE is clearly driving her crazy.

MARLENE: Either that or he thinks a hell of a lot of you to take time off from work. (*She laughs*) I know this much, if I rang Roy at eleven o'clock in the morning to say I could come home, I'd be still stuck here till the end of his shift. And then perhaps he'd go home and have a bit of food first.

Pause.

MARLENE: Doing well for himself, is he? This Robert?

JUNE: (*With difficulty*) He runs his own garage.

MARLENE: I knew it. I knew it. I said to Roy last night. I said, that man works with his hands, I said. You can always tell, can't you? Well I can anyhow. They've got that worn look about 'em, haven't they? And of course there's always the dirt under the fingernails. No matter how hard they try, they never seem to get it all out, can they? Can always see a little bit of black, can't you? Mind you, I like it myself. Always a good sign of a man's man. (*She pauses and quickly eyes*

7

JUNE up) I'm surprised you like a bit of rough, though. I had you down for the more professional type. You know – teacher... accountant. Somebody in a suit.

JUNE moves to the right of Marlene's bed, empties the contents of her sponge bag on it and throws them at MARLENE. MARLENE moves to the left and collects up the things as they are thrown at her, delighted.

MARLENE: Oh lovely. Cotton wool balls?

JUNE resignedly throws a plastic bag of cotton wool balls.

MARLENE: I'll share them with Grace if you like.

BEV enters with two nurses. They wheel on another bed, which contains LUCY. LUCY is in her sixties. Her hair is pulled back very neatly from her head. BEV moves June's bed table centre. JUNE moves centre with her, taking her suitcase and the television. NURSE 1 collects June's locker and passes it to NURSE 2, who takes it off stage. NURSE 1 and BEV move June's bed out of the way, down right.

BEV: Gangway, girls. Sorry, June, my love, but I've got to chuck you out. You're just about ready anyway by the look of it. One in, one out.

BEV and NURSE 1 wheel Lucy's bed into position. NURSE 1 exits.

BEV: It's all go in this place. (*To LUCY*) I'll be back with you now, my love. (*To JUNE*) Come on then, June. Let's get you on the road.

JUNE: I'm waiting for my lift. I'm sure he won't –

BEV: He's here. He's waiting for you down in the day room. Come on... let me give you a hand with that.

She picks up the television and exits.

MARLENE: (*Moving towards JUNE*) It's none of my business, of course –

JUNE: (*Sharply*) No. (*Less sharp*) You're right. (*She pauses; she means 'it is none of your business'*) You're absolutely right.

MARLENE: Believe me, love, no good'll come of it. I know.

JUNE just stares at her.

MARLENE: Not that I've ever had a fling, mind. Not since I've been with our Roy – had plenty before – but not since. One dog one bone, that's me now, love. (*She pauses*) See, it's bad enough under normal circumstances but when you're friends with the wife as well... you're too nice and too soft, I s'pect, which is probably how it all started in the first place.

Pause.

MARLENE: Well, am I right?

JUNE stares into space.

MARLENE: If you were the sort that didn't give a damn you might stand a chance – but you're not see, love, are you? Either way, in my book you're going to end up –

JUNE: Say goodbye for me to the lady at the end.

JUNE exits.

Pause. MARLENE has a good look at LUCY.

MARLENE: (*Referring to June*) Lovely girl. (*She starts putting away all the things on her bed.*)

LUCY watches her.

MARLENE: She insisted on giving me these few things, see. I told her I didn't have any use for them. Any way – (*introducing herself*) Marlene. Marlene Morgan.

LUCY: Lucy Collier.

GRACE: (*Callling from behind her curtained bed*) Excuse me, but I need a nurse.

GRACE is seventyish. A little grand. She had money once but it has all gone now.

MARLENE: (*Crossing to Grace's bed*) Finished, have you, Grace?

GRACE: I would like someone to come and see me.

MARLENE: Beverley will be here now. She's got to come back to get rid of this other bed.

GRACE: I don't want her, I want someone else!

MARLENE: (*To LUCY, as she crosses back to her bed*) She don't like her for some reason. I don't know why 'cos she's marvellous with her. My own daughter wouldn't do for me what she's done for her. You got children?

LUCY: Only one.

MARLENE: Two, I got. The girl is mine by Roy – that's my husband – but the boy is a love child. I was only seventeen.

LUCY: Raymond will be forty this year.

MARLENE: (*Referring to GRACE*) She haven't got any kids. She pretends to like 'em but she hates 'em really. My sister's kids can't stand her. She called them over to her when they came to visit me on a Sunday and they didn't want to go. They're frightened of her. She doesn't look well, mind. (*Quietly*) She's gone – she looks awful and I haven't got the heart to tell her, see. And it wouldn't be so bad if she didn't ask me. But that's all she does. She'll ask you too, I s'pect. She's asks everybody. Obsessed with how she looks, she is. You get fed up with her after a bit 'cos that's all you'll get out of her. 'How do I look?' 'Do I look all right?' You feel you don't know what to say to her in the end. (*She moves to the right of her own bed.*)

LUCY: Have you been in long?

MARLENE: Just over a week.

LUCY: It's nearly a month for me. I've had my stitches out over a fortnight ago.

MARLENE: Why are they keeping you in then? What was the matter?

LUCY: (*With relish*) I couldn't keep anything down. I'd have something to eat and ten minutes later I'd have it all back.

MARLENE: I'm like that, see – only not all the time. Some days I can eat like a horse. Others I can't even look at an egg without having it back. Did they say what was wrong?

LUCY: Some sort of blockage.

MARLENE: They haven't told me nothing yet. I'm still having tests. (*She crosses to Lucy's bed*) Between me and you I've had just about a gut's full here, though. They take so long to tell you anything. And they don't care what they put you through. Do you know, there isn't a part of me that haven't had something or other shoved up inside it. Oh I'm not complaining, mind. In fact, some of it was quite pleasant – (she winks) if you know what I mean. I wouldn't show them that though. Mind you, I had to go and have one of them barium enemas last Tuesday. I didn't enjoy that. Have you ever had one of those?

LUCY: I've had everything. I've been back and fro here for eighteen months.

MARLENE: Almost a resident then? They told me yesterday I might have to have a bag. No, I said, not unless I can have a pair of shoes to match. (*She laughs at her own joke*) Oh you've got to laugh, haven't you? (*She pauses*) Grace have been in a long time. (*Raising her voice*) Haven't you, Grace?

GRACE: I beg your pardon, dear?

MARLENE: (*Crossing down right of Grace's bed*) I said you've been in here a long time.

GRACE: Yes. Is someone getting me a nurse?

MARLENE: We've had a new one in, Grace.

GRACE: Ask her to come and tend to me then, will you, dear? I really do want to get back into bed.

MARLENE: I mean a patient. Little June have left. We've got... what's your name again?

LUCY: Lucy.

MARLENE: We've got Lucy in her place.

GRACE: Is she SRN?

MARLENE: She's not a nurse. (*To LUCY, as she moves centre*) She always gets the wrong end of the stick.

GRACE: (*Insisting*) SRN. I don't want to be seen by anyone less qualified.

MARLENE: You only want someone to wipe your arse. (*She pauses*) Shall I come and do it for you?

GRACE: Certainly not! I prefer a member of staff.

MARLENE: What's the matter? Don't you trust me or something?

GRACE: I'd rather wait!

MARLENE: (*Not really offended*) Please your bloody self then. (*To LUCY*) I've offered. Can't do anything else, can I? (*She moves towards Lucy's bed*) I've always fancied myself as a bit of a nurse. I've got the stomach for it, see. Takes a special kind of person somehow – doesn't it? And I've never minded a bit of... shall I prop you up a bit? You're sinking by the minute by there. (*She pulls LUCY into a sitting position, very roughly.*)

13

LUCY: Thank you. I was going to ask someone when they come to take the bed.

Pause.

LUCY: I haven't asked about going home. I'm not in any hurry.

MARLENE: I can't wait to go home, I can't. I had a sound scan yesterday and once they've had the result of that I'm hoping they're going to let me go. Live on your own, do you?

LUCY: I buried my husband. Raymond comes down as often as he can but it's not easy to get away. Not with his job. And of course there's Hazel, that's his wife. She's very good to me. I rarely see her but she's very good to me. She seldom misses sending a birthday or Christmas card. Raymond has invited me up – they live in Surrey – but it's not a big house, they say, and I wouldn't like to put the girls out. I've got two granddaughters. Eighteen and twenty-one. Need a lot of space at that age, don't they? I've got photos. I'll show you when they bring my things. (*She pauses*) I wish they'd write to me though. (*She smiles*) Boys. That's all they're into now.

MARLENE: Well I can't say nothing about that. I was exactly the same at their age. And you were too, I s'pect.

LUCY: Only one man I ever had and we didn't meet until I was well into my twenties.

MARLENE: Never. Good God, I had twenty before I left school. It wasn't as if I was fast or loose or anything like that. It's just that I hated girls. They bored me to death. I couldn't stand all that girl talk and giggling. I'd rather flirt with a boy any day.

BEV enters with Lucy's locker. She sets it in position.

BEV: Sorry I've been so long, girls.

MARLENE: Oooh hey, Bev – Grace is waiting for you. She needs a hand – literally.

BEV: (*Raising her voice a little*) Won't be a minute, Grace. Just going to get rid of the bed.

She goes to the empty bed, pushes it off and enters.

MARLENE: (*To BEV*) She has been waiting for a long time. (*She moves to the foot of Lucy's bed.*)

BEV: We're short this morning, Ma. We're two down.

MARLENE: Haven't had the chance to see if my results are back then?

BEV: Marlene, I've been dying for a pee for the past hour and a half. I'm hoping to put one in now about eleven o'clock.

MARLENE: Point taken. But you will let me know as soon as they're here, won't you?

BEV: They *are* here.

MARLENE: What?

BEV: Doctor Fairwater is going to come and have a word with you this afternoon.

15

MARLENE: Oh, I can't wait that long. You can have a peek for me can't you, and tell me if everything's all right?

BEV doesn't answer. She turns to leave the ward.

BEV: (*Calling to GRACE*) Be back in a minute, Grace.

BEV exits.

Pause; MARLENE stands motionless.

MARLENE: Why did they take so long? All my other results came back the following day. (*She crosses to the side of Lucy's bed, left*) Are you under him as well? Fairwater?

LUCY nods.

MARLENE: I've *got* to be home for next week. My daughter's getting married a week on Saturday. Lucky, I saw to most of the arrangements before I came in. I'd have said no otherwise.

LUCY: To what?

MARLENE: (*Moving to the foot of Lucy's bed*) Coming in for tests. I said to Roy, I said, 'Trust 'em to send for me now,' I said. I've been waiting for 'em to get in touch for weeks. 'Go in and get it sorted, with a bit of luck you'll be out for the big day,' he said. (*She tries to laugh*) I miss this wedding and I'll bloody crown him. (*She laughs again but she is very worried.*)

LUCY: Does he know about the wedding? The doctor, I mean?

MARLENE: They all know. I made sure I told every bugger the day I came in.

LUCY: I'm sure they'll do what they can.

MARLENE: I paid a fortune for my outfit. (*She moves back to the left side of her own bed*) It fitted perfect when I bought it. I'll have to have it taken in a bit now – I've lost a bit of weight lately.

BEV enters and heads straight for Grace's bed.

MARLENE: (*Stopping her before she disappears behind the curtains*) You've already seen 'em, haven't you?

Pause.

BEV: Doctor will explain it better than me.

MARLENE: I'd rather hear it from you.

BEV: It's nothing to worry about at this stage.

MARLENE: What's it all about then?

BEV: He wants to do more tests.

MARLENE: (*Relieved*) Oh is that all. You had me going... you frightened me a bit by there then.

BEV: Well, it's more of an investigation really.

MARLENE: You mean they want to open me up?

BEV: It's the only way of being absolutely sure, Marlene.

MARLENE: Of what?

Pause.

BEV: Well, like I said... the doctor can explain it better than me.

MARLENE: So it's not an operation then?

BEV: Oh yes. Well, you'll have anaesthetic and that. They'll do tests on the operating table and they might decide to operate, depending on what they find.

Pause.

MARLENE: I see. (*She pauses*) When am I having it done?

Pause.

BEV: Monday.

Pause.

GRACE: (*Calling from behind the curtains*) Nurse!

BEV: All right, Grace... it's your turn. You've got a choice this morning. Which hand do you want... my right or my left? (*She disappears behind the curtains.*)

MARLENE gets into her bed and sits up straight. She looks over to LUCY, then looks out front, a worried expression on her face.

Black-out. Music: District Nurse.

Scene Two

The same.

The following Monday, about 11am.

The lights come up and MARLENE is discovered lying on her bed, now wearing a theatre gown and a surgical paper hat.

BEV draws back the curtains around Grace's bed and exits.

GRACE sits upright, putting on make-up. She wears a wig. LUCY is also sitting upright, reading a letter from her son. A photograph of him and his family is now proudly displayed on her bedside cabinet.

LUCY: (*Excited*) They're coming down. They all are – Raymond, Hazel *and* the girls. (*She continues reading her letter.*)

GRACE: (*Referring to her compact*) There used to be a mirror in this.

LUCY: When is the twenty-third?

GRACE: Why has someone taken the mirror out of my compact?

MARLENE: It's the sixteenth on Saturday.

LUCY: They can't make it before because of the car... it needs servicing and the garage can't fit it in for a week.

MARLENE: That sounds like a load of old bull to me.

LUCY: No, he's very careful with things like that. He won't drive it a mile over what it's supposed to.

MARLENE: What's the matter with the train then? The car needing a service wouldn't stop me from seeing *my* mother.

LUCY: It would cost a lost of money for them all to come by rail. And if it means I'm going to see the girls, I don't mind waiting an extra week.

MARLENE: You are soft in the head, you are – you know that, don't you?

GRACE: I can't see what I'm doing. Sit up and have a look, will you?

Pause.

MARLENE: You talking to me, Grace?

GRACE: I want to know how I look.

MARLENE: Tell her how she looks, Luce.

LUCY: You look lovely.

GRACE: I want the other woman to see.

MARLENE: I've had my pre-med, Grace. I don't know if I can lift my head.

GRACE: Well try, there's a dear.

MARLENE: (*Sitting upright without any effort*) I shouldn't feel like this.

LUCY: What's the matter?

MARLENE: I don't feel any different. I don't think it have taken. I've been waiting here so long I bet the bloody thing have worn off.

LUCY: Come to think of it, you have been waiting a long time.

GRACE: (*To MARLENE*) Well? Tell me the truth. How am I looking?

MARLENE: (*Looking towards GRACE; saying it even though GRACE looks pretty dreadful*) Beautiful. You're looking beautiful. A lot better today, honest. (*She gets off her bed.*)

LUCY: I don't think you should get off the bed.

MARLENE: I'm only going to comb her hair.

MARLENE crosses to the left side of Grace's bed and takes the powder compact. During the following, she rubs some powder from GRACE's face and puts a little rouge on her cheeks, and maybe some lipstick on her lips. Then she makes a little adjustment to GRACE's hair.

LUCY: I think I might be going home.

MARLENE: Why?

LUCY: Raymond's coming for a reason. Perhaps they're going to air the house or something.

GRACE: (*To MARLENE*) What's the matter with the one on the end?

MARLENE: Lucy?

GRACE nods.

MARLENE: She's had an operation.

GRACE: (*Impatiently*) Yes yes, I understand that, but why? What has she had done?

MARLENE: She had a blockage.

GRACE: Where?

MARLENE: I'm not sure. The bowel, I think.

GRACE: Large or small?

MARLENE: I don't know.

GRACE: Has she had everything taken away?

MARLENE: I'll have 'em come and take you away, you keep on.

GRACE: They say that's what they've done to me. I'll soon be on the mend, they said, but I still feel as ill as ever. (*She pauses*) Gilbert tells me I'm coming on in leaps and bounds – but I feel just as ill as before – worse even. Are you sure I look all right?

LUCY: (*Still reading her letter*) That's funny.

MARLENE looks over to her.

LUCY: They're coming on a Friday. They've never done that before.

MARLENE: Think there's something up, do you?

LUCY: I don't know.

MARLENE: Are they on the phone?

LUCY: Yes, but I haven't got their number.

MARLENE: (*Amazed*) What?

LUCY: Raymond rings me once a week. He says he doesn't want me to run my bill up by ringing him... and Hazel said that the number is too long for me to cope with. It is on the long side, what with the area code as well.

MARLENE: So you can't give them a call then?

Pause.

LUCY: Not really.

MARLENE: Do you know their address?

LUCY: I have it written down. (*She looks for it in her handbag.*)

GRACE: (*To MARLENE*) Is Gilbert coming today?

MARLENE: Gilbert comes every day.

GRACE: Then why isn't he here?

MARLENE: Because it's only quarter past eleven and he doesn't come until the afternoon. (*Finishing with the make-up*) How's that?

GRACE: I wish I had a mirror. You wouldn't have one I suppose?

MARLENE: Yes love, I got one. (*She goes to her bed to get her make-up bag.*)

LUCY: (*Noticing MARLENE*) Er... no. (*To MARLENE; confidentially*) I wouldn't. They try not to.

MARLENE: (*Softly*) What?

LUCY: It's best she doesn't. It's an awful shock sometimes.

MARLENE: (*Nodding, realizing the situation*) Er... sorry Grace – I don't know where I've put it, love.

GRACE: Not to worry. They've probably taken yours too.

This hadn't occurred to MARLENE. Panicked, knowing what it might mean if it has been taken, she desperately looks for it in the bag. She finds it, much to her relief. She puts the bag back in her locker.

MARLENE: If they don't hurry up I'm going to have something to eat.

LUCY: You can't do that.

MARLENE: I haven't ate bugger all since eight o'clock last night. I'm starving.

LUCY: You mustn't – not with the anaesthetic. You won't be able to have your investigation.

MARLENE: I don't care anymore. It's not fair to keep me waiting all this time.

GRACE: (*Very grand*) Gilbert never keeps *me* waiting.

MARLENE: I bet he'd never dare.

GRACE: Always on time. I like that.

MARLENE: (*Moving to the left of Lucy's bed*) If I kept Roy waiting when we were courting – and I did more than once – he wouldn't hang about. I always knew where to find him though. I'd only have to look for the nearest pub.

BEV enters, sporting a beautiful black eye.

BEV: Marlene! What are you doing on your feet?

MARLENE: I got fed up laying on my back.

BEV: I heard that was your favourite position.

MARLENE: Who told you that?

BEV: Treorchy Rugby Club. Come on – on the bed please.

MARLENE jumps on to her bed and BEV pulls a blanket over her.

MARLENE: Is this it, then? Have you come to fetch me?

BEV: No. We've had an emergency. I'll find out exactly what's happening now, but I think we might be cancelling you until tomorrow.

MARLENE: No – you can't do that.

BEV: It's out of my hands, love.

MARLENE: If I don't have it done today that means I'll have to have it tomorrow.

BEV: That's right.

MARLENE: But that'll bugger things up good and proper.

GRACE: Nurse?

BEV: Yes, Grace?

MARLENE pouts as she takes in the full consequence of the possible delay.

GRACE: How do I look?

BEV: (*Moving to GRACE*) What have you done to yourself?

GRACE: That common woman came and combed my hair.

BEV moves around Grace's bed, tidying it as she goes.

GRACE: She reminds me of someone. How long before Gilbert arrives? (*Remembering*) I know – I had a charlady like her.

BEV: Two o'clock is about his time. You've got a couple of hours yet. Everything else all right otherwise?

GRACE: I have a constant feeling of nausea.

BEV: Do you want me to get you something?

GRACE: Would you?

BEV: (*About to leave*) I'll be back in a tick.

GRACE: You're not getting me a receiver, are you?

BEV: I'm getting you an injection.

GRACE: Oh dear... not another prick.

BEV: That you should be so lucky, love.

LUCY: (*Calling to BEV*) Nurse, have you heard if I'm being discharged?

BEV: (*Crossing to her*) No, not a dickie bird.

LUCY: My son is coming down from Surrey. (*She gives BEV the letter*) I thought perhaps he was taking me home.

BEV hands it back with a sad smile and a slight shake of the head. A slight pause.

BEV: What about you, Marlene? Can I get anything for *you*?

MARLENE: (*Sitting up*) I'd either like a trolley to take me to theatre, or I'll have pie and chips.

BEV: I reckon that's half your trouble – too much greasy food.

MARLENE: The trolley then. (*She lies down and takes her hat off.*)

BEV: (*Turning as she goes*) I won't be long, Grace.

She exits.

MARLENE: I'm going to scream if I don't end up having it done today.

LUCY looks at her.

MARLENE: They know how important it is for me to have it now. (*She sits up*) Saturday will be here before we know it.

Pause.

LUCY: No one have said anything about the nurse's eye.

MARLENE: She'll have another bugger to go with it if I don't get down that theatre today.

LUCY: It's not her fault.

MARLENE: (*Sighing*) No, I know.

LUCY: I wonder how she had it.

MARLENE: Ask her. I'm sure she'll tell you.

LUCY: Oh no – I wouldn't have the nerve.

MARLENE: It's looking awful sore with her. She should have had a day off.

LUCY: She didn't work over the weekend. She probably hasn't got another day coming.

MARLENE: She could have a day sick.

LUCY: Good thing she didn't. They're short-staffed already. Didn't you hear her say?

MARLENE: This hospital will be here after her. There's nothing wrong in having a day for the queen. She do work hard, that kid do. Apart from her eye she's been looking shattered lately. I wouldn't mind betting she spent the weekend in bed.

LUCY: No – she was going away. She did say, but I can't remember where.

MARLENE: She's got a caravan in Mumbles.

LUCY: That's it – Mumbles.

MARLENE: I wonder if she lets it out? Perhaps she'll let it to me. I wouldn't mind a little week away – help me over this little lot, if I ever have it.

LUCY: When Raymond was small, we used to have a caravan every year in Porthcawl. It was never a holiday for *me* though. It wasn't for any woman. Still isn't as far as I know.

MARLENE: Ooooh, I've told our Roy – I'm not washing a bloody dish when I get out of here. He's going to have to do the lot for at least a month. It's not so bad for him *now* 'cos our Louise is there – but she'll have her own house to take care of after Saturday.

GRACE: It's a shame you having to miss her wedding.

LUCY: She's still keeping her fingers crossed.

MARLENE: It's only Monday *now*, Grace. If I end up having it done today and everything turns out all right, I should be out by Wednesday at the latest.

GRACE: I wouldn't put your mind on it.

MARLENE: I'll get to see her on the day either way, she said. If I end up having some sort of op and I got to stay in, she said she's coming here first with her father, and then coming back after the reception with Wayne.

Pause.

GRACE: My mother never came to *my* wedding. She didn't approve of Gilbert.

MARLENE: Roy threatened not to come to ours. If it wasn't that my father owned an airgun, I don't think he'd have bothered.

GRACE: Your husband doesn't approve of firearms?

MARLENE: Not when they're sticking into the back of your neck – no. I'm the *best* thing that's happened to Roy though. And he'll tell you that himself – when he's drunk. God knows how he'd have turned out if it wasn't for me. Alcoholic, I shouldn't wonder.

GRACE: She grew to like him eventually of course.

MARLENE and LUCY turn to look at her.

GRACE: Gilbert. (*She pauses*) My mother. He nursed her right up until she...

Pause.

MARLENE: Roy's been good to me too, mind. And he's always worked – I'll say that for him. He's never had a lot of brains, but there's nothing wrong with a bit of brawn now and again. What do you say, Luce?

LUCY coyly covers a smile.

MARLENE: And he's never once laid a finger on me. I'll put up with a lot but I won't stand for that. It wouldn't pay him to give me a clout, anyway – I'm bigger than he is. Or I was – I've lost a bit of weight lately.

Slight pause.

GRACE: Gilbert and I used to knock each other about rather a lot. It was our form of foreplay.

MARLENE: Roy's idea of foreplay is half a dozen pints of lager and a game of darts.

BEV enters.

BEV: (*Going to Marlene's bed*) Guess what, Marlene? It's on.

MARLENE: What is?

BEV: I've got a porter outside waiting to take you down.

LUCY: (*To MARLENE*) There you are – everything's failing into place. I'll keep my fingers crossed for you.

MARLENE: Ay – and everything else.

BEV: (*To MARLENE*) Are you ready? Shall I send him in?

MARLENE: Let me put my hat on first. (*She does.*)

BEV: Very nice, too.

MARLENE: Bugger off.

BEV: Fit?

MARLENE: If I was fit I wouldn't be done up like this.

BEV: Now, you're not worried or anything now, are you?

MARLENE: Worried? I'm bloody shitting myself.

BEV: Want me to come down with you?

MARLENE: (*Shaking her head*) No need for that.

BEV: Two hours and you'll be back in bed.

MARLENE: What time do you knock off?

BEV: Oh, I'll come and see you and make sure you're all right before I go home, don't you worry.

MARLENE: Come on then... let's get this show on the road.

BEV: (*Opening the door and calling to the porter*) She's ready when you are Mr DeMille.

Black-out. Music: Doctor Kildare.

Scene Three

Twenty-four hours later.

The lights come up. MARLENE is sitting in an armchair. She is attached to a drip – her investigation turned into a more serious operation. She is a little weaker than she was, but still as sharp as ever. GRACE is also sitting in an armchair, reading a magazine. Lucy's bed is empty and unmade – she is out of the ward at present. After a second or two BEV pops in. Her eye is not as bad as it was.

BEV: It's very quiet in here. How's my favourite girls do in 't?

MARLENE: Favourites? I bet you say that to every bugger.

BEV: No I don't.

MARLENE: I've heard you in the other wards.

BEV: Yeah but I mean it with you two. (*She checks the drip.*)

MARLENE: How long have I got to be attached to this thing?

BEV: If this stand had a mouth, Marlene, it would probably ask me the same thing. (*She has a little laugh*) Only a day or two – that's all I expect.

MARLENE: I want to get back into bed, Bev.

BEV: (*Checking her watch*) Try and stick it for another ten minutes.

MARLENE: I couldn't believe it when they got me out of bed this morning.

BEV: Aaahh, we don't hang about these days.

MARLENE: That's a nasty black eye you've got.

BEV: It's going now – thank God.

MARLENE: Lucy was wondering how you got it.

BEV: And you weren't?

MARLENE: It had crossed my mind.

BEV: I fell down stairs.

MARLENE: Ay – and I got wings sprouting out of my back.

BEV: (*Insisting*) I did. (*She tidies up around Marlene's bed.*)

MARLENE: If I believe that, I'll believe anything. And anyway, caravans don't have stairs.

BEV: (*Smiling*) How do you know I've got a caravan?

MARLENE: Never mind how I know – tell me what happened to your eye.

BEV: My stair carpet was a bit loose. Luckily I fell *up* the stairs and not down, or I would have had more bruising than this.

MARLENE: Hang about a minute by here now. *You* just said you fell *down* the stairs.

BEV: No I didn't.

MARLENE: Yes you did.

BEV: Well I meant up.

MARLENE: I can't swallow that, somehow.

BEV: You can't swallow anything at the moment, Marlene – that's why you're on a drip, love. (*She has another little laugh.*)

MARLENE: You know exactly what I meant.

Pause.

MARLENE: Somebody have been giving you a clout, haven't they?

BEV: It's nothing I can't handle.

MARLENE: You're a lovely girl and I don't like the thought of you being knocked about. If anyone's giving you trouble let me know. Our Darren used to be in the TAs.

BEV: Ooohhh, a soldier – give me his name and address.

MARLENE: Handsome boy. Big lump of a thing. He's seventeen and a half collar. He's into all this 'body beautiful'.

BEV: Oh, I'm going before I come over all funny. (*She makes to leave.*)

MARLENE: No, don't go – stay here a minute.

BEV sits on Marlene's bed.

MARLENE: Look, I know I got a bit of a chops on me, right? But me an' you get on OK, don't we? What I mean is – if you need somebody – just to listen like – I wouldn't interfere – you know where I am. Got me?

BEV: (*Smiling and nodding*) Got you.

Pause; BEV starts to leave, then stops by GRACE.

BEV: You all right, Grace?

GRACE: I'd like a word.

BEV kneels beside her.

GRACE: Something's wrong.

BEV: What's the matter?

GRACE: I didn't see Gilbert yesterday.

BEV: It's a lot to come every day, Grace. He's probably having a break.

GRACE: No. It's not like him. Not without telling me. And he would have rung – said something to someone. No – something isn't right and I'm concerned.

BEV: Fair enough – no more said than done.

GRACE: What will you do?

BEV: Wave my magic wand, what else?

MARLENE: Well you're the first bloody fairy I've seen with a black eye.

BEV: Then you haven't lived, Marlene. My God you haven't lived.

BEV exits, laughing.

MARLENE: Oh she's a girl, i'n' she?

Pause.

MARLENE: Don't worry, Grace. She'll sort it out for you if anybody will.

GRACE: He's never missed coming before – not once.

MARLENE: Pity he didn't have anyone to share it with. Like Bev said, see – it's a lot for the one to keep coming all the time. And I mean he's like you, i'n' he – Gilbert now, I mean. He's no spring chicken, is he? Mind you – the way I'm feeling this morning I think I'm past the sell-by date myself.

GRACE: (*Half listening*) We don't eat chicken. Gilbert and I are vegetarian.

MARLENE: I wish Roy was – I'd save a fortune. It's nothing for me to spend fifteen pounds on meat – and that's just for the weekend.

GRACE: (*Amazed*) Just for Sunday lunch?

MARLENE: No no – Saturdays is in that as well. Then there's the cooked meat, see. And he eats faggots like he's eating grapes. I've told him – it's you who should be in here, not me, I said. His bowel system is like Trawsfynydd Nuclear Power Plant. *And* it smells like it sometimes.

GRACE: Flatulence is nothing to be ashamed of.

MARLENE: Oh he's *not* ashamed of it. He'll tell you himself, he's proud of most of 'em.

Pause.

MARLENE: Lucy's been gone a long time.

GRACE: (*Pathetically*) I wish *I* could have a bath.

MARLENE: (*Encouragingly*) Why don't you ask 'em then? Bev will sort it out if you ask her tidy.

GRACE: (*Shaking her head*) There's mirrors in there. I have realized they're keeping them from me. I'm sure I must look dreadful.

MARLENE: You look all right to me.

GRACE: Do I really?

MARLENE: If I could get out of this chair on my own, I'd come over and comb your hair for you.

GRACE: You do realize it's a wig.

MARLENE: But it's a very good one, Grace.

GRACE: I lost it all you see – with the treatment. Bit of a mess, is it?

MARLENE: It'll be all right if it had a comb run through it.

GRACE: If only *I* could come to you.

MARLENE: Don't try it. You stay where you are. Bev will comb it nice for you now when she comes back.

GRACE: Do you have a comb there?

MARLENE: Yes – I'll throw it to you.

GRACE: No – better I throw it to *you*.

GRACE takes off her wig and tosses it over to MARLENE. It lands on Marlene's bed. Poor GRACE looks strange now, with only wisps of hair here and there.

MARLENE: (*Reaching for the wig and combing it*) It's a lovely one, Grace. Bet you paid a lot of money for this.

GRACE: They wanted to give me a hospital issue, but when I put it on Gilbert thought I looked like Joan of Arc. I thought I looked more like Rin-tin-tin. Gilbert insisted on my having something decent.

MARLENE: It's nice – you only get what you pay for see, don't you? I bought a wig once. Remember when they were all the go in the Seventies? Roy used to make fun of it. I kept it for years. I gave it away in the end.

GRACE: Charities are usually grateful for anything like that.

MARLENE: I gave it to a boy across the road to make a Guy. Come to think of it *that* looked a bit like Joan of Arc as well.

GRACE: And I presume it suffered the same fate.

MARLENE: I don't think Joan of Arc was pushed around by a gang of kids in an orange box.

LUCY enters. She has just had a bath. She hangs her towel over the back of her chair.

MARLENE: There you are. I was beginning to wonder if they'd drowned you.

LUCY: I'm sure they forgot me. Still, I enjoyed the soak.

MARLENE: I'll be glad when they'll let *me* have a bath. I can't see it happening for a bit yet, though. Not till I've had my stitches out at least. And there's something to be said for a blanket bath – even if it *is* only the nurses that do it. What do *you* say, Grace?

GRACE: I won't even undress in front of Gilbert. We've been married fifty-four years and he has never once seen me naked.

MARLENE: Oh, you're one of these that likes the light out, are you?

GRACE: I insist on it. Well I used too. There hasn't been any point for such a long time now.

MARLENE: Do me a favour, Luce, and put this back on for Grace?

LUCY turns and is shocked to see GRACE without her wig. She reluctantly takes the wig from MARLENE and places it on GRACE's head.

LUCY: I've just seen Doctor Fairwater.

MARLENE: Yes, I heard he was here. I'm waiting for him to come round. I want to ask him about the wedding.

LUCY: Oh, I think he's gone.

Pause.

MARLENE: What do you mean?

LUCY: He's finished for the day, I'm sure.

MARLENE: But he haven't set foot in here.

LUCY: I heard Sister say, 'See you tomorrow, then,' as he disappeared through the double doors.

MARLENE: (*Shrugging it off*) Oh he's probably told her it's all right for me to go. A busy man like him – no need to see me to tell me that see, is there?

LUCY: (*To GRACE*) There you are. All right?

GRACE: How do I look?

LUCY: Very nice.

GRACE: If only I could see for myself.

MARLENE: I think I'll try and get up.

LUCY: Do you think that's wise?

MARLENE: If I show 'em I can get about – that's bound to help 'em make up their mind. In case they're not sure what to do.

LUCY: I'd stay where you are if I were you. Apart from the operation, your body is still full of the anaesthetic.

MARLENE: I'll be all right. (*Referring to the drip*) I can always hang on to this thing. (*She grabs hold of it and manages to scramble to her feet.*)

LUCY: (*Crossing to the foot of Marlene's bed*) Oh, be careful.

GRACE: Stay where you are, you silly woman!

MARLENE: You got to show 'em what you can do. They'll keep you in her till God knows when otherwise.

GRACE: You'll do more harm than good.

MARLENE: (*Determined*) I'm not missing that wedding, Grace. Not for all the tea in China, I'm not. (*With great difficulty she manages to walk to the foot of the bed. Pleased with herself*) How's that?

LUCY: How do you feel?

MARLENE: Buggered up.

LUCY: Leave it at that. Perhaps you can go a bit further tomorrow.

MARLENE: (*Resting her behind on the end of the bed*) I'll be all right. I'll just have a spell by here a minute.

LUCY: Let me help you back to your chair.

MARLENE: No, I'll be all right... I'll be all... (*She is in such pain that she falls forward.*)

LUCY: (*Panicking*) Oh... (*To GRACE*) What should we do now?

GRACE: Buzz for a nurse.

LUCY crosses to the right of her bed and presses her buzzer.

GRACE: Silly thing ought to have known better.

MARLENE: (*Still in the same position*) I'm all right – don'tpanic, I'm all right.

GRACE: Anyone with any common sense will know *she's* not going home at the weekend.

LUCY: (*Crossing back to GRACE*) Oh don't say that.

GRACE: Well it's true, and she's only fooling herself to think otherwise.

LUCY: You've got to have a goal.

GRACE: Even in this ward?

LUCY: Especially in this ward. It's pointless just sitting back and letting things happen – it's good to have something to aim for.

GRACE: I've gone through all that. There's no way out in the end.

LUCY: Don't talk like that.

GRACE: It's all right for you now. You wait until it's *your* turn.

Pause.

LUCY: Don't you have any faith?

GRACE: I lost it around about the same time I lost my hair.

LUCY: There's no need to be cynical.

GRACE: It makes you like that after a time.

MARLENE attempts to move from the bed.

LUCY: No Marlene – don't move. Wait till someone gets here.

MARLENE: (*Exhausted*) Lucy – you can help me back in my chair, if you want to. Don't let 'em see me like this. I'm all right – I'm not hurting. But don't let 'em see me like this.

LUCY helps MARLENE back into her chair then sits on her own bed.

MARLENE: Oh thank you – thank you. Don't say nothing now, will you? When they come, keep your mouth shut, right?

GRACE: They ought to be told. You may have done yourself a serious injury.

MARLENE: I'll do *you* a serious injury if you say anything. Got me?

GRACE: I'm only thinking of your own good.

MARLENE: I know what's good for me. If I can be in that church on Saturday... (*she pauses to get her breath*) being there is going to do more for me than a couple of days' rest in this place.

GRACE: The whole event will be too much for you.

MARLENE: I think *I'll* be the judge of that.

GRACE: But you're not. The situation is out of your hands.

MARLENE: When it comes down to it the final decision is mine.

LUCY: (*Scornfully*) Marlene! You'd be silly not to listen to the doctors.

MARLENE: Only one daughter I've got, look.

LUCY: I don't think Roy would let you sign yourself out anyway, if that's what you're thinking.

MARLENE: *Roy* wouldn't have a say in it, either.

LUCY: You're trying too hard. (*To GRACE*) Maybe they'll allow her home in a wheelchair.

MARLENE: That's right – a wheelchair. That'll do. I don't care how I go as long as I get there.

GRACE: Why didn't they postpone?

MARLENE: They didn't know I was going to be stuck in here, did they? Nobody knew. Could hardly cancel with a couple of days to go.

LUCY: I still don't think it's out of the question.

GRACE: Well I do.

MARLENE: (*To LUCY*) Just don't say anything about what's happened.

LUCY: I'm not.

MARLENE: That goes for you too, Grace. You open your gob and you can comb your own hair in future.

GRACE: I don't have a future.

LUCY: (*To MARLENE*) Oh God, she's down today.

GRACE: (*Insisting*) No I'm not. I'm not at all depressed. I'm a fair age. I have no complaints. I just wish I'd stop this shilly-shallying and go. I can't bear anything dragging on.

LUCY: I don't know what to say to you anymore.

GRACE: You can tell me the truth.

LUCY: I've never lied to you, Grace.

GRACE: You're lying now. You humour me, that's all you do. You and that one there.

LUCY: (*Giving up; turning to MARLENE*) Let me put a blanket over you. (*She attempts to do so.*)

MARLENE: No – I don't want it. I don't want anything that might make me look worse.

BEV enters.

BEV: Somebody buzzed?

No one answers.

BEV: Somebody buzzed?

LUCY: Well er...

MARLENE: No.

GRACE: Yes.

Pause.

GRACE: I was wondering about Gilbert.

LUCY is relieved, but would still like to be out of the situation. BEV crosses to Grace's bed and plumps up her pillow.

LUCY: I think I'll just pop down to the day room and swap my magazine. Marlene – what about you?

MARLENE: Yes, I wouldn't mind a read. (*For BEV's benefit*) I'm feeling a lot better today.

LUCY: Grace? Would you like something?

GRACE waves her hand dismissively.

LUCY exits.

GRACE: (*To BEV*) Do you have any news?

BEV: Not yet, but Sister have rung the police station.

GRACE: (*Alarmed*) Police station?

BEV: They're sending someone round. They'll ask your husband to ring you so as you don't worry.

GRACE: When?

BEV: Straight away, I imagine.

GRACE: But you haven't heard anything yet?

BEV: I'll let you know the minute I do, Grace, OK? (*She makes to leave.*)

MARLENE: Doctor Fairwater have been and gone then?

BEV nods.

MARLENE: He didn't show his face in here.

BEV: (*Moving to Marlene's bed*)No, but he's gone over your notes with Sister.

MARLENE: I wanted to see him.

BEV: He's a very busy man, Marlene.

MARLENE: What's going to happen now, then?

BEV: I'm not with you.

MARLENE: About me. Have he said if I can go home or what?

BEV: Sister is going to have a word with you when she's got a minute.

Pause.

MARLENE: She's going to tell me I can't go, isn't she? (*She pauses*) I feel marvellous, honest I do.

BEV: (*Sitting on the side of the bed and holding MARLENE's hand*) Sister did mention about Saturday to Doctor... but he wouldn't hear of it, love. He wouldn't take the responsibility of discharging you.

MARLENE: Then I'll take it myself.

BEV: Look... I know you're disappointed.

MARLENE: Two hours – that's all I want to go out for.

BEV: Have a word with Sister when she comes.

MARLENE: (*Trying not to be upset*) What's the point? She's only going to come and say the same thing.

BEV: Better to stay and get well, Marlene.

MARLENE: (*Crying now, but silently*) But I wanted to be there.

BEV: Of course you did.

MARLENE: (*Still crying*) She needs me see, Bev. All daughters need their mother on their wedding day.

BEV: I'm sure she'd rather have you better so she can need you another time.

Pause.

BEV: Well am I right?

BEV hands MARLENE a tissue. MARLENE nods, blows and dries her nose.

LUCY enters with two magazines. She puts one down at the foot of Marlene's bed as she passes it.

MARLENE: I suppose I knew all along they wouldn't let me go.

BEV: (*Standing up*) Another week and you might have swung it.

Pause.

MARLENE: You can tell Sister she haven't got to bother to come and see me. She's a busy woman and I don't like her very much anyway. I'm glad it come from *you* though.

LUCY: Yes. You've got a way about you.

BEV: Oh go on.

LUCY: (*Insisting*) No, you have. (*To GRACE*) Haven't she Grace?

GRACE: I beg your pardon?

LUCY: I said Bev have got a way about her.

GRACE doesn't answer.

LUCY: I bet you love your job, don't you?

BEV: You've got to. You'd never be able to stick it otherwise.

LUCY: Everybody likes you.

BEV: Now you're embarrassing me.

LUCY: No they do. You've only got to listen to 'em talk in the day room. No one has a bad word to say about you. Mind you, it wouldn't pay them to or they'll have Marlene to reckon with.

BEV makes a face as she moves to go.

MARLENE: No don't go. Have five minutes with me?

BEV stays. Pause.

MARLENE: Hey listen... what are you working on Saturday?

BEV: I'm not, I've got it off.

MARLENE: (*Disappointedly*) Oh, I thought you'd be here when our Louise comes.

BEV: I will if you want me too.

MARLENE: Will you? You can see her dress then... and you might get a look at her brother if he comes with her.

BEV: That settles it. Wouldn't miss it for the world.

MARLENE: (*With new enthusiasm*) Well, if I can't go to the wedding, I can't go.

LUCY: (*Sitting on her bed*) That's the spirit.

MARLENE: But I'm still going to have my hair done though.

BEV: That'll be nice.

LUCY: Perhaps we all will.

GRACE: Even me.

MARLENE: Can we, Bev, what do you think?

BEV: I don't see why not.

MARLENE: We will then. I can still make a bit of a fuss even if I am stuck in here.

LUCY: Of course you can.

GRACE: I'm quite looking forward to it.

MARLENE: Will you ask Sister if we can have clean covers? That'll make it look a bit better, won't it, and I'll make sure we've all got some nice fresh flowers. Oh I hope to God the weather'll stay nice for her.

LUCY: Oh and me.

MARLENE: We'll have a couple of photos done too, so you make sure you're here now, Bev – I want you to be in them as well. (*She gets really excited*) Oooh, I'll dress up to the nines.

BEV: You can put your new outfit on.

MARLENE: Oh you should see it Bev, it cost a fortune, mind – I look a million dollars in it.

BEV: I bet.

GRACE: And she paid over forty pounds for her hat.

MARLENE: I did yes, so I think I'd better wear that as well, don't you? What you think girls? Go the whole hog, i'n' it? (*Shouting*) Yeah.

The lights begin to fade slowly as everybody shouts, joining in with MARLENE.

Music: Emergency Ward 10.

Black-out.

Act Two

Scene One

The same.

The following Saturday afternoon, about 3.20pm.

As the house lights fade we hear the last few bars of Stand By Your Man.

RADIO VOICE-OVER: And that was for Marlene Morgan, whose daughter Louise got married earlier today...

There is a sudden and loud burst of church bells as the lights come up.

All three women are lying on their beds, sleeping and snoring. GRACE and LUCY are both wearing their dressing-gowns, while MARLENE is wearing her wedding outfit, complete with gloves and her forty pound hat. She is not attached to the drip any longer. Louise's bouquet is on the bedside cabinet – she and her new husband visited MARLENE earlier and left some time ago. MARLENE now has a portable television by her bed.

After a moment, a DOMESTIC enters wheeling a tea-trolley. Throughout the following, the DOMESTIC takes tea to MARLENE, then LUCY, then GRACE. Once that is finished, she takes bread and butter to them in the same order. When that task is completed, she strikes water jugs from each bedside. She is about to place a cup and saucer on Marlene's locker when MARLENE wakes.

MARLENE: Oh... tea, is it?

DOMESTIC: Bread and butter?

MARLENE: Oh God no, nothing to eat. Listen to these two.

LUCY and GRACE continue to snore.

MARLENE: I'm lucky to sleep a wink. What time is it?

DOMESTIC: Twenty past three.

MARLENE: Is it indeed. I've been laying for nearly an hour trying to drop off. Were you here earlier on?

DOMESTIC: I've been here all day. Just coming to the end of my shift now though.

MARLENE: Saw my daughter then, did you?

DOMESTIC: (*Nodding*) Oh, she looked beautiful.

MARLENE: She paid a thousand pounds for that dress. I told her when she bought it, 'It's lovely,' I said. 'It's beautiful, but you're off your head paying that kind of money.' (*Amazed*) A thousand pounds. 'Think what you could have done for your house with that,' I said. She haven't got a washing machine. 'I'll bring my dirty washing over to you,' she said. (*She laughs*) I don't mind – I've got an automatic so it's only a question of shoving it in. I've told her, 'You can do your own ironing though,' I said. I don't mind helping out but you've got to draw the line somewhere see, haven't you? (*She pauses*) You thought she looked nice then?

DOMESTIC: All brides are lovely, aren't they?

MARLENE: I wasn't. Oh I thought I was done up like a dog's dinner at the time – but when I think of it now.... You should have seen me. I got married in a loose-fitting salmon-pink crimplene two-piece suit. Kids today don't know they're born, do they? I mean, for a thousand pounds she could have furnished her house from top to bottom. But they won't have second-hand these days. If it's not new they don't want to know. She had the chance to buy a beautiful fridge for forty pounds. No. I'd rather go without, she said. You should have seen it — there wasn't a mark on it — a real cop. I said to Roy, I said, if ours wasn't working so well I'd have bought it myself, I said. (*She pauses*) Listen to me chopsin' by here. If I don't let you get on every bugger else's tea will be cold.

The DOMESTIC makes to go.

MARLENE: Er... where have you come from now? What I mean is... have you been to ward six or are you on your way there?

DOMESTIC: No, I've been.

MARLENE: How's her husband doing? (*She nods in GRACE's direction.*)

DOMESTIC: Who is he?

MARLENE: Bed fourteen. Gilbert 'arris. Or *H*arris as she likes to say. He fell in the house a couple of days ago.

DOMESTIC: I know – broken femur, but he's fine I think.

MARLENE: I'll tell her now when she wakes up. She'll be glad to hear that. See you tomorrow then, is it?

DOMESTIC: God willing.

She exits.

MARLENE takes a sip of tea. LUCY and GRACE continue to snore.

MARLENE: I can't stick this much longer. (*Calling to LUCY*) Oi! Rap up, will you?

LUCY: (*Gently opening her eyes*) Oh... did I drop off?

MARLENE: Drop off? You were snoring so much I thought you were in a coma.

LUCY: I don't snore.

MARLENE: (*Looking at GRACE*) She don't think *she* does either.

LUCY: I'm glad you woke me, though. I wasn't having a very nice dream. I dreamed I was going home – but when I got there my house wasn't there. No matter how hard I tried I couldn't find it. People I knew didn't recognize who I was... it was awful.

MARLENE: Oh, there you are then. There's a cup of tea by there. Drink it. You'll feel better after that.

LUCY: (*Sitting up to drink her tea*) I wonder what it means. They say all dreams have meanings.

MARLENE: Do they? I dreamed I was playing the piano like hell last night and I can't read a word of music.

LUCY: Perhaps you've always wanted to. Deep down.

MARLENE: Do you think so?

LUCY nods.

MARLENE: Oh I don't know.

MARLENE takes the bouquet from the locker and admires it.

LUCY: It really is lovely, isn't it?

MARLENE: Have a guess how much.

LUCY: I wouldn't have a clue.

MARLENE: Forty-seven pounds fifty.

LUCY: Good God.

MARLENE: Lot of money i'n' it? She could have bought a second-hand fridge for that. Mind you, she'd have looked bloody funny walking down the aisle with a fridge on her arm. (*She laughs.*)

Pause.

LUCY: She's a beautiful girl.

MARLENE: Well, you know, *I* like to think so.

LUCY: She isn't like you at all, is she?

MARLENE is gobsmacked for a second.

LUCY: What I mean is, I hadn't noticed until this morning how like your husband she is.

MARLENE: Now you're not the first to notice that. When she was younger she was his spittin' image.

Pause.

MARLENE: Didn't notice anything else this morning, did you?

LUCY: Like what?

MARLENE: With Roy. (*She pauses*) I thought he was a bit quiet.

LUCY: It was probably nerves. I mean he's never given away a daughter before.

MARLENE: No it wasn't that. (*She pauses*) He was staring at me. And every time I caught his eye he looked away. Not straight away, like – he wasn't that obvious, but it must have happened at least half a dozen times. And then when he came back here after the reception... (*she breaks off*) he didn't seem himself at all. Something's wrong.

LUCY: He seemed all right to me.

MARLENE: He hadn't had a drink. Just the toast. That's all he said. He haven't touched a drop of beer.

LUCY: That's what it was then – he was sober.

They both have a laugh, but it is clear MARLENE is concerned.

Pause.

MARLENE: It wasn't just this morning, mind. I've noticed it before. He's been a bit strange for a day or two, now.

LUCY: Well, you know him better than anybody.

MARLENE: Louise was all right, and Darren seemed OK – it's just Roy that didn't seem right.

LUCY: I'm sure it's nothing to worry about.

MARLENE: You do though, don't you? You've got all the time in the world to worry in this place.

LUCY: You're probably over-reacting.

MARLENE: And now he've said he's not going to the do tonight. They got a disco and a running buffet for two hundred and fifty people. Couldn't ask them all to the wedding, see, so they've had them to the fling in the night. Roy was looking forward to it – now he's not going.

LUCY: He probably feels it wouldn't be the same without you.

MARLENE: And the strangest thing of all is, he said he's coming back here. 'No need for that,' I said. Well I think you heard me, didn't you? 'You go and enjoy yourself,' I said. I'm not funny like that, see. But no – he've insisted. Back here he's coming and back here he's going to stay, he said.

LUCY: I think he's missing you.

MARLENE: (*Suspiciously*) Well it all seems bloody funny to me. I mean Roy's not that type. To miss me, like. Or if he is he'd never show it – not for a minute. He's *never* been able to show feelings like that. He does have 'em. He just can't express 'em, that's all.

LUCY: Which is why he's coming back here tonight and not going on to the celebrations.

MARLENE: Maybe. (*She pauses*) Do you know something? He's never once told me he loves me? Not once. Not once in twenty-five years. Oh he've been jealous, mind. Stopped me doing the gypsy tango with Jackie Turner from the Non Pol once – so I suppose he shows he cares in *that* way. It's just that it would be nice if he actually came out and said it. God, I'd be grateful if he wrote it down. (*She pauses*) Do you know what he wrote on my anniversary card last year? It was our twenty-fifth. 'To Marlene, Happy anniversary – all the best – Roy.' Didn't even have a bloody kiss on the bottom. Didn't even have a card till our Louise went out and got him one. (*Slight pause*) He's always been the same though – never made a fuss. See all these by here? (*She points to all the 'Get Well' cards displayed on the headboard of the bed*) Not one is from him. It's not that he's tight or doesn't want to send me one. (*Mimicking him*) 'What do you want a card from me for? I'd feel so bloody soft, mun.' (*She tries to laugh*) I can hear him now.

LUCY: There's a lot of men like that. I blame it on their mothers.

MARLENE: How's that?

LUCY: It's the way they're brought up.... School is to blame, too. We're taught early on to play roles, aren't we?

Boys have to be tough and play cowboys and Indians and girls, shop and house.

MARLENE: Not me, love. I'd rather play cowboys any day. A regular Annie Oakley – that's me.... You're right though, I s'pose. Perhaps it does all 'ark back to school days.

Pause.

MARLENE: He doesn't even say he loves me when we're... you know.

LUCY looks vague.

MARLENE: (*Persisting*) You know... I'm glad then though, mind. It would be easy to say it at a time like that. I'd rather hear it out of the blue. It would mean a lot more then... He nearly told me once. Years ago now, before our Louise was born. We were on a bus of all things. It was Palm Sunday and we were coming back from the cemetery... I lost a little boy, see. Christopher. He was only four months. Spit of Roy.... None of us said anything for a long time. I was staring out of the window and I don't know where Roy was looking, but our minds were together. We turned and looked at each other at the same time. Uncanny it was. I knew he wanted to say he loved me then – I could see it in his eyes. It was in his mouth – on the tip of his tongue. (*She pauses*) We stared at each other for a long time. Is he going to say it, I thought? Yes he is – no he's not, yes he is – no he's not – (*very excited*) yes he is! Then the bus screeched, swerved, ran over a sheep and *that* put pay to *that*.

GRACE stops snoring and wakes up.

GRACE: What time is it?

MARLENE: Awake at last, are you?

GRACE: I feel quite horrid.

MARLENE: There's a cup of tea by there for you. Gone cold now though no doubt.

GRACE: (*Sitting up*) Did someone say the time?

LUCY: It's twenty-five to four.

GRACE: Is it still Saturday?

MARLENE: Good God, you haven't been sleeping that long. (*She goes to GRACE*) Ooohh, hey – I was talking to the domestic when she brought the tea and I asked her about Gilbert. She said he's doing all right but he's broken his femur.

LUCY: Oh that *is* a shame.

MARLENE: I think it's marvellous – it could have been his neck.

GRACE: I told him to leave the damn decorating alone.

MARLENE: It's always the same, i'n' it? Just when you're doing all right life comes and kicks you in the shin.

GRACE: He had a thing about me coming home to a freshly decorated bedroom – and now look where it's led to.

LUCY: He only wanted to make everything comfortable for you.

GRACE: (*Suddenly*) What about Boris?

MARLENE: Who's Boris? (*She sits on the edge of the bed.*)

GRACE: He can't be left in the house by himself.

LUCY: (*To MARLENE*) She always said she didn't have any family.

MARLENE: (*To GRACE*) He lives with you then, does he, this Boris?

GRACE: Did Gilbert mention anything? Perhaps he's made arrangements. Oh dear....

MARLENE: Listen, Gilbert was by himself in the house when they found him. (*To LUCY*) Ring for Sister. Somebody had better ring this Boris and explain, like. He'll be wondering what the hell has happened to Gilbert. Is he your side of the family or his?

GRACE: Boris is our cockatiel.

MARLENE: Your cock what?

LUCY: It's a bird.

MARLENE: (*To GRACE, laughing*) Is that what you're on about? A bloody bird?

GRACE: He might have enough food and drink for a few days – but with a broken femur, Gilbert is going to be in here for months.

MARLENE pulls out a bed stool from under Grace's bed and sits on it.

LUCY: Would he have left a key with anyone? A neighbour looks after my cat.

GRACE: We've had him for seventeen years.

MARLENE: Look, don't worry about it. I'll go up and see Gilbert after. Ten to one he've done something about him.

LUCY: They're a bit like cats in a funny sort of way, aren't they? Birds.

MARLENE and GRACE look at each other, then at LUCY.

LUCY: I mean they're not like dogs at all.

Pause.

MARLENE: No, Luce – I'll say that – a dog is nothing like a cat or a bird.

LUCY: Dogs are so much more dependent.

GRACE: I hope he's still in his cage. Gilbert likes to let him out as often as he can. It's just possible he was flying around when Gilbert had his fall. If that's the case, heaven knows what might have happened to him.

LUCY: They're a worry, aren't they? Pets.

MARLENE: They're good company though. Dog I got. Nothing posh, like – Heinz fifty-seven that's all he is, but I can't move for him. Under my feet all day. Even follows me to the toilet.

LUCY: (*To GRACE*) Does the bird talk?

GRACE: Can't utter a syllable – but he sings his heart out.

LUCY: You think it would say something after seventeen years.

GRACE: It's the hens do all the talking.

MARLENE: Just like us then in other words. (*She laughs*) No bugger can get a word in edgeways once *I* start.

GRACE: Yes, that's true.

MARLENE: I've always been the same. Never short of something to say, me.

GRACE: But sometimes it's nice not to hear anything. (*She pauses*) So much can be said with just a look.

MARLENE: Now I know exactly what you mean by there.

GRACE: You get quite a lot of that in this place – and not only from the staff. Your own family get to do it in the end. (*She pauses*) Nothing of any seriousness is ever discussed. It's all hidden away in touch or a smile. Everything is said in the gaps and the glances.

MARLENE: I hope you're not getting morbid again, are you?

GRACE: Nobody understands, but there comes a time when certain things have to be talked about. Arrangements will eventually have to be made, but no one is prepared to speak about it. You notice that. (*She pulls herself together*) Everything has to be in apple pie order or you just don't rest.

MARLENE: I'm sure Gilbert have got everything sorted out.

GRACE: I hope so. If he hasn't he's not going to be able to do anything about it now.

LUCY: Don't you have any other family at all?

GRACE: We have a godson. William. But he's in Detroit, that's in America. We keep in touch. We usually write to each other about once a month. He knows I'm in here but he has no idea why. He thinks I'm having digestive problems, which isn't exactly a lie.

LUCY: Wouldn't you like to see him again?

GRACE: Oh of course – but it's such a long way to come. We had a letter from him last week. Gilbert brought it in but I haven't felt up to reading it yet. (*She gestures towards the cabinet where it is*) He's such a dear boy – works terribly hard.

MARLENE: Doing well for himself, is he?

GRACE: He's very successful. Runs a company that manufactures mobile homes. Caravans to you.

MARLENE: You're pretty close then, even though he lives so far away.

GRACE: He's the nearest thing I'll ever have to a son.

MARLENE: Well I think you're cruel.

GRACE: Pardon, dear?

MARLENE: If he's as close to you as you say you are to him, I think it's awful he haven't been told how bad you've been.

GRACE: What's the point of worrying him?

MARLENE: What's going to happen now with Gilbert stuck in here as well?

GRACE: It's his femur he's broken not his wrist.

Pause.

MARLENE: I suppose he gets everything, does he, when something happens to you and Gilbert?

LUCY: Marlene! You shouldn't be asking things like that.

MARLENE: I'm only asking to make a point. (*To GRACE*) Well am I right? Does he get the lot?

GRACE: Everything, yes. Lock stock and barrel.

MARLENE: Well I'd be mortified if I found out that someone I cared for had been awful bad and they never showed me. You might have got your reasons for not wanting him to come and see you, but have you thought about him and his feelings? No – mortified I'd be if anything was to happen and all I thought was wrong with you was you couldn't swallow. If he knew the score I bet he'd be over here like a shot.

GRACE: (*Quietly*) Oh I'm sure he would – but Gilbert and I have decided not to tell him and that's an end to the matter.

Pause.

MARLENE: You're afraid, aren't you? For him to see you.

Pause.

GRACE: I looked so healthy when he saw me last.

MARLENE: Do you think he'd care for a minute what you looked like?

Pause.

GRACE: *I* care.

MARLENE: But you look all right. Doesn't she, Luce?

LUCY: You're looking a lot better today.

GRACE: You don't understand, do you? If he were to walk in here this minute, as much as I'd like him to – and he were to see me... I'd see my reflection in his face... and I would die.

A pause.

MARLENE slowly moves back to her bed and sits on it, left.

Suddenly BEV rushes on, dressed in off-duty clothes. She hides a small package behind her back.

BEV: Here you are, Marlene – a prezzy for you. (*She reveals it.*)

MARLENE: For me? What you got?

BEV: Open it and find out.

MARLENE: Oh I love presents, I do.

BEV hands the package over and MARLENE opens it.

MARLENE: Photos? (*Very excited*) Not of Louise? How did you have 'em so quick?

BEV: I took them into town. Only takes an hour.

LUCY: Oh can I have a look as well?

MARLENE, BEV and LUCY sit on the end of Marlene's bed. GRACE gets up and starts to make her way over.

MARLENE: (*Excited*) Oh look at me by there.

BEV: There's a better one than that.

MARLENE: Nice one of you, Luce. (*She hands it to her.*)

BEV: (*To MARLENE*) That's it – look at you in that one.

MARLENE: (*Screaming with laughter*) I look bloody awful. You caught me looking funny by there and the flash made my eyes red. It's a nice one of Louise, though. And you've come out nice, Bev. You take a lovely photo you do. Oh and there's one of us all together, look. Don't Louise look something in that dress? Worth every penny in the long run, see. Oh God – (*she screams*) look at Roy in this one. (*She laughs.*)

All four are in very high spirits as they pass the photos around. Plenty of ad-libbing, etc. GRACE is confused by one of the photographs and points it out to MARLENE.

GRACE: Who is that?

MARLENE: (*Looking at it*) Well that's me, that is. And Bev, look. We're all in that. Who took that one I wonder?

BEV: Roy, I think.

MARLENE: (*Still looking at the same photograph*) And there's Lucy standing next to Darren – and Bev by there see, looking quite jealous.

BEV: (*Laughing*) Go on.

MARLENE: Yes you are. Say the truth – you couldn't take your eyes off him.

GRACE: But who is this here? (*She points.*)

MARLENE looks at the photo then at BEV. BEV turns her head to see who it is. There is a very awkward moment as they both realize GRACE is asking about herself.

Slow fade to Black-out. Music: St Elsewhere.

Scene Two

The following Thursday, 9.00pm.

When the Lights come up, MARLENE is nowhere to be seen. LUCY and GRACE are both in bed. Marlene's portable television is on and the music for the BBC's Nine O'Clock News *is heard.*

LUCY: (*To GRACE*) Shall I turn it off?

GRACE doesn't reply.

LUCY: I think I will. (*She gets up and turns off the television, then hovers about*) I can't it watch these days – it's always so depressing. I can remember when they always used to slip in some light-hearted things. Now it's one mugging after the other – when they're not showing you starving children and burnt out cars on the M4. (*She shrugs*) Oh, perish the thought.... Raymond will be using that motorway tomorrow. Still – he's a very careful driver. (*She goes over to GRACE*) Are you all right, Grace?

There is no answer.

LUCY: (*Taking hold of GRACE's hand and touching her forehead*) Grace?

Still no answer.

LUCY: Would you like anything?

GRACE: (*Quietly*) I wish I could go to sleep and never wake up.

LUCY: (*Gently scorning her*) Grace... no, don't say that.

GRACE: I'm tired and I've had enough.

LUCY: You mustn't give in. You're a fighter – don't let it get the better of you now.

GRACE: Everything has gone wrong. It was all right before Gilbert was ill.

LUCY: Gilbert is doing all right – (*she sits on the bed stool*) there's no need to worry about him.

72

GRACE: They don't tell you everything. They said it's only a broken femur but heaven knows what else it might be.

LUCY: That *is* all that's wrong with him, Grace, honestly. Marlene has seen him, remember. If there was anything else to worry about *she'd* know what it was. Don't you think?

GRACE: She wouldn't tell me if there *was* anything.

LUCY: Maybe not, but she'd tell me and she hasn't said a word. There really isn't anything to be bothered about. Even that nice little ambulance man is taking care of Boris.

GRACE: Do you think that's true? They say so many lies here in hospital.

LUCY: I'm sure they don't.

GRACE: Oh nothing malicious. I know they do it to protect you.

LUCY: It's Gilbert who told Marlene about Boris, remember. You don't think *he'd* lie to you, do you?

Pause.

GRACE: No – perhaps not.

Pause; LUCY makes to move away.

GRACE: (*Sighing weakly*) Oh dear...

LUCY: (*Turning back to her*) What is it?

GRACE: I feel so ill.

LUCY: Are you in pain?

GRACE: I'm sure I'm due for another injection. I'll try and hang on until then. She's been gone a long time. Where has she gone?

LUCY: (*Sitting down again*) Who knows. Probably making tea for the entire wing.

GRACE: Well her heart's in the right place.

LUCY: Yes.

GRACE: Shame about her mouth.

LUCY: (*Smiling*) Grace!

GRACE: She talks too much. She's not a bad old thing but she talks too much.

LUCY: She keeps us going anyway, doesn't she?

GRACE: It would be a duller place here without her, I'm sure. Why am I so hot?

LUCY: Shall I buzz and ask for a fan?

GRACE: I feel really... odd.

Pause.

GRACE: Something strange happened earlier on. I'd dozed off – but then I woke up. I could hear you talking, but I couldn't open my eyes. I was wide awake, and aware of everything but my eyelids remained closed. I couldn't even move my limbs.

LUCY: Maybe you were only dreaming you were awake. I've heard it happens sometimes.

GRACE: (*Insisting*) No I *was* awake, I tell you. I can even repeat what you were talking about. She (*she means MARLENE*) was pumping you for information about your son. And you were telling her how he owns your house. How he bought it for you several years after your husband passed on. I heard it all but I could do nothing but lay here... I relaxed, thinking... well if this is some kind of coma perhaps I'm on my way, so to speak. I couldn't tell myself to close my eyes because they were already shut. I thought I may just as well give in and not fight it when I must have dropped off to sleep again. When I eventually woke up everything was back to normal. Isn't that strange?

LUCY moves back to her own bed.

GRACE: You *were* telling her about your son and your house, weren't you?

LUCY: Yes – yes I was.

GRACE: And it's happened before. That is about the fourth time this week.

MARLENE enters, pushing in a portable telephone (on a trolley).

MARLENE: (*Revealing it as if she was a magician's assistant*) Darra!! (*To LUCY*) Look what I found. All I got to do is plug it in for you and you're away.

LUCY: *I'm* away?

MARLENE: Well I brought it for you.

LUCY: I don't want to make a phone call.

MARLENE: You haven't *said* you want to make one, but I can read between the lines. I'm a mother myself. I know you're dying to talk to him really.

LUCY: To who?

MARLENE: To Raymond. Don't try and tell me it's not eating you away.

LUCY: What's not?

MARLENE: Tomorrow. His visit. Why he's coming down. Go on – tell me it's not bothering you.

LUCY: Of course it's bothering me – but I can wait until tomorrow.

Pause.

MARLENE: Well no harm in ringing.

LUCY: I don't know the number.

MARLENE: Directory enquiries. You can have a little chat to him anyway. (*She plugs the phone in.*)

LUCY: No.

MARLENE: Perhaps *he's* got something to tell *you*.

76

LUCY: Whatever he has to say, he'll say it tomorrow.

MARLENE: Well it's up to you of course... but don't you think it'll be better to know what it's all about *now*? What do they say – forearmed is forewarned?

Pause.

LUCY: I've been thinking about it. Whatever his reasons for coming down I'm sure it's nothing to worry about.

Pause; MARLENE ponders what to do next.

MARLENE: (*Moving round in front of the phone*) Look, it's no good – I've got to tell you.

LUCY looks at her.

MARLENE: I'm quick see, Lucy. I've always been sharp like that.

LUCY: What are you talking about?

MARLENE: I don't know how to tell you this... I've had an idea there was something up for a bit now. *And* of course you do tell me little bits now and then like –

LUCY: What are you trying to say?

Pause.

MARLENE: I know where you live, right? I already knew the street but I didn't know the number till you said it the other day. I asked our Roy to go past it on his way down here, like, you know – when he was coming to visit me?

Pause.

MARLENE: It is number sixty-two, i'n' it?

LUCY nods, not knowing what to expect.

MARLENE: Elizabeth Street?

LUCY nods again.

MARLENE: That's right then.

Pause.

MARLENE: Well he's got it up for sale, love.

LUCY sits on her bed.

MARLENE: Lanyons Davies and Evans are handling it. Thirty-seven and a half thousand. Roy phoned 'em this morning. You're leaving all your carpets and curtains, but you're taking the light fitting in the front room.

There is a terrible pause.

LUCY: I'm leaving most of the furniture too.

MARLENE: What?

LUCY: Well I won't be needing it, will I?

Pause.

MARLENE: You mean you know about it?

LUCY: I've been asking him to sell it for months. He wouldn't put it on the market until he'd finished the alterations to his house. He's making his study bigger and turning it into a bedroom for me.

Pause.

MARLENE: Oh, there you are then.

LUCY: I wouldn't be at all surprised when he comes tomorrow if I don't end up going back with him.

MARLENE: So you did know about it then?

LUCY: What?

MARLENE: The sale of the house.

LUCY: Yes. But it's not *my* house remember.

MARLENE: No. (*She pauses*) Still don't want to ring him?

LUCY makes a face as she smiles and nods her head.

MARLENE: (*Incredulously*) Oh well, there you are then. (*She pushes the phone trolley to the foot of her bed. Pause. She crosses to GRACE*) How arc you. Grace? All right?

GRACE: No, I'm dreadful.

MARLENE: What's the matter? Anything I can do?

GRACE: I'd like a paper hanky.

MARLENE: (*Looking through the locker*) You've run out. Don't worry though – I got plenty.

GRACE: No. There is another box inside.

MARLENE: (*Finding a new box of Kleenex, then a letter*) Oh... look at this. (*She takes the letter out and shows it to GRACE*) You've got a letter by here.

GRACE: It's from William.

MARLENE: I guessed it was, 'cos of the airmail. (*She opens the box of tissues and hands one to GRACE*) Here you are. (*She pauses*) Shall I read it to you?

GRACE: Would you?

MARLENE: Yes, love. I don't mind at all as long as I can understand his handwriting. Just let me get my glasses. (*She gets them, then sits on the bed stool next to Grace's bed, then opens the letter. Reading with an American accent*) 'Hi there!' (*She, laughs then resumes in her own accent*) 'Got your letter last week and was glad to hear that everything is OK now with you, Grace, and that you're out of hospital at last.' (*She looks up at GRACE.*)

GRACE: Go on, go on.

MARLENE: 'I was only saying to Mim' – who's Mim?

GRACE: His wife.

MARLENE: Funny name.

GRACE: Just get on with it.

MARLENE: (*Reading*) 'I was only saying to Mim just a few days ago how worried I was getting. But I guess I can ease up a little now that you're home and doing just fine. Things have been really hectic here – sales have gone through the roof, so needless to say it's a very busy time for me right now. Things should ease up in a couple of months and only then will normality be restored.'

LUCY dozes off.

MARLENE: 'Mim and I plan a vacation then so you can be sure we'll come over and visit. Six years is a long time and we're anxious to see you both. We went to Jaynie's graduation since I wrote you last. She looked beautiful – I know if you'd seen her you'd have been proud. We took a couple of shots and I've enclosed one.' There's a photo.

She places it in GRACE's hand but GRACE doesn't look at it.

MARLENE: 'Maybe we'll bring her over with us when we come. Mim and I thought we'd hire a car and take you both up to the Lake District for a week, maybe. Wouldn't that be just great?'

GRACE's head falls sharply to the left.

MARLENE: 'Well it's something for the two of you to think about. Maybe you can let me know your thoughts when you next write. Anyhow, I'm going to sign off now. Mim has cooked a meal and the whole house is full of its wonderful smell. Lots of love and kisses, William, Mim and Jaynie.' Ahhh. (*She looks up*) I wonder what she cooked.

Silence.

MARLENE: Grace?

There is no reply. MARLENE calls her again, louder this time. LUCY wakes and moves to left of Grace's bed.

MARLENE: Grace – can you hear me?

LUCY: What's wrong?

MARLENE: I thought she was upset 'cos of the letter – but she doesn't look right to me.

LUCY: Press the buzzer.

MARLENE: You saw her. She was all right just now, wasn't she? (*She presses the buzzer*) Mind you, saying that, she've been going down hill a bit lately.

LUCY: Ever since they brought Gilbert in.

MARLENE: Well thereabouts. (*She tosses Grace's letter on to her own bed.*)

LUCY: It is only the femur with Gilbert, isn't it?

MARLENE: As far as I know. Why?

LUCY: She was worried about it. Said to me earlier on that she was afraid it was something more.

MARLENE: No – it's just the femur. Anything else I'd have found out by now.

LUCY: That's what I said. It's a shame they can't get together and see each other. But I don't suppose it's possible to get her up to his ward.

MARLENE: I don't know – but they'd never be able to bring him here. Not in the state he's in. In a couple of weeks perhaps...

LUCY: I think that might be too late then, don't you?

MARLENE: They're stopping the treatment now, did she tell you?

LUCY: Why are they doing that?

MARLENE: The body can only take so much, see, Lucy. It doesn't sound very good, does it?

LUCY: Careful! Don't let her hear you.

MARLENE: I don't think she can hear anything.

LUCY: No – she might be having one of her turns. She was telling me about them just now.

MARLENE: She looks completely gone to me.

LUCY: You mean she's –

MARLENE: No, she's still breathing. She's just out for the count, that's all.

BEV enters.

BEV: What's the problem, girls?

MARLENE: (*Grabbing her*) Come and have a look at Grace.

BEV quickly examines GRACE then takes her pulse.

MARLENE: She was all right one minute, and the next –

BEV: How long have she been like this?

MARLENE: Oh I don't know... about five minutes? It is about five minutes, Luce, i'n' it?

LUCY nods.

MARLENE: Yes, about five minutes. I buzzed you straight away – I didn't hang about.

MARLENE leans right over GRACE and lifts her eyelid.

BEV: Don't do that, Marlene.

MARLENE: You want to check her eyes. Have a look and see if they've dilated.

BEV: Why don't you go to your bed, Marlene.

Pause.

MARLENE: Are you being funny to me?

BEV: Course I'm not. I don't like the look of this.

MARLENE: I was saying to Lucy – well we were both saying – she haven't been looking right for a couple of days. (*She lifts GRACE's wrist and checks her pulse.*)

BEV: I'm going to have to insist you go back to your bed, Marlene. (*She takes MARLENE by her elbow and moves her towards her bed*) I want to have a proper look at Grace and I don't want you under my feet. (*She goes back to Grace's bed and draws the curtains around it so that neither she nor GRACE can be seen.*)

MARLENE: She *is* short with me – I don't care what she says. I can tell in a minute, I can.

LUCY: She's only doing her job.

MARLENE: Well I wasn't going to stop her. Helping her – that's all I was doing. (*She lies down.*)

LUCY: They don't like anyone interfering.

MARLENE: (*Outraged*) Bloody good job I *did* interfere. God knows how long she'd be left laying like that if I hadn't noticed and buzzed to tell 'em.

LUCY: There's no need to be offended.

MARLENE: *I'm* not offended. But it would be nice to be appreciated now and again. This sort of thing goes on all the time, you know.

LUCY: What sort of thing?

MARLENE: Patients keeping an eye on each other. Some of these nurses wouldn't know what was going on half the time if it wasn't for people like me. Oh I'm not saying I want 'em to thank me every two minutes – but like I said see, Lucy, it wouldn't do 'em any harm to realize how much they depend on patients like us.

Pause.

MARLENE: Do you know something?

LUCY: What?

MARLENE: I *am* offended.

LUCY: She only asked you to go back to your bed.

MARLENE: Yes but me and her are butties. I could take it off any other nurse.

LUCY: Well it's about time someone put you in your place.

Pause.

MARLENE: What do you mean?

LUCY: I know you're trying to be good, but you go too far sometimes.

MARLENE: (*Amazed*) I do?

LUCY: People don't always need it.

MARLENE: What?

LUCY: That little push you always want to give them. I know you mean well but –

MARLENE: If you've got something on your chest I think you'd better come out and say it.

LUCY: I don't want to quarrel with you –

MARLENE: I know what it is. (*She gets up and crosses to LUCY*) You didn't like it because I brought you the phone. That's it isn't it?

LUCY: I didn't mind you bringing the telephone at all. I *did* mind though, you asking Roy to have a look at my house. It's none of your business. It's got nothing to do with you but you still had to go and poke your nose in!

Pause.

MARLENE: (*Quietly*) You didn't know he put the house up, did you?

Pause.

LUCY: No. But I'm sure I'm right. I will be going to live with him when I leave here.

BEV appears from behind the curtains and starts to leave.

MARLENE: (*Leaping back on to her bed*) Everything all right, 'Nurse'? I don't want to interfere – I'm only concerned, that's all.

BEV: I'm going to get Sister. I'm concerned about her as well.

She exits.

LUCY: (*Confidentially*) Do you think she's taken a turn for the worst?

MARLENE: *I'm* afraid to open my mouth gone.

Pause.

LUCY: Peer in. See what she looks like.

MARLENE: You do it. I might get accused of something.

LUCY: I hope we're not going to fall out.

MARLENE: I thought I was doing you a favour.

LUCY: I'm sure you did.

MARLENE: I'll learn my lesson though.

LUCY: Do you think so?

Pause.

MARLENE: (*Laughing a little*) I can't help myself. That's me – that's how I am and there's nothing I can do about it.

LUCY: You'll get in hot water one day.

MARLENE: Oh I hope so – I haven't had a bath since I've been here.

They both laugh.

LUCY: I hope nothing is going to happen to her.

BEV returns with SISTER. They speak to no one and walk briskly to Grace's bed. MARLENE gets up and goes towards GRACE but SISTER quickly shuts the curtains to prevent her from looking in.

MARLENE: (*Turning back to LUCY*) It would have to be her!

LUCY: Oh, she's all right.

MARLENE: It must be me then, 'cos Bev won't have nothing said about her either.

LUCY: Bev won't have anything said about anyone.

MARLENE: True. She's good like that, i'n' she. I've asked her to come and visit me and Roy when I get out of here. I don't know whether she will, mind.

LUCY: Did she say she would?

MARLENE: She didn't say she wouldn't.

LUCY: Well she probably will then.

MARLENE: 'You don't live that far from us,' I said. It's only twenty minutes over the mountain in the car. She got a Fiat Panda.

LUCY: What's that?

MARLENE: You've seen the trolley that comes round with our food?

LUCY nods.

MARLENE: Well it's a bit like that with doors. Big enough for her though, no doubt. It's only her and her fella see, i'n' it? (*She moves to Lucy's bed, pulls over a chair and sits in it*) She was telling me the other night, when we were having a cup of tea together in the solarium, that things have come to a head.

LUCY: With who?

MARLENE: Her and that boy she's with. I opened a packet of McVitie's half-covered and she told me everything. Spilt the lot, she did. She's been having a hell of a life with him, I s'pose. And the best part about it, it's her house. Chuck him out, I said. I wouldn't put up with it. (*She pauses*) He's still there though from what I can gather. She haven't done anything about it yet as far as I know.

LUCY: She probably still thinks a lot of him. It's hard to let go if you still feel like that. When you love someone it's easy to let them get away with murder.

MARLENE: Well it's never easy but I know what you mean. It doesn't matter what they do behind your back – he's still your son and you'll always love him. Well am I right or am I right?

Pause.

LUCY: I wonder how Grace is.

MARLENE: I can't see Gilbert lasting long if anything happens to her, can you?

LUCY: No, they are devoted, aren't they?

MARLENE: I wonder why they never had kids.

LUCY: She told me that she was one of nature's little treasures.

MARLENE: What did she mean by that?

LUCY: I don't know, and I didn't like to ask.

Pause.

MARLENE: She should have someone with her... you know, family like, at a time like this.

LUCY: Having children is no guarantee that they'll be there for you when you need them.

MARLENE: Well I'd like to think that *my* two would be around.

LUCY: All mothers hope that. The truth is that it doesn't always happen.

MARLENE: Well let me put it this way... God help our Darren and Louise if they're not there for *me* when I need 'em.

LUCY: You stand a better chance than some. The odds go up a lot if you've got a girl.

Pause.

MARLENE: If I was seriously ill like Grace, I'd want somebody close to be with me, wouldn't you?

LUCY: Oh yes. It's not a time for being on your own.

MARLENE: Right, well that settles it then. (*She gets up, tucks the chair under Lucy's bed, gets the phone, takes it centre, plugs it in and then dials the international operator.*)

LUCY: What are you doing?

MARLENE: Get a pen and paper, will you? I want you to write this down.

LUCY: (*Getting a pad and pencil from her handbag*) What are you up to now?

MARLENE: Pass my purse out of my locker too. This is going to take a couple of fifty pences.

LUCY: (*Getting Marlene's purse and handing it to her*) Tell me what you're doing.

MARLENE: I'm running some hot water, right? And if I scald myself I scald myself.

LUCY stands next to MARLENE, pencil and paper at the ready.

MARLENE: (*Into the phone*) Hallo. Operator? Yes. Get me the code for Detroit!

Black-out. Music: The Young Doctors.

Scene Three

The following Saturday, around 11am.

When the lights come up, the curtains are around Grace's bed. Almost immediately they are opened (by BEV), to reveal JUNE lying on the bed, wearing a dressing-gown, and BEV, who, having asked some preliminary questions, is writing on the record sheet. She has a fairly large white envelope tucked under one arm. MARLENE is not in the ward. She is about to be discharged, and her weekend case is on her bed, packed. LUCY is sitting in an armchair near her bed. She looks trance-like, staring into mid air.

BEV: (*To JUNE*) ...Oh and religion – I've forgotten to ask you that.

JUNE: I don't believe.

BEV: (*Writing*) OK – atheist. Right, well you're down for an X-ray. I have sent for a porter so it shouldn't be too long. Anything you want to ask me?

JUNE shakes her head.

BEV: You know my name. I'm Bev. You remember me from last time, don't you?

JUNE: Yes.

BEV: If you need anything, just buzz. (*She replaces the records on the foot of the bed. To LUCY*) No idea where Marlene went, Lucy?

LUCY: She might have said where she was going, but I didn't take much notice.

BEV: (*Crossing to LUCY*) Oh what's the matter, love? You don't seem your usual self this morning.

LUCY: Oh I'm all right – you don't have to worry about me.

BEV: (*Remembering*) Of course... I know what it is. You're disappointed because you weren't able to go home with your son yesterday.

Pause.

BEV: Oh never mind – it was nice to see him anyway, wasn't it? And between me and you I don't think you'll be too long in here now. Maybe a week at the most.

Pause.

BEV: I see she's got her case out. Is she all packed and ready to go?

LUCY: She's been ready for about two hours.

BEV: I expect you'll miss her too, won't you? We all will.

MARLENE enters. She is wearing a shell-suit and a pair of trainers. She seems a little out of sorts.

BEV: Talk of the devil....

MARLENE: I thought I just saw Roy going into the Sister's office.

BEV: (*Crossing to MARLENE*) Yes... Doctor Fairwater wants to explain your medication.

MARLENE: So he's come to fetch me, has he?

BEV: Nice little surprise, isn't it?

MARLENE: When was all this arranged then? 'Cos the last thing I said to Roy was to book a taxi to fetch me at quarter past eleven. There was no mention of him taking a day off work yesterday.

BEV: Sister had a quick word after visiting last night.

They share a look. MARLENE knows there's more to all this. BEV doesn't offer any more information.

BEV: (*Handing her the envelope*) Look. I got this for you. It's from Roy.

MARLENE: From Roy? What is it? Is never a card?

BEV: Open it.

MARLENE: (*Opening it; moving to her bed*) What's he sending me a card for? (*She reads it, obviously touched*) 'Welcome Home'. (*She opens it to read what's inside, then looks up at LUCY and BEV.*)

LUCY: (*Sitting on her bed*) What does it say?

MARLENE: (*Fighting back a tear*) 'To Marlene. Welcome home, all the best... Roy.' (*She blows her nose*) Guess what... I got a kiss this time. Only one, but it's a start. (*She pulls herself together and smiles as she reads the front of the card again*) 'Welcome Home'. (*Trying to make light of it*) That's a laugh. I bet I can't get in the kitchen for dirty dishes.

BEV: It's like a palace there – he told me.

MARLENE sighs and unzips her case to put the card inside. BEV starts to strip Marlene's bed.

MARLENE: I've been to see Grace.

LUCY: How is she?

MARLENE: Not very good. That's what they told me, anyway – they wouldn't let me in.... I went to say so long to

Gilbert too. I wasn't going to mention nothing about Grace but he already knew all about it 'cos of the godson.

LUCY: Fancy coming all the way from America.

MARLENE: Nice of him to come in here and thank me, wasn't it? (*To LUCY*) Handsome boy, i'n' he? What he sees in that Mim though, I *don't* know. Still – one man's meat, I s'pose.... (*To BEV*) Do you think he meant it when he asked me to come and visit him in America?

BEV: I don't think so.

MARLENE: Why not?

BEV: Well it wasn't a real invitation.

MARLENE: (*Insulted*) What do you mean?

BEV: As I remember it, Marlene, you more or less invited yourself.

MARLENE: No way I did.

BEV: I was here, Marlene. I heard it all.

MARLENE: Did he or didn't he say that me and Roy can come over and stay with him any time?

BEV: What *he* said... or rather what *you* said went something like this – 'Oh... Detroit. I've heard such a lot about it. Do you know – and this might sound a bit of a coincidence – but I've always wanted to go to America? Funny i'n' it? And I was only saying to Roy the other day, I said, 'The airfare isn't a problem,' I said. But you've really got to have someone out there to go to, haven't you? Family like, you know. Or a friend. Or even a friend of a friend. Someone who'd be kind enough to meet you off the plane, put a roof over your head and show you the sights.' And to that he said – well, if ever you find yourself over there, give him a call and maybe you can all meet up. Now that's hardly an invitation to stay with him in Detroit.

MARLENE: (*Crossing her legs*) Well it's good enough for me. Anyway, it wouldn't be for a year or two.

They look straight into each other's eyes.

MARLENE: Apart from all the expense I've just had with the wedding, I've got to get out of the woods first.

Pause; the stare continues.

MARLENE: I need a little break though, so I thought I might book your caravan for a week. How does that grab you?

BEV: (*Smiling*) I don't normally let it out.

MARLENE: Now you know I'd look after it.

BEV: It's nothing grand.

MARLENE: Well that's all right 'cos I wouldn't want anything posh – not with Roy and the dog.

Pause.

MARLENE: Well, are you going to let me have it or not?

BEV: You are a human bulldozer, you know that, don't you?

MARLENE: I take it that means yes then, does it? We can talk about the details when you come and see me next week.

BEV: Oh, I'm coming next week am I?

MARLENE: Well you'll have to if you want your deposit for the van. Don't just turn up though. Let me know when you're coming so's I can make too Darren is around.

BEV: You're naughty, you are.

MARLENE: Go on, I know you like him, and he can't take his eyes off you when he's here.

BEV: I've got to get on.

MARLENE: I haven't given you my address.

BEV: I'll be back. You'll see me before you go, don't worry. You don't need to give me your address anyway – I'll get it from records.

She exits, taking the dirty sheets with her.

MARLENE: (*Sighing*) Hell of a girl, see. (*She takes down all the 'Get Well' cards which are displayed around her bed.*)

LUCY: She told me *I'll* only be about a week.

MARLENE: (*Pleased to hear it*) Oh, there you are.

LUCY: At least that's time enough for Raymond to make his arrangements.

MARLENE: (*Going to her*) Listen, love – there's nothing wrong with sheltered accommodation. Roy's mother was in it for years. Loved it, she did. Five pounds for a television licence and a warden at your beck and call, you won't know you're born.

Pause.

MARLENE: Oh I know it's not what you had in mind – but, well, I wouldn't want to leave the valleys, anyway. Between me and you you can shove Surrey up your arse. Wouldn't give you tuppence for it. Take it from me, you'll be better off down here.

Pause.

MARLENE: S'cuse me a minute. (*She goes to JUNE, still with the cards in her hand*) I hope you won't be offended or anything.

JUNE looks up from a magazine.

MARLENE: But I was wondering if you'd like to have these. (*She holds up the cards*) Only I noticed when you were in here last that you didn't have any.... To be honest with you they're not all mine. Three or four of 'em was still on the bed when I came in. (*She puts some of them on the headboard of June's bed*) Shall I put 'em up by here for you? I won't say nothing if you won't. Let 'em think you're popular, i'n' it? (*She displays more cards*) Still having problems then, are you?

JUNE: Pardon?

MARLENE: I had a shock to see you back in so soon... Same trouble I s'pose?

JUNE doesn't answer.

MARLENE: Remember Grace? She was in this bed up till last Thursday. They got her in a little room on her own now. She took a turn for the worst. It's only a matter of time. Come in by ambulance, did you?

JUNE: (*Firmly*) Yes.

MARLENE: What was the matter with Robert then? It is Robert, i'n' it? I remembered his name right – Robert? Not convenient, I take it.

JUNE: I wonder would you do something for me?

MARLENE: Yes love – anything – what do you want?

JUNE: (*Shouting*) Will you just fuck off!

MARLENE is gobsmacked. She looks over at LUCY and then back at JUNE.

MARLENE: Want me to leave you alone, do you?

JUNE doesn't answer.

MARLENE: (*Crossing to Lucy's bed*) She's a bit upset. Thought she'd seen the last of this place see, I s'pect.

Pause.

LUCY: They're going back home today. Raymond and Hazel.

MARLENE: Oh... what time are they coming?

LUCY doesn't answer.

MARLENE: They are calling in before they go?

LUCY: They said they would, but I don't think they will.

MARLENE: Why not?

LUCY: They know in their hearts what they're doing is wrong.

Pause.

LUCY: He needs the money, he said.... He'll lay low for a bit now. If I know him, he'll ring the hospital and leave a message saying that he's had to go home straight.

MARLENE: Kids – I don't know. Do they never stop breaking your heart?

LUCY: I always thought Hazel was behind it all. I used to think she was behind everything he did – but she's not. He's doing what he's doing and he is what he is without any help from her... it's all his doing, and that twists the knife that little bit more.

MARLENE: Well try and look at it this way, Luce – you don't live with 'em, you've got bugger all to thank 'em for.

Pause.

MARLENE: I reckon he'll be here, anyway. I can't see him phoning without saying so long.

BEV enters with a wheelchair.

BEV: June? You ready, love?

JUNE gets up from the bed and sits in the wheelchair.

BEV: Right then, let's get you off to X-ray. (*To LUCY*) Ooh, Lucy, there's been a phone call for you. Your son wants you to give him a ring. Sister's office is still busy or you could use the phone in there. I'm sure I saw the portable down in the day room though. OK June... fasten your seatbelts – it's going to be a bumpy ride. (*She winks at MARLENE.*)

She exits, wheeling JUNE.

Pause; MARLENE and LUCY look at each other.

MARLENE: (*Crossing to LUCY*) Well... you going to ring him?

LUCY: It's only to tell me he's not calling in.

MARLENE: What if it's not? Perhaps he's ringing to say he's not going to sell the house after all. He could have had second thoughts.

LUCY: (*Shaking her head*) If that was the case he wouldn't have left a message. He'd have been here in person.

MARLENE: So you're not going to ring him then?

LUCY: Oh, I probably will. I'd rather I didn't but I probably will.

MARLENE: Got ten pences?

LUCY: There's plenty in my purse.

MARLENE: Going to go now, are you?

LUCY: Just as well. (*She reaches for her purse on her locker.*)

MARLENE: I expect I'll be gone by the time you come back.

LUCY: Yes... well take care of yourself.

MARLENE: And you.

Pause; they hug each other. They are both genuinely touched.

MARLENE: Don't take any bloody nonsense off him now mind. If you're right and he's not coming to see you before he goes – tell him straight. Only one mother he's got and you might not always be here.... None of us are here for ever, love.

They share a look.

LUCY exits. As she goes she passes BEV coming in.

BEV: All done?

MARLENE: The doctor finished with Roy?

BEV: Not quite.

An awkward pause.

MARLENE: Is he all right? Roy?

BEV: I've just come from there and he's fine. (*She touches MARLENE's arm*) He's very positive about it and I think *you* should be too.

MARLENE: Oh I am. If anybody's going to beat this thing it's *me*.

BEV: (*Smiling*) I bet you are.

Another awkward pause.

MARLENE: When are they going to start treatment?

BEV: That's what he's telling Roy now. I think in about a fortnight.

MARLENE: (*Trying to make light of it*) I wonder should I buy one my own colour or should I go for a change. (*She touches her hair.*)

BEV: You're going to be all right.

MARLENE: I know I am.... What about you?

Pause.

BEV: I took your advice. There was one almighty row, but I told him to be gone by the time I come home from work today.

MARLENE: Good for you. You're too nice to be treated like that. You won't be sorry.

BEV: (*Making a face – not knowing if she agrees*) I don't like coming home to an empty house.

MARLENE: Nor our Darren.

They look at each other and laugh.

BEV: You don't give up, do you?

MARLENE: It wouldn't pay me to, love.... Well... I'm ready. (*She gets her suitcase from her bed.*)

BEV: Give me that.

MARLENE: There's nothing in it, hardly.

BEV: I'll take the telly then.

MARLENE: No, I'm not having it now. I told Lucy she can have a lend of it while she's still in. You can put it by there for her if you like.

BEV picks it up and puts it by Lucy's bed.

MARLENE: She said she'd give me a ring when to fetch it.

Pause.

BEV: Right then – come on – I'll walk out with you.

MARLENE: Er, no... I'm not being funny or anything but I'd rather go on my own. I walked in by myself and I want to walk out the same way... silly, i'n' it?

BEV: Not at all.

Pause.

BEV: I'll see you then.

MARLENE: When?

BEV: Soon.

MARLENE: When?

BEV: Friday.

MARLENE: You won't forget?

BEV: You won't let me. (*She turns to leave.*)

MARLENE: (*Remembering; just as BEV reaches the door*) Er...
Darren does weights on a Friday.

BEV: Thursday?

MARLENE: Great.

BEV: Half-past seven.

MARLENE: I'll have the kettle on.

They stare at each other as BEV smiles and nods.

BEV exits.

*MARLENE is alone in the ward and the place seems strangely quiet.
After a short moment, she takes her case, has one last quick look
around and walks out, quite determinedly. As soon as she is out the*

door she starts talking with all the energy and verve that is still so much part of her character.

MARLENE: (*As she goes, then off*) Hallo Emrys, how are you? Back again I see. Having another inch cut off are you?

We hear her laughter off, as Shirley Bassey sings This is My Life.

Black-out.

Curtain.

Erogenous Zones

First performed by the Sherman Theatre Company
Sherman Theatre, Cardiff, 17th September 1992.

Cast:

Lesley – Kathryn Dimery
Alison – Erica Eirian
Andrew – Geraint Morgan
Tom – Brendan Charleson
Michael – Stuart Hulse

Creative Team:

Director – Phil Clark
Designer – John Elvery
Lighting Designer – Keith Hemming
Company Stage Manager – Maggie Higgins

"*Erogenous Zones* takes a funny yet poignant look at the ups and downs of being in or out of a relationship.... Vickery's play did what it was supposed to do: entertain, enlighten and uplift."

theatre-wales.co.uk

Act One

Scene One

Lesley's kitchen, Alison's flat, Michael's flat. Friday night on a May bank holiday weekend.

The set is in three areas. There is the kitchen of a semi-detached house on a modern estate and two flats in a large Victorian house: the living-room and bedroom of a ground-floor flat and, above all this, the living-room of an upstairs flat. Left, is the front door to the building. Centre, there are four steps which lead to Michael's flat upstairs.

When the curtain rises, the stage is in darkness. Music begins (perhaps Queen singing Somebody to Love*).*

During the first eight bars or so, the cast enter and take up their positions on stage. Andrew sits on the sofa in Michael's flat reading a holiday brochure. LESLEY stands motionless in her kitchen with a suitcase in her left hand and her right hand out stretched placing a note to the front of the fridge. ALISON sits on her bed with her arms wrapped tightly around TOM's waist. He stands very close to her with his hands up in the air away from her. There has been a struggle between them and, for the moment at least, they are frozen. MICHAEL stands centre.

The music stops playing. A spot comes up on MICHAEL. A very low soft light comes up on the set. After a moment MICHAEL addresses the audience.

MICHAEL: Saturday night, bank holiday weekend. Michael Bennett. Thirty-one and unemployed. I live at 23b Pontcanna Street. That's the flat upstairs. I've lived there for three years. Before that I was with my parents. I'd still

111

be with them now if they hadn't realized my lifestyle and asked me to leave. Actually they threw me out. Oh, by the way, it's just as well to mention at this point that this (*he opens out his arms slightly*) is more or less the end of the play. Have a look round (*he turns round to look at the three areas*).

A soft light gently comes up on each area.

MICHAEL: Take everything in. (*Facing the audience*) All will be revealed in two hours, I promise. There is a plane leaving the airport in (*checking his watch*) three hours and I've got no idea at this point if I'm going to be on it or not. Oh I've got my ticket bought and paid for but... things haven't gone exactly as I'd hoped. Something's come up: I won't tell you what, you'll find out soon enough and I really don't know if he's gone without me. I've got a terrible feeling he has.

Suddenly Abba sing Take a Chance on Me. *The music begins immediately and the lights change from their previous state to flashing coloured circles which move all over the three acting areas.*

LESLEY leaves her kitchen. She takes her suitcase and her note with her. ANDREW places the brochure under the coffee table and leaves the living-room of the upstairs flat, and TOM and ALISON leave the bedroom. MICHAEL trots upstairs to his flat and switches on a small table lamp. The music stops immediately.

MICHAEL: (*To the audience*) Friday night. (*He presses the button of his stereo cassette and some very nice relaxing opera music is heard, a female voice. He lounges on the sofa. After a moment he reaches for the brochure. Reading aloud*) 'Barcelona, Spain's city of the sea. Barcelona is rich in medieval architecture especially amongst the narrow alleyways of the Gothic Quarter, where you will find the Cathedral of Santa Eulalia and the majestic courtyard of the Episcopal Palace. A short stroll from here you will find the succession of streets called *Ramblas* full of shops, cafés, restaurants and flower stalls. Down by the sea is the colourful Barceloneta quarter with its inexpensive fish restaurants and cafe bars and famous monument to Christopher Columbus. Two hundred and nineteen pounds for seven nights.'

The music stops.

MICHAEL: (*To the audience*) I could just about manage that.

There is the sound of running water.

MICHAEL: Trouble is, I don't want to go by myself. God knows I've dropped enough hints. He's either deaf or he's just not interested. I suppose he's just not interested. I say he, I mean Andy. Or Andrew as he prefers to be called. He's my flatmate. He's in the shower at the moment. Can you hear the water? (*He listens*) Hear it?

The water stops.

MICHAEL: It's stopped now. (*After a slight pause*) I lost my job about four months ago. Things were tough for a while, so to help ease things financially I took in a lodger.

ANDREW enters. He is wearing a suit and is carrying a sports bag.

MICHAEL: I'd no sooner advertised when there was a ring at the door.

ANDREW rings the doorbell. The Lights change. MICHAEL stands at the top of the stairs.

113

ANDREW: Hi. Michael Bennett?

MICHAEL: Yes.

ANDREW: Andrew Duggan. I've come about your ad.

MICHAEL: (*A little taken aback*) I only put it in this morning.

ANDREW: Have to act fast these days. Can I come in?

MICHAEL: Of course, yes. Sorry. (*He steps back to let ANDREW inside.*)

ANDREW: It hasn't gone, has it? You seemed a bit vague.

MICHAEL: No.

ANDREW: For a minute there I thought someone had beaten me to it.

MICHAEL: No, you're the first I didn't expect a reply so soon.

ANDREW: (*Looking around*) It's not bad, is it? (*He places the sports bag down on the floor just outside the bathroom.*)

MICHAEL: It's only a one-bedroom flat. You do understand that?

ANDREW: (*Moving behind the sofa*) So it's twin beds then, is it? (*He laughs.*)

MICHAEL: Er, no.

They share a look.

MICHAEL: I have the bedroom. You have the settee. It pulls out.

ANDREW: That's fair enough.

MICHAEL: If you take it I think it should only be for a month.

ANDREW looks at him.

MICHAEL: Better see how things work out... then we'll take it from there.

ANDREW: Oh it'll work out. I'm sure of it.

MICHAEL: Really.

ANDREW: Yeah. (*Turning to face him*) I've got this gut feeling, you know?

They stare. MICHAEL smiles.

ANDREW: When can I move in?

MICHAEL: We haven't talked terms.

ANDREW: What are you asking?

MICHAEL: Half the rent.

ANDREW: Which is?

MICHAEL: Sixty quid a week.

ANDREW: That's all right.

MICHAEL: And half the running costs: light, heat, telephone and so on.

ANDREW: Meals?

MICHAEL: Buy your own, cook your own.

ANDREW: (*Smiling*) Tomorrow then. I'll be around about ten. Shall we shake on it? I wouldn't like to be gazumped.

MICHAEL: I wouldn't do that.

They shake hands. Maybe ANDREW holds on a little too long.

MICHAEL: There's not a lot to see but I'd have a look round if I were you, before you finally commit yourself. (*Indicating*) Kitchen's through there, bathroom there, and that door is my room.

ANDREW: I'll have a quick browse then, but there's no problem. (*Goes off into the kitchen.*)

MICHAEL: (*To the audience*) It was only supposed to be a month. He's been here three. I like him. He's all right but – I'm still not sure I did the right thing. We get on fine but he's a bit like Jekyll and Hyde. One day he's everything a room-mate should be – more, even – and the next he's completely indifferent to me.

ANDREW begins to sing in the shower, off.

MICHAEL: If I thought he was using me I'd ask him to leave... so I'd rather not think about it. His money helps – and I don't like living by myself. Maybe I'm using him.

At this point ANDREW comes into the living area having just that minute stepped out of the shower. His hair is damp and he is wearing a large white towel around his waist. He goes to his sports bag which is next to the door and takes out a can of anti-perspirant. He shows MICHAEL what he is taking out of the bag and shakes it vigorously as he turns to go back into the bathroom – singing as he goes. 'You wanna be in my gang my gang my gang–wanna be in my gang, wo ho ho ho....'

MICHAEL: (*To the audience*) Handsome little bugger, isn't he? He's showered but he's not going out. I've just been to the fridge and he's stocked up. He's bought a chicken, garlic and breadcrumbs – and I think it's Chicken Kiev. He's even chilling a bottle of plonk.

ANDREW: (*Off, shouting*) Mike?

MICHAEL: Yeah?

ANDREW: (*Off*) Got any plans for tonight?

MICHAEL: Nothing special, no. (*To the audience*) Perhaps this would be a good time to come straight out and ask him. The worst he can say is no. (*He reads the brochure.*)

ALISON comes on, left. She is carrying a bag of groceries. She goes into her flat and puts the groceries down near the table.

MICHAEL: (*To the audience*) That's Alison. She's late tonight. (*He picks up a small toffee hammer and taps on a pipe which leads directly to the flat below.*)

ALISON hears this and taps her radiator in response then takes off her coat and throws it on the bed and goes out.

117

TOM walks into his kitchen, (the modern one) carrying a pile of exercise books and a glass of milk which he has half drunk. He sits at the table and begins to mark the books.

During the following, MICHAEL runs down the stairs and into Alison's flat.

LESLEY comes into the kitchen carrying a tray of tea things.

TOM: How did she do?

LESLEY: She picked at it. (*She sees that TOM has left a considerable amount too.*) Have you finished?

He nods.

LESLEY: I don't know why I bother. (*She takes his plate and empties it along with the other one from the tray into a pedal bin.*)

TOM: I didn't see you eat anything?

LESLEY: I ate earlier.

MICHAEL is now in Alison's flat.

MICHAEL: (*Calling*) Al?

ALISON: (*Off*) I won't be a minute. Put the kettle on.

MICHAEL: You're late tonight. (*He goes off into the kitchen.*)

ALISON: (*Off*) I had a meeting.

LESLEY is about to take TOM's glass of milk but he grabs it back almost without looking up.

TOM: I haven't finished that.

LESLEY begins to tidy things away.

TOM: It's still off then, is it?

She looks at him.

TOM: My game of squash.

LESLEY: I told you yesterday I was going to a cane party.

TOM: Sounds erotic. Why can't Rachel sit with Mother?

LESLEY: I don't think it's fair to ask. She didn't do well in her 'mocks'. Apparently she has an enormous amount of work to do if she has any hope of passing the nine. At least that's what her mother says.

TOM: Couldn't she swot here? It would only be for an hour. You should be back by then, shouldn't you?

LESLEY: (*Raising her voice*) I'm out for the evening, Tom. Joanne has laid things on. They usually do at those sort of get-togethers.

TOM: What things?

LESLEY Drinks and that.

TOM: (*Sighing*) Well, fair enough then. I was only checking. I didn't want to let Colin down unless I absolutely had to, that's all.

LESLEY: Haven't you told him you can't make it?

TOM: Yes... of course I have, yes. But I said I'd let him know if there were any last minute change of plan.

LESLEY: (*Snapping*) Ring him then! Play your bloody precious game of squash. Leave her on her own, it doesn't bother me – she's your mother not mine, remember.

LESLEY empties the washing machine during the next few lines.

ALISON enters.

ALISON: I could murder a coffee.

MICHAEL: (*Off*) You've had a visitor.

ALISON: Who?

MICHAEL comes in from the kitchen.

MICHAEL: Twice.

ALISON: Tom?

He nods.

ALISON: Did you speak to him?

MICHAEL: The second time.

ALISON: What did he say?

MICHAEL: I told him I didn't know where you were. There was no message.

LESLEY goes off out into the garden with the linen basket. Immediately she disappears TOM picks up the telephone and dials.

ALISON: (*After a slight pause*) I bet it's off. He called to cancel.

MICHAEL: He never said.

ALISON: It must be, to call twice.

MICHAEL: He could ring and do that.

ALISON: Oh no he couldn't. He rang and cried off the last time. He wouldn't know how to tell me a second time on the telephone.

ALISON's telephone rings. She answers it. MICHAEL hurries to stand next to her in order to listen in. ALISON speaks into the telephone immediately before TOM has a chance to speak.

ALISON/MICHAEL: (*Together*) Hallo, Tom.

ALISON pushes MICHAEL away slightly.

TOM: (*Quietly*) How did you know it was me?

ALISON: It wasn't difficult. Why are you whispering?

TOM: I'm in the kitchen.

ALISON: What?

TOM: (*A little louder*) Lesley's in the garden, I'm in the kitchen. I called to see you.

ALISON: Yes, I know.

TOM: (*After a slight pause*) Listen, I may have to hang up quickly. When Lesley comes back I'll...

ALISON: Yes yes, I understand. (*Slight pause*) Did you want something?

TOM: It's difficult for me on the telephone.

ALISON: Then why did you ring?

TOM: You weren't there when I called. (*Pause*) Umm... it's about tonight.

ALISON: You're not coming. (*She looks at Michael.*)

TOM: I'm afraid not, no.

ALISON: (*Determined*) I've planned a meal. Done all the shopping for it.

TOM: I just can't get out of it, Al, honest. It's just that Lesley has this wicker and cane thing and someone has to stay with Mother.

ALISON: What about the kid next door? Gretchen?

TOM: (*Correcting her*) Rachel. Lesley doesn't think we should ask her.

ALISON: (*Trying to tempt him*) Sod Lesley, I've got Chicken Kiev.

TOM: Maybe I can swing something for tomorrow.

ALISON: If you don't turn up for this meal, Tom, there's only going to be one thing swinging tomorrow and that's you.

TOM: Look, try and understand.

A pause.

ALISON: This is not on, you know.

LESLEY comes in from the garden. TOM hangs up.

MICHAEL: He's crying off?

ALISON: (*Putting her hand over the receiver*) You wouldn't believe the excuse he's got. (*Back into the telephone*) Look, Tom... Tom?

LESLEY: (*Putting the empty linen basket on top of the washing machine*) There's a yoghurt in the fridge – take it to her. Maybe she'll eat that. (*She exits.*)

ALISON: (*To MICHAEL*) He's hung up. Sixteen pounds I spent in that shop.

MICHAEL: Well you will go to Marks and Sparks, won't you, luv?

They pause.

Meanwhile, TOM gets a yoghurt from the fridge and takes it to his mother.

ALISON: There's too much of it to waste.... What are you doing tonight? Do you fancy...

MICHAEL: I'd love to eat with you, Al, but Andrew's got something planned.

ALISON: For the two of you?

MICHAEL: Well I presume so. He wouldn't go to all that trouble just for himself.

ALISON: So it's just you and him then?

MICHAEL: Yeah, I think I might have cracked it at last.

ALISON: It's odd, isn't it? You want to get into a relationship, and I think I want to get out of mine.

MICHAEL: Oh yeah, that was obvious from the way you practically put a gun to his head to get him to come over.

ALISON: That's my point I shouldn't have to do that.

MICHAEL: Who cares as long as he comes.

ALISON: I do. It never used to matter before but it does now. Why is that?

He shrugs.

ALISON: I'm getting older I suppose and some things just aren't good enough anymore. (*Slight pause*) You know something? I don't like my life very much.

MICHAEL: OK, so do something about it. Have you told Tom?

She shakes her head.

124

MICHAEL: Then tell him how you feel. Talk to him, you idiot.

ALISON: I hardly see him. That's part of the problem. Mind you, we don't talk much when we do see each other.

MICHAEL: (*Smiling*) Oh?

ALISON: He's usually in such a knot when he gets here, all he wants to do is unwind.

MICHAEL: You mean undress.

ALISON: I mean both. (*Slight pause*) I don't know what I feel for him anymore. He still hurts... and you can only be hurt by people you still care about, right?

He smiles.

ALISON: If he didn't mean anything then it wouldn't matter that we don't see each other that much... so I suppose I do still care. I'm just not sure these days how much.

MICHAEL: Enough to commit yourself to him and you would.

ALISON: (*After a slight pause*) I'm not very happy.

MICHAEL stands behind ALISON and puts his arms around her.

MICHAEL: Who is? You show me two happy people and I'll show you at least one liar.

ALISON: That's a bit cynical.

MICHAEL: It's true. It's very rare two people are happy at the same time. (*He sways her from left to right*) It oscillates.

ALISON: I don't want to be the other woman anymore.

MICHAEL: (*Letting ALISON go*) Look luv, take the knocks and enjoy the good bits for what they are.

ALISON: There aren't any good bits these days.

MICHAEL: You've got to keep bouncing back. You're getting a case of Mistressitis.

ANDREW comes out of the kitchen door. He is fully dressed now.

ALISON: So what can I take for it?

MICHAEL: A deep breath? It'll pass.

ALISON: And if it doesn't?

They look at each other. He doesn't have an answer.

ANDREW taps on the radiator above then immediately goes back into the kitchen.

MICHAEL: That's for me.

ALISON: Enjoy your meal.

MICHAEL: I will. (*He goes.*)

ALISON stares after him for a brief moment then goes off into the kitchen.

When MICHAEL gets into his flat, ANDREW obviously isn't there. MICHAEL sits down on the sofa.

LESLEY comes into her kitchen with an arm full of washing (bed sheets). She is putting them into the washing machine when the telephone rings.

LESLEY Hallo? (*Surprised*) Oh... Joanne. (*She glances towards the kitchen door*) No, nothing. I didn't expect you to ring that's all.... A what? Wicker and cane party. (*Under her breath*) I don't believe this. Er... nothing, I was talking to Tom. Well, I'm not very keen on those sorts of things. It's difficult anyway... Tom has arranged a game of squash and I know he can't get out of it.... That's all right, thanks for asking me anyway. Bye. (*She hangs up and continues to busy herself with the washing machine.*)

ANDREW comes from the kitchen.

ANDREW: Listen... I've bought a couple of things, I'm going to cook a meal.

MICHAEL: Yes, I saw the fridge.

ANDREW: Wouldn't do me a favour and help me out?

MICHAEL: Of course I will... only go easy on the garlic.

ANDREW: No – I was going to ask you to go out. A film or something.

MICHAEL: Oh... all right, yeah I don't mind.

ANDREW: Are you sure?

MICHAEL: No, what do you fancy?

ANDREW: No, I'm not going out I meant just you.

MICHAEL: Hang on. You want me to go out while you stay in and cook me a meal?

ANDREW: No – not cook you a meal. I've invited someone round. (*He sees MICHAEL's reaction.*)

ANDREW: I know perhaps I should have asked first, but I didn't think you'd mind. You don't mind, do you?

MICHAEL: You want me out of the way.

ANDREW: Only for a couple of hours.

MICHAEL: Christ, I had it all wrong.

An awkward pause.

LESLEY goes out into the garden.

ANDREW: Is it all right?

MICHAEL: No it's not all right. This is my flat and if you want to screw in it you ask me first.

ANDREW: Yeah, I know I should have, but I...

MICHAEL storms off into his bedroom, slamming the door. There is a pause. ANDREW ponders what to do. He looks at the telephone, then at Michael's bedroom door. He goes and taps on it.

ANDREW: Mike, this is stupid. (*Slight pause*) Look, I've arranged everything. It'll be embarrassing if I back out now. Please? Is it all right? (*Slight pause*) Just for tonight? (*Slight pause*) If you don't answer I'll take it that it's OK then. (*Slight pause*) Is it OK?

MICHAEL: (*Off*) Fuck off!

ANDREW: What's the problem? If it's money I can lend you a couple of quid.

MICHAEL opens his door and comes out. He is furious.

MICHAEL: Lend? You want to lend me money to get out of your way?

ANDREW: Have it then. I'll give it. Keep it. (*Reaching for his wallet*) Is a fiver all right?

MICHAEL: And you'd expect me to take it too, wouldn't you?

ANDREW: Look, make it ten. Call in and have a Chinese on the way home.

MICHAEL looks at him incredulously before slamming the door again. ANDREW stands there with his money in his hand. After a pause he puts it back into his wallet. He goes to the telephone and dials. The phone in Lesley's kitchen rings.

LESLEY and TOM rush into the kitchen: LESLEY from the garden, TOM from the house. LESLEY gets there first. TOM sits at the table and continues to mark his books.

LESLEY: Hallo?

ANDREW: It's me – Andrew.

LESLEY: I think you must have got the wrong number.

ANDREW: It is Lesley, isn't it ?

LESLEY: (*Strained*) Yes.

ANDREW: Thank God for that. Look, something's come up. Tonight's off. I'll be in touch. (*He hangs up and goes to the sofa.*)

LESLEY: (*Into the telephone*) No, this is seven-three-eight-five-two-one. That's all right. (*She hangs up.*)

TOM: Who was that?

LESLEY: It wasn't anyone. A wrong number.

TOM: (*Looking up from his books*) Male or female?

LESLEY: (*After a slight pause*) Female. Why?

TOM shrugs his shoulders and shakes his head. Slight pause.

LESLEY: Listen. Joanne rang just now. A few people have cried off and cancelled for tonight. You can play your game of squash.

TOM: Can I.

She nods. A slight pause.

TOM: Maybe I should stay in tonight.

She looks at him.

TOM: Maybe we need a night in together.

LESLEY: Don't be silly – ring Colin.

TOM: We can open a bottle of wine... talk... laugh.

He puts his arm around her and pulls her towards him.

TOM: We haven't done that for a while.

LESLEY (*Pulling away*) We can do all that anyway. You go and have your game of squash and I'll chill a bottle in the fridge.

TOM: (*After a slight pause*) Well... if you're sure.

LESLEY: Ring him, go on.

TOM: (*Returning to his books*) There's plenty of time.

LESLEY: (*Insisting*) You may as well do it now, otherwise he might have made other arrangements.

A pause. He reluctantly goes to the telephone but dials Alison's number. LESLEY sits at the table with her back to TOM for the moment.

ALISON comes out of her bedroom to answer the telephone.

TOM: Hallo, Colin?

ALISON: Who?

TOM: I can make it tonight after all.

ALISON: (*Delighted*) Tom, it's you.

TOM: That's right.

ALISON: You sound strange. Lesley's there.

TOM: Of course.

ALISON: Right, I see. So it's back on then, is it?

TOM: Lesley's arrangements have fallen through.

ALISON: Oh what a shame. What time shall I expect you?

TOM: What time did you book the court?

ALISON: Seven-thirty?

TOM: I'll see you there on the hour then.

ALISON: Bye.

TOM: See you.

They both hang up.

ALISON goes off into her kitchen.

TOM smiles rather uncomfortably at LESLEY.

TOM: I'd better go and spend half an hour with Mother. (*He leaves.*)

LESLEY stays in the kitchen.

MICHAEL comes out of his bedroom. ANDREW is sitting on the sofa reading the holiday brochure.

MICHAEL: (*To ANDREW*) I've changed my mind.

ANDREW: What?

MICHAEL: You heard.

ANDREW: Why?

MICHAEL: I'm being silly and stupid. (*A slight pause*) No don't try and tell me I'm not because I am. I will go out, but I won't take your money though.

ANDREW: I want you to.

MICHAEL: I couldn't.

ANDREW: Are you sure?

MICHAEL: Yeah.

ANDREW: OK then. Where will you go?

MICHAEL: Don't worry about it.

ANDREW: Will you see a film?

MICHAEL: Maybe.

ANDREW: Eleven o'clock should be all right.

MICHAEL: For what?

ANDREW: To come back.

MICHAEL: Eleven o'clock, right. (*Slight pause*) Thinking of going somewhere?

ANDREW looks up, not understanding what he means.

MICHAEL: The brochure.

ANDREW: Oh... no. Well yeah. Spain perhaps. I've got a week coming. Don't fancy going by myself though.

MICHAEL looks up at the audience before going to tap on the radiator.

TOM comes back into the kitchen.

ANDREW goes to the telephone and dials. MICHAEL goes downstairs to see ALISON.

TOM: (*To LESLEY*) She's dropped off. Mother's dropped off.

LESLEY: (*Sharply*) Wake her or she won't sleep tonight.

TOM: She's only cat-napping.

LESLEY: (*Insisting*) Wake her, Tom. It's not you who has to get up when she calls at three in the morning.

TOM: Let her have an hour. She's exhausted.

LESLEY: I'm the one who's exhausted. (*Shouting*) Wake her!

They stare at each other for a brief moment. TOM goes off to wake his mother. The telephone rings. LESLEY answers it.

LESLEY: Hallo?

MICHAEL: (*Going into ALISON*) Alison, you'll never guess.

ANDREW: It's Andrew.

ALISON comes out of the kitchen.

ALISON: What?

LESLEY: Don't keep ringing.

MICHAEL: I am able to eat with you.

ANDREW: Can we talk?

ALISON: You are?

LESLEY: Make it quick.

MICHAEL: Is it all right?

ANDREW: It's back on for tonight.

ALISON: Well...

LESLEY: What do you mean?

MICHAEL: It's not.

ANDREW: Change of plan – it's back on.

ALISON: Tom rang back. He's coming round.

LESLEY: (*Desperately*) No it's not – it can't be.

MICHAEL: I see.

ANDREW: (*Insisting*) Yes, I've managed to sort things out.

ALISON: What's happened with you?

LESLEY: (*Can't believe it*) I can't come.

MICHAEL: (*Making to leave*) Oh, I'll explain tomorrow.

ANDREW: Oh no, don't say that.

ALISON: Don't go – what's wrong? Isn't Andrew cooking?

LESLEY: When you called it off I told Tom he could play squash.

MICHAEL: Oh yeah, he's cooking...

ANDREW: Tell him you've changed your mind.

ALISON: Then what's the problem?

LESLEY: I can't do that.

MICHAEL: It's not for me – it's for someone else.

ANDREW: Why not?

ALISON: Oh Michael.

LESLEY: He's made his arrangements.

MICHAEL: I'll see you in the morning.

ANDREW: Can't you come anyway?

ALISON: No wait...

MICHAEL is outside her flat now.

LESLEY: I wish I could. I'm desperate to talk to you. There's Tom. (*She hangs up abruptly*) Shit!

ALISON: Shit!

ANDREW: (*Hanging up*) Shit!

MICHAEL: Shit!

Blackout.

Scene Two

The same. Later that evening.

The Lights come up in Alison's flat and in Lesley's kitchen.

ALISON is sitting at the table facing the audience. TOM is putting his squash kit in his sports bag. He is wearing a short jacket.

TOM: (*To the audience*) Tom Medford. Thirty-four. School teacher. Married, no children, dying mother. She's very demanding and has never liked Lesley – that's my wife – from the start. She's lived with us now for four years and she still hasn't changed her mind about her. Lesley suffers her for my sake and for that I'm truly grateful although I rarely show it. (*Thinking about what he has said*) In fact I've never shown it. That often happens though, doesn't it? Often when you've been married for several years almost without realizing you start hiding things... little insignificant things. Well I did anyway. You start off by lying, actually, but over a period of time you eventually progress to that. (*He has finished packing his bag and places it on the floor to his left. He sits at the table.*)

ALISON: (*To the audience*) Tom and I have known each other a long time. We were in teacher training college together. That's where we met. We were almost engaged once. We split up before we both qualified. After college I didn't see him for almost six years. I was having lunch out one Saturday and there he was... two tables away.

She looks over at TOM but he is not looking in her direction.

ALISON: I recognized him immediately. Physically he hadn't changed at all. He kept looking over once or twice. (*Smiling*) I can see his face now. It took ages for the penny to finally drop.

The Lights change: now only the two areas are lit in a tight circle. Music plays.

TOM gets up as he recognizes ALISON.

TOM: Alison?

ALISON: (*Getting up*) Hallo, Tom.

TOM: I wasn't sure. I'm sorry, I've been staring. May I?

They walk nearer to each other until they are standing a few feet apart.

TOM: How are you?

ALISON: Fine.

TOM: Teaching?

ALISON: Of course.

TOM: (*After a pause*) Do you live near or what?

ALISON: Ten minutes away by bus.

TOM: Still don't drive then?

ALISON: I never went back to it, no.

There is an awkward pause. ALISON breaks it.

ALISON: Well, it was very nice seeing you again, Tom.

TOM: Can we meet?

ALISON: I don't think so. You're married.

TOM: Just for a drink and a chat.

ALISON: Will you bring your wife?

TOM: If you'd like me to.

ALISON: I would, yes.

TOM: You will then?

She nods.

TOM: When?

ALISON: (*Immediately*) Wednesday.

TOM: Do you know the Millers Arms?

ALISON: I'll find it.

TOM: There's a quiet lounge. Say about eight?

ALISON: I'll look forward to seeing you... both.

TOM beams at her before he turns and exits, taking his sports bag with him.

The Lights change: only Alison's flat is lit.

ALISON: (*To the audience*) I was early. I didn't plan it that way, in fact I would have preferred to have been a little late. Bang on eight o'clock he walked into the lounge... alone. He fed me some cock and bull story about his wife not being able to make it. Half of me didn't really believe he would bring her and the other half was hoping he wouldn't. I made the customary effort to leave – he insisted on me staying for at least one drink and ten years later here we are. Older. Maybe a little wiser, certainly a lot more discontented, I'm speaking personally of course. We all change and ten years is a long time. I know I'm not the same person I was in those days and Tom certainly isn't. (*Slight pause*) He was never able to stay the night but we had some wonderful times together. I used to think he was mad. He was never very careful not to let things slip with Lesley. He was so irresponsible – but somehow that made it all the more exciting. He used to have me anywhere. I remember once, he had me here on this table. And just to add extra spice he insisted on having the door open. He didn't really want to be seen – it was just the thought of the possibility of being caught. (*Slight pause*) Time is said to be a healer... but sometimes I think it's got one hell of a lot to answer for. (*She goes into the kitchen.*)

The Lights come up on Michael's flat.

ANDREW comes out of the bathroom wearing shorts and a vest. He is carrying a towel.

ANDREW: (*To the audience*) Great night this is turning out to be. Michael never came back after he went downstairs to see Alison, so I never had the chance to tell him that Lesley couldn't make it after all. I'm cooking the meal anyway, so he'll probably get some when he comes in. (*He begins to do press-ups on the floor*) I thought tonight was going to be perfect, and a damned sight cheaper than the hotels we've been using. Lesley's great though. She insists on paying half. I don't like to take it but it's OK to go Dutch these days. (*Slight pause*) I've never been with a married woman before. Anyone who has will know that it's different. The apple is always sweeter when it's stolen, right boys? OK so you're out with your wives tonight – but you know what I mean, Lesley is searching for something. I don't think she's going to find it in me, but I'm having a hell of a lot of fun helping her look. (*Slight pause*) Michael's searching too. I suppose we're all after something, that's what makes the world go round. And if I can make it go a bit faster for someone (*he speeds up his press-ups*) – or a little slower (*he slows them down*) – so what? All in a day's living, right? (*The telephone rings. He stops the press-ups and wipes his neck in the towel*) And you see, I've got this theory. (*Going to the telephone*) If you can help someone, and at the same time do a good turn for yourself – why waste your time being obstructive? (*Answering the telephone*) Hallo? Lesley. Where are you? Fantastic. Well, if you're at the bus station you get a twenty-five. Ask the driver to put you off at Cathedral Road.... That's right. It's halfway down on the left. (*He remains on the telephone but continues his conversation in mime.*)

ALISON comes out of the kitchen, followed by TOM.

TOM: Yes well there it is. (*Slight pause*) You haven't been listening to me.

ALISON: I have.

TOM: I get the feeling you're not taking anything in. Somehow I don't seem to be getting through.

ALISON: Don't be silly.

TOM: You're short with me. Ratty almost. You're not about to come on, are you?

ALISON sighs and makes a face.

TOM: See what I mean?

ALISON: What?

TOM: You're aloof. Speaking's an effort. You make a fuss to get me here and all I've done since is listen to the sound of

142

my own voice. All right, you have chipped in the odd word
– given the occasional nod...

ALISON: I wish I didn't have to do that.

TOM: What?

ALISON: Make a fuss.

TOM: It was awkward for me.

ALISON: But you're here. I've known you come when it
was impossible.

TOM: (*Going to her and holding her to him*) The longer I know
you the less I understand you.

ANDREW comes off the telephone and goes off into the bathroom.

The Lights change: only Alison's flat is lit now.

ALISON: It always seems I have to fight to see you these
days.

TOM: I have to fight too.

ALISON: Lesley?

TOM: Who else?

ALISON: It's always the same.

TOM: And it always has been.

ALISON: I remember a time – not so very long ago, when I used to win a lot more than I do now.

TOM doesn't reply.

ALISON: Who comes first with you, Tom?

TOM: I've had to skip a couple of nights and you feel threatened – that's what this is, isn't it?

ALISON: I don't feel threatened at all.

TOM: What is it then?

ALISON: I think I'm scared.

TOM: Of what?

ALISON: I'm losing you and I'm scared because I think I want to. (*Annoyed with herself*) Oh why do I only think I want to?

TOM: Because you need reassuring.

ALISON: I need more than that.

TOM: Proof then? Let me prove it to you.

He kisses her; music plays: maybe If You Don't Know Me By Now. *They move into the bedroom and begin to undress each other, still kissing as they're doing it. TOM is down to his underpants and ALISON to her bra and knickers. They get into bed and pull the covers over them. After a moment ALISON's hand reaches up and switches off the light. The music stops at the same time as the lights fade to Blackout. A spotlight comes up, left.*

144

LESLEY walks into it. She is wearing a light coat.

LESLEY: (*To the audience*) I was nineteen and pregnant when I married Tom. We were married on December nineteenth and on January the eighth I miscarried. I used to think he'd have married me anyway in those days – but I don't suppose I'll ever know for sure. It was a good marriage once. Fourteen years is a long time to be with someone and I don't care who you are, people do drift in all kinds of directions. Oh, they might not have affairs... but mentally I was beginning to leave Tom months before I met Andrew. (*She exits.*)

The spotlight fades. The Lights come up in Alison's bedroom. ALISON and TOM are 'at it'. TOM's movements are energetic at first then he begins to slow down.

TOM: (*Absolutely exhausted*) Hurry up, for Christ's sake. (*He tries to continue.*)

ALISON: It's no good – get off.

He does.

TOM: What happened?

ALISON: Nothing.

TOM: That's what I mean. Why?

ALISON: (*ratty*) I don't know.

TOM: We haven't done it for ages.

ALISON: You don't have to tell me.

TOM: If you didn't feel like it you should have said.

ALISON: I did feel like it. I still feel like it.

TOM: What's the problem then?

ALISON: Why are you asking me?

TOM: (*Getting out of bed, pulling up his underpants with his back to the audience*) I gave my all.

ALISON: You're saying it's my fault?

TOM: It's your climax.

ALISON: You create it.

TOM: You're blaming me? After all that effort you're blaming me?

ALISON: It shouldn't be an effort. Yours wasn't.

TOM: No, and do you know why? It's because of the effort I put into it.

ALISON: So you're saying I didn't put anything into it?

TOM: You were blocking me – it!

LESLEY comes on, left, dressed as before. She has a small piece of paper in her hand. She is looking for Andrew's address.

ALISON: (*Shouting*) Oh I'm sorry. But it's just not possible for me to feel loved and assured and locked in ecstasy when you're shouting down my ear, 'Hurry up, for Christ's sake'.

There is a ring at Alison's door. It is LESLEY. ALISON and TOM dress very quickly. As they are doing this, LESLEY realizes she has rung the wrong bell. She presses the correct one and the lights come up in Michael's flat.

ANDREW comes out of the kitchen to answer the door.

ANDREW: I was beginning to think you were lost.

LESLEY goes into Michael's flat. The minute she disappears ALISON is at her door. There is no one there. She goes back inside.

TOM: Who was it?

ALISON: It wasn't anyone. I'm going to check the chicken.

ALISON goes into the kitchen. ANDREW and LESLEY kiss passionately.

LESLEY: (*After a slight pause*) Something smells good.

ANDREW: Chicken. I hope you haven't eaten?

LESLEY: When you said you were cooking I didn't bother.

ANDREW: So you're hungry then?

LESLEY: Starved. Nice flat.

ANDREW: I was lucky to find it.

LESLEY: (*Eyeing up the room*) Very cosy.

A slight pause.

ANDREW: Plonk? Medium, sweet or dry. I wasn't sure which you'd like so I got one of each.

LESLEY: God knows how many times we've been out for a drink and you're still not sure what wine I like.

ANDREW: It's medium, isn't it?

LESLEY: It's dry.

ANDREW: Of course. I'll just get the glasses. (*He goes off into the kitchen.*)

LESLEY slips off her coat and shoes and then sits in the armchair. TOM comes out of the bedroom.

ALISON comes out of the kitchen with two glasses and a bottle of wine. She places them on the table and pours.

TOM: So you blame me because you didn't come.

ALISON: (*Without looking at him*) Don't worry about it.

TOM: But I do.

ALISON: Why? Has it happened before?

TOM: I've never had any complaints.

ALISON: Neither have I.

TOM: Stop this!

ALISON: What?

TOM: We're playing games.

ALISON: No we're not. (*Slight pause*) It hurts, doesn't it? Knowing you didn't satisfy me?

He doesn't answer. He sits in a chair at the table.

ALISON: Ego bruised a little?

TOM: Why didn't you fake it?

ALISON: You'd have preferred that?

TOM: (*Shouting*) Yes!

ALISON: Oh poor Tom. Why should I make it easy for you? Faking it isn't going to help us.

TOM: And this is?

ALISON: I have faked it, Tom. For the last six or seven times I've faked it. (*She goes back into the kitchen. As she goes*) Tonight I just wasn't up to it.

LESLEY: I don't know why... but I imagined it to be bigger.

ANDREW comes in from the kitchen with the glasses and the wine.

ANDREW: What?

LESLEY: The flat.

ANDREW: Big enough for one. (*He pours the drinks.*)

LESLEY: What is it (*indicating the doors*) – bathroom and bedroom? (*She gets up to have a look.*)

ANDREW: That's right. I'll give you a grand tour later.

LESLEY: (*Opening the door to what she believes to be the bedroom*) Oh...

ANDREW: That's the bathroom.

She has a quick peep into the bedroom.

LESLEY: (*To ANDREW*) A double bed?

ANDREW: I'm a restless sleeper.

LESLEY: It's not a bad size really.

He hands her a glass of wine.

LESLEY: Two could be quite happy here. (*A slight pause*) You keep it very well. If I didn't know better I'd say it had a woman's touch.

ANDREW: (*Smiling*) No no... I do it all myself.

LESLEY: (*Looking at her watch*) Can I use the telephone? I said I'd ring and check that everything is all right with Rachel – my dragon sitter.

She picks up the telephone and rests it on the back of the sofa. She dials and while she is waiting for a reply she and ANDREW kiss more. She has to break away when Rachel comes on the other end.

LESLEY: Hallo Rachel? Lesley. Everything all right? (*Firmly*) Wake her up.... No, don't let her sleep.... Well talk to her – stick pins in her, anything, only keep her awake.... Yes, fine. I've just bought a beautiful wicker-basket. I won't be late. Bye. (*She hangs up.*) That woman gets more and more nocturnal by the day. (*Laughing*) Or should I say by night.

ANDREW: You told me she was on her last legs.

LESLEY: Apparently she is. They only gave her eighteen months and that was four years ago.

ANDREW: (*Getting up*) Listen. We've got a while yet. Still waiting for the chicken. (*He gets the bottle of wine and his glass*) Do you want to have another drink out here or shall we take the bottle in there? (*He bumps the bedroom door with his bottom.*)

They both laugh then rush into the bedroom.

TOM is still sitting – brooding. ALISON comes out of the kitchen.

ALISON: If anyone has the right to brood then it's me.

TOM: I'm not brooding.

ALISON: What are you then?

TOM: Hungry.

ALISON: You always are after sex.

A slight pause.

TOM: Have you really faked it before?

She smiles.

TOM: It's important to me that I satisfy you.

ALISON: Is it?

TOM: Oh come on.

ALISON: What about my other needs?

TOM: You're not satisfied?

ALISON: Seeing you once in the last fortnight? No. Having a quickie one lunch-time the month before that – is not what I'm into. And it's not what you're into either – or at least it never used to be. We're not seeing enough of each other, Tom. If you want to satisfy me –

TOM: I do love you... you know that.

ALISON: Then do something about it.

TOM: I have other responsibilities.

ALISON: (*Raising her voice*) Your mother is going to live for years, Tom. She's outwitted every doctor in BUPA already. She'll see you in your grave, take it from me.

TOM: I can't leave while she's like she is.

ALISON: What about Lesley?

TOM: (*after a slight pause*) I don't want to hurt her.

ALISON: (*Shouting*) Then what are you doing here? (*She answers herself*) Hurting me.

TOM: If I'm that much of a bastard why do you want me?

ALISON: (*Turning to look at him*) For once I can't answer you.

TOM: I thought we were happy.

ALISON: You show me two happy people and I'll show you at least one liar.

A slight pause. LESLEY comes out of the bedroom and sits on the floor at the coffee table.

ALISON: It doesn't bother me that you still care for Lesley. I can handle that as long as I believe you care more for me. (*A slight pause*) There was a time when if I'd said that you'd have put your arms around me and told me that everything was going to be all right.

TOM: You haven't answered my question.

ALISON: I've forgotten what it was.

TOM: No you haven't.

ALISON: (*Determined*) Yes I've faked it a few times, yes. (*Going to the kitchen*) And I don't just mean the sex!

ALISON goes into the kitchen. Simultaneously ALISON and ANDREW come out of their kitchens carrying two dinner plates complete with meals plus a Goldspot spray. They place the plates on the tables.

ANDREW: (*Announcing*) Chicken Kiev!

LESLEY: God, I can't eat garlic.

ALISON: Why not?

TOM: What will I tell Lesley?

ANDREW: Don't worry – like a good boy scout, I'm all prepared.

ANDREW places the Goldspot on the table. So does ALISON. LESLEY and TOM pick it up immediately.

LESLEY: What is it?

ALISON: Goldspot.

ANDREW: Guaranteed to leave your breath fresh and sparkling.

TOM: Are you sure about that?

ANDREW: He'll suspect nothing, I promise.

Both couples sit down and begin eating.

ALISON: Wine?

LESLEY: Not too much.

They pour.

ANDREW: Enough?

TOM: Fine.

There is a pause while they eat.

ALISON: Is it all right?

LESLEY: Delicious. You'll make someone a lovely wife.

ALISON: (*Snapping*) Oh very bloody funny!

TOM: Sorry, sorry, bad joke. I shouldn't have said that.

Pause.

ALISON: Why are you rushing?

LESLEY: I didn't realize I was.

ANDREW: There's no need.

ALISON: Take your time.

LESLEY: I can't stay too long.

ALISON: Why not?

TOM: A game of squash doesn't take all night.

ALISON: By the time you shower – presumably have a few drinks with Colin.

TOM: If I leave at ten... that should be all right.

She gives him a long hard look before returning to her meal.

LESLEY: Can I ask you a favour? (*Pointing to the basket beside the armchair*) That wicker waste-paper basket. Can I have it?

ANDREW: (*Amused at this request*) What?

LESLEY: Will you give it to me?

ANDREW: What do you want that for?

LESLEY: I'm supposed to be at a wicker party. It will look a bit suspicious if I don't go home with anything.

ANDREW: It's a bit awkward, actually.

LESLEY: Isn't it yours?

ANDREW: Oh yes it's mine. (*Trying to think of a good reason for not giving it to her*) Only it was a gift from an aunt. When I moved in.

LESLEY: Does she visit?

ANDREW: (*Awkwardly*) Not very often, no.

LESLEY: Well she won't miss it then, will she?

ANDREW doesn't look very happy about it.

LESLEY: Please? I'll just feel a lot more comfortable going home with something.

He looks at her for a brief moment then grabs her and pulls her down with him on to the sofa. More kissing.

TOM and ALISON have finished eating and are staring at each other.

TOM: (*After some time*) Say something.

ALISON: There's no future for us is there, Tom?

He can't answer.

ALISON: I know we both knew that in the beginning, but neither of us cared then. You're not enough for me anymore. I want something permanent. I'd like to have it with you... (*she trails off*). I'm thirty-six, I'm not unattractive. I'm still young enough to go shopping and old enough to count the change.

TOM: You're part of my life.

ALISON: A very small part.

TOM: I need you. I need to come here whenever I can.

ALISON: No, Tom. That's how it used to be. You even used to come here when you couldn't – and those were the best times. Remember? Now you come here when you think you should – and not always then.

TOM: That's not true.

ALISON: But it is. And it's not good enough anymore.

TOM: (*After a slight pause*) You're saying you want to finish it?

ALISON: I'm saying it's up to you. It's time to decide, Tom. You're going to have to make a choice.

An uncomfortable continuous sound begins, starting quite low but growing in pitch. As it reaches a peak it stops quite abruptly. Immediately it stops, LESLEY and ANDREW part physically.

ANDREW: (*Unable to believe his ears*) What?

LESLEY: I'm pregnant.

A slight pause. ANDREW gets up from the sofa.

ANDREW: What are you going to do?

LESLEY: What do you want me to do? It's yours.

ANDREW: Don't think I'm trying to get out of this but how do you know it's mine?

LESLEY: Because I haven't had sex with Tom for the past six months. We've been seeing each other for three and I think I'm two months gone.

ANDREW: Think?

LESLEY: I've missed a month. That's something I've never done.

ANDREW: It's not official then? I mean you haven't had a test or anything?

LESLEY: I'm pregnant, Andrew. You can put money on it. (*Slight pause*) I wasn't going to tell you until I'd seen a doctor... but tonight seemed the right time.

158

ANDREW: (*Frantically thinking what to do*) I'll give you money.

She looks at him.

ANDREW: You don't want to keep it? The kid, do you?

She starts to cry and empties her handbag on to the sofa in order to find her handkerchief. She has her back to ANDREW. We don't hear her cry but we see her wipe her eyes.

ANDREW: Look... um... well it's the only thing to do, isn't it?

LESLEY: (*Not really agreeing*) Of course.

ANDREW: I'll pay. I'll pay for it all.

LESLEY: I thought maybe you'd want it.

ANDREW: Keep the baby you mean?

LESLEY: I would if you would.

ANDREW: (*After a slight pause*) That would mean you'd have to leave Tom.

LESLEY: (*Raising her voice a little*) Well he'd hardly want me with someone else's child. (*A slight pause*) You don't want me to leave him?

ANDREW: (*After a slight pause*) Er... no. I don't, no. (*Slight pause*) Look, it's difficult not to appear the rat here but... we have a good thing going, right?

She doesn't answer.

ANDREW: Why spoil it all? No commitments – that's what we said, wasn't it? All right, we've got a problem but nothing that can't be sorted.

LESLEY: What am I going to tell Tom when I disappear for a few days?

ANDREW: You could be visiting someone.

LESLEY: Who?

ANDREW: (*Screaming*) Anyone! (*A pause*) Don't you know anyone?

LESLEY: Please. Stick by me on this?

ANDREW goes to LESLEY and holds her.

ANDREW: Of course I will. (*Turning her to face him*) It's our problem, right? We'll sort it out. Then everything will be as before. I promise.

LESLEY: (*After a slight pause*) I've got to ask you this. I know you've never told me, not once, ever... but now I really need to know. (*Slight pause*) Do you love me?

ANDREW: (*After a slight pause*) I don't think I've ever loved anyone.

LESLEY: (*Swallowing hard*) I see.

ANDREW: I love being with you. I love going to bed with you... (*Slight pause*) But I'm not in love with you.

LESLEY looks at him.

ANDREW: Would you rather I lied?

LESLEY: (*Shouting*) At this moment – yes! I think so.

ANDREW: It would only make you feel better until you asked me again. I wouldn't have lied twice.

LESLEY: If we lived together you might –

ANDREW: It wouldn't work.

LESLEY: You don't know till you give it a try.

ANDREW: Where would we live?

LESLEY: Here. It's big enough.

ANDREW: No.

LESLEY: If it worked out we could always look for something bigger –

ANDREW: (*Shouting*) Lesley don't!

LESLEY: When I divorce Tom I'll get half. We'll be able to buy something –

ANDREW: (*Shouting*) Don't! Don't do this to yourself. (*Pause*) Look, when we've solved our problem, when things are back to normal, I want to go on as we were. Good times – no commitments. You wanted that as much as I did. Nothing's changed.

LESLEY: Except I'm pregnant.

ANDREW: That shouldn't make any difference.

LESLEY: But it does!

ANDREW: Only until you do something about it. Oh Les... you feel vulnerable now, but it'll pass. (*Slight pause*) Shall I tell you something?

She looks at him.

ANDREW: You've never told me you love me either.

LESLEY: But I've wanted to. You haven't.

LESLEY goes off into the bedroom.

ALISON is now facing away from TOM downstage. TOM is facing front.

TOM: I'm sorry.

ALISON: I promised myself I'd never ask you to choose between Lesley and me. I always knew I'd get the short straw.

ANDREW: (*Calling into the bedroom*) Are you sure you're all right?

LESLEY: (*Off*) Yes.

ANDREW: I'd rather walk you some of the way.

LESLEY comes out of the bedroom.

LESLEY: No, I'll be fine. (*She puts on her shoes.*)

Pause.

ANDREW: I'll be in touch then?

She nods hesitantly.

ANDREW: Ring me.

LESLEY: No. You ring me.

There is another awkward moment when they are both not sure whether to kiss. It becomes obvious it's not going to happen. LESLEY turns to get her bag from the sofa. ANDREW remembers the wicker basket and bends to pick it up. By the time LESLEY turns to face him he is holding it out towards her. She almost snatches it from him. She makes to leave, taking her coat.

ANDREW: Wait. (*He picks up the Goldspot and throws it into the basket.*)

She is halfway down the stairs.

ANDREW: (*Calling after her*) See you.

LESLEY stops for a moment. She takes the Goldspot from the basket, sprays it into her mouth once or twice, then walks off.

ANDREW hovers for a moment before going off into the kitchen.

ALISON is sitting at the table. TOM is standing behind her.

TOM: I don't know what else to say. (*He puts his hands on her shoulders.*)

ALISON: (*Shrugging him away*) No don't.

TOM: Why spoil it by wanting more?

ALISON: (*Holding up the Goldspot*) Go away, Tom.

Pause. TOM takes his coat from the back of the chair then takes the Goldspot from ALISON. He leaves. Outside her flat he pauses before spraying the Goldspot into his mouth. Having done this he storms off.

ALISON is obviously upset. She gets up from the table and in a fit of frustration sweeps everything off it before tipping it up on its side. She then goes off into her bathroom.

ANDREW comes on from the kitchen with wine. He drinks it straight from the bottle. He lays down on the sofa, drinks and eventually goes to sleep.

LESLEY, still carrying the wicker basket, enters her kitchen and switches on the light. She puts down the basket and grabs a quiet moment to herself.

A door slams.

LESLEY: (*Calling*) Tom? (*She busies herself.*)

TOM comes in wearing his coat and carrying his sports bag.

LESLEY: How did it go?

He looks at her.

LESLEY: The squash?

TOM: Oh, fine. Fine. (*He starts emptying his bag on to the table.*) Mother all right?

LESLEY: She's watching *Newsnight*.

TOM: Been all right then, has she?

LESLEY: As far as I know. Joanne rang back after you left. The wicker party was all back on. I told her it was difficult for me but you know Jo. I asked Rachel to come in. (*She has a sneaky squirt of Goldspot.*)

TOM: Well that's rich. You didn't think she should be asked to sit for me.

LESLEY: It was for Joanne. You know how neurotic she is. If I hadn't gone I think that she would have had a nervous breakdown. (*She takes the clean sheets from the washing machine.*)

TOM: Mother had her Horlicks? (*He has a sneaky squirt of Goldspot.*)

LESLEY: Ten minutes ago. (*Slight pause*) Er... listen. I've been thinking. Holiday. We haven't had one since God knows when, why don't we make arrangements for Mother and go off somewhere. Spain or something.

TOM: What's brought all this on?

LESLEY: Nothing. (*Slight pause*) Well it was Jo, actually. Something she said. What do you think? Is it a good idea?

No answer.

LESLEY: I think it would be good for the two of us to get away – spend some time on our own. (*Slight pause*) Well, shall I arrange something? (*Quickly*) Why are you looking at me like that.

TOM: Is there anything wrong?

LESLEY: Wrong? (*She puts Tom's squash clothes into the washing machine.*)

TOM: It's all so out of the blue. What was it exactly Joanne said?

LESLEY: I just fancy the idea of spending some time away, that's all... fancy spending some time together. (*Slight pause*) Fancy spending some time together?

No answer.

LESLEY: Look – I know things have been a bit strained between us this last couple of months... well they haven't been right, anyway. The truth is neither of us have been very happy.

TOM: You show me two happy people and I'll show you at least one liar.

LESLEY: A short break together would do us the world of good. Clear the air. Recharge the batteries.

Pause as they look at each other.

LESLEY: What do you say?

He doesn't say anything. He half smiles and nods ever so slightly.

LESLEY: Good. Perhaps you can call into the travel agents tomorrow and see what's available.

TOM: But you can do that, can't you?

She looks very uncomfortable. She half nods. She picks up the linen basket of clean washing and is about to take it out into the garden.

TOM: Will you sit with Mother for quarter of an hour? (*He goes to the door*) I'm going to have a shower.

LESLEY: Didn't you shower at the centre?

TOM is caught briefly for an answer.

TOM: They weren't working. Can you believe that?

TOM half turns to leave. LESLEY does the same. Both sneak one last spray of Goldspot before going off.

ALISON comes out of her bathroom. She is wearing pyjamas. She is still upset. She looks at the mess in the living area before going into her bedroom. She sits on the bed.

MICHAEL enters, left. As he passes Alison's flat he stops briefly and thinks about knocking but changes his mind. He goes up into his flat. He sees ANDREW fast asleep on the sofa. He goes to him and shakes him gently. ANDREW mumbles but doesn't wake.

MICHAEL: I'm back.

ANDREW stirs again.

MICHAEL: You haven't made up your bed.

ALISON gets under her duvet.

MICHAEL: The settee – you haven't pulled it out. You haven't made your bed.

ANDREW: (*Still very groggy*) It's all right... it's all right. Don't worry about it.

MICHAEL: Shall I give you a hand?

ANDREW: I'm too tired. I can't be bothered.

Music starts to play: maybe I'm Not In Love.

At this point TOM comes into his kitchen wearing his dressing-gown. During the following he looks in a cupboard for a bottle of shampoo. He finds it and leaves.

MICHAEL: Do you want to come in with me?

No reply.

MICHAEL: Andrew?

Still no answer.

MICHAEL: You can share with me if you...

He realizes it's hopeless. He takes off his short jacket; for a moment we think he might be joining ANDREW on the sofa, but he places the jacket over him. Dejected, MICHAEL goes to his bedroom, putting the light out as he goes.

Keeping the same position on her bed, ALISON stretches up and switches off her light.

As TOM leaves the kitchen he does the same.

Black-out.

Curtain.

The same. The following morning: Saturday 9.15am.

Tom's kitchen is brightly lit giving the impression of a sunny day. There are no breakfast things about so it looks as if they've been up for some time – although no one is around. ALISON is still asleep. We see her form under the duvet in her darkened room. Her living area has some light. She didn't completely close the curtains the night before and there is a shaft of sunlight through the gap. The room is exactly as she left it, with all the remains of the dinner still on the table and floor.

Michael's flat doesn't look very tidy either. Things have not been cleared away. ANDREW is not on the sofa – the room is empty.

After a moment MICHAEL comes out of his bedroom. He has not dressed. He is wearing just a dressing-gown and underpants. He looks at the mess, then at the sofa, then back at the mess.

MICHAEL: I shouldn't have to clean up this mess. Do you have any idea what you're doing to me? (*Putting the empty bottles and glasses on a tray*) You show me no respect. But do you know what hurts most? I let you treat me like that. I let you because I'd rather be hurt by you than ignored by you. The thing is – most of the time I'm both by you. It doesn't make sense. I should leave all this for him. It's Saturday, he's got a half-day but I can't bear to look at it until twelve o'clock. (*He carries the tray off into the kitchen.*)

A small coloured light comes up in Alison's living area for the dream sequence.

TOM briskly walks on, left. He goes straight into Alison's flat and stands in the middle of the living area.

TOM: (*Calling out*) Can I come in?

ALISON stirs slightly.

TOM: I came over to talk.

ALISON: I thought we said it all.

TOM: I've changed my mind. I made a mistake. You put me on the spot and I made a mistake. I want you.

ALISON: I don't want an affair, Tom.

TOM: I know. I understand that. I haven't come back to ask you to go on as before. Things have come to a head, I realize that. Walking home last night and lying awake in bed I had time to think – about you – about me, and Lesley. For years I've dreaded the time when you'd ask me to leave Lesley. I knew if we were together long enough it would come up and sure enough last night there it was. I panicked. I panicked and made a wrong decision. I made a mistake and I'm asking you to let me put it right.

ALISON: How?

TOM: By leaving.

ALISON: Lesley?

TOM: Of course.

She smiles briefly into the pillow before looking up again.

ALISON: Tom, I've been thinking a lot too.

TOM: Come on, don't let's play games. I've put my cards on the table. Just answer me one simple question. Do you want me or not?

ALISON: (*Quickly*) Yes.

She kneels on the bed. TOM rushes into her.

ALISON: Yes yes yes yes yes!

They embrace.

ALISON: When will you leave?

TOM: A week? Next Wednesday? Today if you like.

ALISON: What about your mother?

TOM: Yes, I'll have to sort something out there, won't I?

ALISON: What exactly?

TOM: I don't know. Sheltered accommodation, something like that I suppose. I don't want you worrying about it. I'm going to take care of everything.

They kiss a few times.

TOM: Do you know what I fancy right now?

She tries to drag him down on the bed but he resists.

TOM: No... no, listen. A coffee.

ALISON: How boring.

TOM: A really strong cup of coffee.

ALISON: Well you know where the kitchen is.

TOM: I thought maybe you'd like to do it for me.

ALISON: (*Affectionately*) Did you now. You move in here all those sort of things are shared.

TOM: Really?

ALISON: Well I might let you off once in a while.

TOM: Shall I start by putting the kettle on?

Suddenly TOM picks her up in his arms.

ALISON: Tom, what are you doing? Put me down.

TOM: Since I'm not going to get the opportunity to carry you over the threshold for some time – I thought I'd carry you into the kitchen instead.

ALISON: (*Very happy*) Oh Tom, it's not going to go wrong, is it? Lesley could make it difficult for us.

TOM: I don't want you worrying about Lesley.

ALISON: What if she won't give you up?

TOM: Yes, I've thought of that and the only thing I can come up with is that you move out of this place – we'll sell the house, and the four of us will live together in a nice big semi somewhere!

She screams at the thought. TOM runs off with her into the kitchen.

Immediately they are off, ALISON screams again and her double (dressed in an identical wig and pyjamas) sits up in bed and puts her hands to her face. She gets out of bed and runs into the bathroom.

The dream sequence ends and the Lights revert to their previous state.

LESLEY comes into her kitchen. She goes to the sink and picks up a dishcloth and proceeds to wipe down the kitchen table. As she is doing this the telephone rings. She is about to answer it when it stops. She ponders for a moment, thinking it might be Andrew. Hesitantly she picks up the phone and dials. Michael's telephone rings.

He comes out of his bedroom to answer it. He is properly dressed this time.

MICHAEL: Hallo?

LESLEY: Andrew?

MICHAEL: No, he's at work. (*Slight pause*) Who is this?

She hangs up. MICHAEL thinks this strange. While tidying the sofa cushions he finds a bunch of keys. He stands and looks at them. There is a key tab on the ring with the owner's name and address. MICHAEL reads it. He makes a decision and runs off into the bedroom.

LESLEY is standing motionless at the table.

LESLEY: (*To the audience*) I worked all my married life up until a few years ago when I stopped to take care of Tom's mother. Three months of her and I was screaming to go back to work. Tom wouldn't hear of it, it would have meant putting his mother into care. But he compromised eventually and I found a part-time job. Going home one lunch time, one of the girls wanted to book a holiday and she asked if I'd come to the travel agents with her. While she was being seen to I browsed through a few brochures. Towards the back of the office there was a rather large desk.

Music: Cavatina. *The Lights change.*

LESLEY: Someone was sitting at it frantically tapping information into a desk computer. Suddenly the telephone rang and he looked up to answer it. We caught each other's eye. He was beautiful. I found myself asking all sorts of questions about a holiday I had no intention of buying. I left my number with him under the pretence of him finding me a more suitable holiday. I waited almost a fortnight for him to ring. He never did. I took to walking home that way from work hoping to bump into him. I shocked myself. I couldn't believe I was behaving in that way. Before the day I walked into his office I was a reasonably unhappy, married woman. Now I started dreaming about him. I'd never seen anyone in my life that I wanted so much. I felt I was being driven by some incredible force. I was quietly becoming obsessed. Almost without thinking I was back in his office again, telling him a pack of lies. I was ashamed of the way I was acting but my feelings were so strong I just couldn't help myself. Eventually, he did ring me at home. Tom was out at the time, thank God – and the rest is history. (*Slight pause*) I don't know to this day why I did it – why I allowed myself to do it. All I know is, from the moment he looked at me, he saw something... some... (*she searches for the word*) some corner of my soul, that until then I didn't know existed. No one I've known has ever been able to do that.

The lights change. Pause.

LESLEY: I don't know what's going to happen to me now, but all I can say is – although I made everything happen – I feel my behaviour was... is, alien to me – and that I... me – Lesley Medford – had very little or nothing to do with it.

She goes off into another part of the house.

MICHAEL comes out of his bedroom. He is wearing a rather short, distinctive blouson-type jacket. He has made up his mind to return the keys. He leaves his flat, running down the stairs and goes straight into Alison's. Just before MICHAEL has entered her flat she comes out of her bathroom, (she has dressed by this time) and in a temper tips over the chairs in the messed-up living area. MICHAEL comes in.

MICHAEL: Jesus. Did you do this?

ALISON: (*Shouting*) Who else lives here!

He tries to clear up.

ALISON: No, don't – leave it. I'll do it later.

MICHAEL: You want to talk about it?

ALISON: No!

MICHAEL: Yes you do.

ALISON: You know what it's about.

MICHAEL: Tom.

She nods.

MICHAEL: Don't tell me he didn't turn up?

ALISON: Oh he turned up.

MICHAEL: (*After a slight pause*) And?

ALISON: One thing led to another.

MICHAEL: Obviously.

ALISON: I just couldn't let it go on anymore.

MICHAEL: You finished it.

ALISON: I made him choose.

MICHAEL: Oh shit!

ALISON: I didn't think he could hurt me anymore.

MICHAEL: (*Thinking what to do*) Coffee.

ALISON: No! You think you're strong – you think you're on top – and although I've known for years he wouldn't choose me, I can't tell you how I felt when I heard him say it.

MICHAEL: Whisky.

ALISON: Shall I tell you what I need more than anything now? Company. I don't want to be on my own.

MICHAEL: Do you want him back?

ALISON: It wouldn't be the same.

MICHAEL: It might even be better.

ALISON: He wouldn't come back – it's over,

MICHAEL: Has he given back his key?

ALISON: No.

MICHAEL: Then it's not over. Believe me it's never over till they hand in their key. (*Slight pause*) I'm sure you can patch all this up.

ALISON: Part of me wants to – and part of me wants to turn away. World War Three is going on inside me and all I really want to be is a conscientious objector.

MICHAEL: What you really want is to win.

ALISON: What can I do?

MICHAEL: Fight. If I wanted someone that much, I'm damned if I'd give him up that easily. Do you really want him?

No answer.

MICHAEL: You've got to know what you want before you go after it.

ALISON: I don't want to go after anything; or anyone who doesn't want to be got!

MICHAEL: Alison, make him want it.

ALISON: If I knew how to do that he'd have chosen me and not Lesley.

MICHAEL: Lesley?

ALISON: His wife.

MICHAEL: (*Almost laughing*) It's ironic how much we have in common. That cosy little meal and bottle of plonk last night was for Andrew and a fella called Lesley.

ALISON: What?

MICHAEL: I found the keys, didn't I. There's a tag with his name and address. Against my better judgement, I thought I'd return them. Fancy a ride on the bus?

ALISON: I don't think you should.

MICHAEL: I know but I want to. I want to see the opposition.

ALISON: It's a bad idea.

MICHAEL: Haven't you ever seen Tom's wife?

ALISON: No, never.

MICHAEL: Well I've made up my mind. Are you coming?

ALISON: I think I'd better stay and clear up this lot.

MICHAEL: I'll see you later then. I won't be long. I'll call in when I get back... let you know how I got on. (*He goes.*)

ALISON: (*Calling*) Just don't come back with a black eye.

MICHAEL exits, left. ALISON starts to clear up her living area.

LESLEY comes into the kitchen followed by TOM. He has his coat on and is about to leave. LESLEY takes the clean bedding out of the washing machine and puts it on the table. Throughout the following scene she folds the bedding.

TOM: Well, shall I or shan't I?

LESLEY: (*Indifferent*) It's up to you.

TOM: I know I said for you to call in and pick some up, but it's nothing for me to do it on my way back.

LESLEY: Do it then.

TOM: Why do I feel it's not what you want?

LESLEY: It doesn't matter to me one way or the other.

TOM: Then you call in. You do it.

LESLEY: If you like.

TOM: Look, what is it with you?

LESLEY: Tom – if you want to call in and pick up some brochures, call in – if you don't – I'll do it.

TOM: Why do I get the impression you'd rather me not go there.

LESLEY: (*Impatiently*) Tom!

TOM: You've changed your mind, is that it?

LESLEY (*Deliberately*) I have not changed my mind!

TOM: Then what's the matter with you this morning? There's something wrong. You're different.

LESLEY: Don't be ridiculous. I'm just busy, that's all. Your mother hasn't given me five minutes this morning.

TOM: Oh no – you can't blame her – not this time. You're completely different to how you were last night. I wish I knew what it was.

LESLEY: I wish you'd get out of my way. Go if you're going.

TOM: Have I said something?

No reply.

TOM: If it's me – tell me.

LESLEY: (*Quietly*) It's not you.

TOM: What is it then?

Pause.

LESLEY: This holiday. A good idea but the timing is all wrong.

TOM: So you don't want to go?

She stops folding a blanket and stands with her back towards TOM.

LESLEY: I need a break, Tom... but I need a break from everything. (*Slight pause*) You included. Oh I don't mean a fortnight in Spain... just a weekend perhaps. Somewhere quiet where I can relax and be alone. I need that more than I need anything.

TOM: That's it. I knew there was something. You haven't looked at me once this morning. Look at me.

She continues to fold the blanket.

TOM: Come on look at me. (*Shouting*) Look at me!

She immediately turns and they stare at each other for a moment.

TOM: We're in trouble.

Repeat the same sound effect from Act One.

A second or two after it begins, ANDREW appears, left. He crosses and goes straight up into the flat. All the time the sound is increasing in pitch.

ANDREW: (*calling*) Mike?

He looks in at Michael's bedroom and then does the same at the kitchen door but MICHAEL is nowhere to be seen. As ANDREW shuts the kitchen door the sound effect stops.

ANDREW: Shit! (*He takes two airline tickets from his pocket and puts them on the coffee table.*)

TOM goes off leaving LESLEY alone in the kitchen.

ANDREW goes into the bathroom.

ALISON is standing behind her table. LESLEY similarly. Throughout the following scene, LESLEY folds the bedding and puts it into the linen basket, and ALISON resets her furniture and makes her bed.

LESLEY: (*To the audience*) My mother used to say that you could always tell if your husband is messing around by the number of times he changes his underwear. There was no advice to the man on the woman. (*Slight pause*) I wonder if I've left any tell-tale signs.

ALISON: (*To the audience*) My father changed his underclothes twice a week every week for his entire married life. He was married for thirty-six years – 'carried on' for twelve and my mother didn't know a thing. Maybe it's the same with Lesley.

LESLEY: The biggest give-away, I think, is 'mood'.

ALISON: I don't think I could hide mine from my partner... well, not successfully, anyway.

LESLEY: It's not easy to deceive – but like everything, the more you do it, the easier it gets.

ALISON: I'm not against a little fibbing. A little lie here and there never did anyone any harm – and sometimes saves a lot of pain.

LESLEY: I hate it. I do it because I have to – but I hate it.

ALISON: But then of course it snowballs, doesn't it? You start off by lying about where you're going – then you lie about who you were going with, then what you were doing and where you were doing – it, so pretty soon you're not only lying to your partner, you start lying to yourself as well because you actually start to believe the lie – and that's where it starts to get dangerous.

LESLEY: Everything should work out OK providing you keep it in check. The trouble is of course, once you're caught in this tender trap, common sense and reason go out of the window. And it's not as if you have any warning. No signals as to what's going to happen. There's no knock on the door so you don't have the opportunity of not answering.

ALISON: Or shutting him out. You're not even aware that he's got one foot over the threshold.

LESLEY: Just suddenly – he's there.

ALISON: Standing in the middle of this space inside you.

LESLEY: You don't know how he got there –

ALISON: And by that time you don't care –

LESLEY: Something tells you you ought to be frightened –

ALISON: Because you feel violated in some way –

LESLEY: But you feel too wonderful to feel threatened.

ALISON: And yet the whole business makes you completely and utterly vulnerable.

LESLEY: (*After a slight pause*) And that's kind of scary.

ANDREW comes out of the bathroom and dials Alison's number.

ALISON: I wonder if she knows. Some women do and ignore it. Some find out and go to pieces. I wonder what Lesley would do.

Her telephone rings.

LESLEY takes the washing out into the garden.

ALISON: (*Into the telephone*) Hallo?

ANDREW: It's Andrew. I don't suppose Michael's there?

ALISON: No, he's not.

ANDREW: Any idea where he is?

ALISON: I'm afraid not, no.

ANDREW: So you wouldn't know if he's due back or anything?

ALISON: Er... no.

ANDREW: Right. OK. Er... listen – when he does come back, if he should pop in to see you first, will you tell him I want to see him?

ALISON: Yes I will.

ANDREW: It's urgent. Bye.

ALISON: Bye.

They both hang up. ALISON goes into her kitchen. ANDREW goes into the bathroom.

MICHAEL enters, left.

MICHAEL: (*Immediately to the audience*) See? I said I wouldn't be long, didn't I? Alison's never going to believe me when I tell her. (*He makes for Alison's flat*) I'm not sure she'll want to believe it. I mean at this stage in her emotional crisis, I don't know whether it's good news or not. (*He steps into her flat*) That's better. At least it looks like a living-room now.

ALISON comes out of the kitchen carrying a plate of fried scampi.

MICHAEL: I'm glad to see that the whole business hasn't put you off your food.

ALISON: This is the first thing I've eaten all day.

MICHAEL: (*Taking a scampi*) Boy, have I got news for you!

ALISON: There's more in the kitchen if you want some. Go and help yourself.

He does. He takes his coat off and leaves it on the back of the chair before going.

ALISON: (*Calling after him*) They're in the freezer but the fat's still hot.

MICHAEL: (*Off*) This news: you'd better sit down.

ALISON: Oh by the way, Andrew just rang.

MICHAEL: (*Off*) Are you sitting?

ALISON: Did you hear what I said? He was looking for you. Wants to see you straight away.

MICHAEL puts his head around the kitchen door.

MICHAEL: Straight away?

ALISON: (*Sitting at the table*) Urgent, he said.

MICHAEL: Well he's just going to have to wait, isn't he? Good, you're sitting. Are you comfortable?

ALISON: Just get on with it.

MICHAEL: Well, bombshell number one. I found the address on the keytab with extreme difficulty. I had to change buses and when I finally got there no one had heard of the address.

ALISON: I hope you're not letting that fat burn.

MICHAEL rushes off back into the kitchen.

MICHAEL: (*Off*) I eventually found it and rang the doorbell.

Lesley's doorbell rings.

MICHAEL: (*Off*) Now I expected some sort of Adonis to be standing the other side of the door, but this piece about thirty-five answered. She didn't look anything special. Where's the master of the house, I asked myself, he's the one I've come to feast my eyes on. Anyway, I explained about the keys and she asked me in.

ALISON: Oh will you please get on with it.

LESLEY: (*Off*) No, please – it's the least I can do.

LESLEY enters her kitchen followed by MICHAEL. He is wearing a coat identical to the one he took off in Alison's flat.

LESLEY: It's kind of you to bring them all this way. You should have rung, I'd have collected them... that would have saved you the trouble.

MICHAEL: It's no trouble. (*Immediately he spots his wicker basket on the floor. He does a double-take. He gives LESLEY a sly look. He then addresses ALISON although she is in her own living area*) She insisted on giving me a drink.

LESLEY: (*Looking in a wall cupboard*) Oh damn! We're not great drinkers... it's only cooking sherry.

MICHAEL: It's all right... don't bother. (*To ALISON*) She offered me coffee instead.

LESLEY: Coffee then. You'll have a cup of coffee.

MICHAEL: (*To ALISON*) I didn't really want one but (*nodding and smiling at LESLEY*) I smiled and nodded. (*To ALISON*) So she flicked on the electric kettle.

LESLEY does so.

MICHAEL: The conversation had gone along quite nicely then all of a sudden there was this awkward pause.

An awkward pause.

MICHAEL: The two of us were frantically trying to think of something to say. She thought of something first.

LESLEY: Do you drive?

MICHAEL: Pardon?

LESLEY: A car?

MICHAEL: Er, no. Well I mean I do... but I don't have one at the moment.

LESLEY: So you came by bus then?

He nods.

LESLEY: Then I must give you the fare.

MICHAEL: There's no need.

ALISON: It's not like you to refuse money.

LESLEY: I can't let you be out of pocket.

MICHAEL: (*To ALISON*) I'm not tight. (*To LESLEY*) It wasn't very much.

LESLEY: (*Setting her purse*) One pound twenty is one pound twenty.

MICHAEL: OK. If you insist.

ALISON: Are you going to go all round the mulberry?

LESLEY hands MICHAEL the money then returns to making the coffee.

LESLEY: Sugar?

MICHAEL: One. (*Slight pause*) It's not a very good idea, you know.

LESLEY looks at him.

MICHAEL: On the keys... the address tag. I could be a thief.

ALISON: You don't look like a thief.

MICHAEL: (*To ALISON*) Shut up!

LESLEY: If you were, you'd hardly be returning them.

MICHAEL: True... but you get my point about key-tabs.

LESLEY: (*Thoughtfully*) Mmmmm.

MICHAEL: (*To ALISON*) She said something earlier that I found a bit odd. I thought it strange she should know the fare.

ALISON: Did you ask her about it?

He nods.

ALISON: What did she say?

MICHAEL: She ignored me at first.

LESLEY: Milk?

MICHAEL: Please.

She pours milk into the cups.

LESLEY: You said you found the keys near the bus station?

MICHAEL: Yes.

LESLEY: Well that's what it costs from there and back.

ALISON: There you are – a perfectly rational explanation.

ANDREW comes out of the bathroom and dials a number.

LESLEY: At least that's what I paid yesterday. I was visiting a friend and I must have lost them as she walked me there last night.

MICHAEL: (*To ALISON*) Did you hear that? Did you hear what she said? I lost them, she said. It suddenly dawns on me that the keys don't belong to her brother at all – they're hers. (*To LESLEY*) They're yours? The keys are yours?

LESLEY: Whose did you think?

MICHAEL: Your brother's, or husband's or something. It says Lesley, I thought –

LESLEY: A lot of people do.

MICHAEL: (*To ALISON*) I was gob-smacked. I mean I'd gone out all that way to get a look at this hunk that he upstairs cooked dinner for last night and I'm looking at her. She is Lesley.

ALISON: What did you do?

MICHAEL: I didn't know what to do. Luckily the telephone rang.

The telephone rings.

LESLEY: Excuse me. (*Answering the telephone*) Hallo?

ANDREW: It's Andrew. Can you talk?

LESLEY: No, well yes.

ANDREW: Are you alone?

LESLEY: No, but it's all right. Look, I'm sorry about ringing earlier. I know you don't like being rung at work but I didn't know what else to do.

ANDREW: It's all right – listen, I've looked everywhere but I haven't found them.

LESLEY: It's all right – I've got them now.

MICHAEL: (*To ALISON*) It's Andrew.

LESLEY: Someone found them near the bus station. He's brought them over. I'm giving him a cup of coffee – he's here now.

ANDREW: Listen, I've got to talk to you.

LESLEY: Now?

ANDREW: Yes – can you take the call in another room?

LESLEY: Not really, no.

ANDREW: I'll have to ring you back then.

LESLEY: I don't know. Perhaps it's better if I ring you.

ANDREW: When?

LESLEY: As soon as I can.

ANDREW: Will you be long?

LESLEY: I don't know.

ANDREW: It's important.

LESLEY: Maybe in an hour or so.

ANDREW: Sooner.

LESLEY: I'll try.

ANDREW: OK. Bye.

She replaces the receiver and looks rather uncomfortably at MICHAEL.

LESLEY: My friend.

MICHAEL nods disbelievingly.

LESLEY: I rang her at work to ask if I'd left them at her house. (*She turns away and pours coffee.*)

MICHAEL: (*To ALISON*) She's not a very good liar.

ALISON: How did you know it was Andrew on the phone?

MICHAEL: (*To ALISON*) I asked her.

LESLEY: Biscuit?

MICHAEL: Look, ummm, I'm afraid I lied to you.

LESLEY: What?

MICHAEL: I don't feel bad about it because you lied to me too.

LESLEY: I don't know what you're talking about.

MICHAEL: I didn't find the keys near the bus station. I found them down the side of a bed-settee at 23b Pontcanna Street.

LESLEY: How do you know that address?

MICHAEL: I live there.

LESLEY: (*After a slight pause*) You know Andrew?

MICHAEL: Oh yes.

LESLEY: You live there with him? I mean you're his flat-mate or something?

MICHAEL: No, he's mine. It's my flat. (*Slight pause*) You look surprised. He's never mentioned me?

LESLEY: (*In a mild state of shock*) No.

MICHAEL: No, he never mentioned you either. Was it him on the telephone just now?

She nods. He gets up.

MICHAEL: You won't mind if I don't have the coffee. I'd better get my bus back.

LESLEY: (*Suspiciously*) Why did you come here?

MICHAEL: Curiosity, I suppose. I thought you were a man.

LESLEY: What does that mean?

MICHAEL: It means I thought Andrew had dinner with a fella last night.

LESLEY: Would it have made any difference to you if he had?

He shrugs his shoulders.

LESLEY: Why hasn't he mentioned you?

MICHAEL: You'd better ask him that.

LESLEY: He definitely gave me the impression he lived alone. Why would he do that?

MICHAEL: Maybe he wanted to block any ideas you might have had about moving in.

LESLEY: (*Snapping*) I had no intention of moving in!

MICHAEL: I only said maybe. (*To ALISON*) Oooh, touched a nerve there, didn't I?

ALISON: The relationship sounds a bit scratchy to me.

MICHAEL: We'd both run out of things to say by this time.

ALISON: So what happened next?

MICHAEL: Bombshell number two. Someone shouted from the hall.

TOM: (*Off*) I'm off.

LESLEY: (*Panicking*) It's my husband.

MICHAEL: And there he was standing at the door.

ALISON: And he's heard her.

MICHAEL: No.

ALISON: Where's this bombshell?

MICHAEL: Guess – guess who is standing in the doorway?

TOM stands in the in the doorway.

TOM: Is there anything else you want while I'm out? I don't fancy making the trip... (*seeing MICHAEL*) twice.

LESLEY: I thought you'd already gone.

MICHAEL: Hallo Tom.

ALISON: (*Throwing her now empty plate on to the floor in amazement*) Tom?

LESLEY: You two know each other?

MICHAEL: Yes.

TOM: (*Jumping in*) From school.

ALISON: (*Screaming*) Bloody liar!

TOM: Michael's a lab technician in the science block – aren't you?

ALISON: (*To MICHAEL*) What did you say?

MICHAEL: (*Suiting the action to the words*) I just smiled and nodded my head slightly.

LESLEY: (*To TOM*) He found my keys. I lost them – I didn't tell you, I knew you'd make a fuss. (*To MICHAEL*) You were just going, weren't you?

MICHAEL: (*To ALISON*) She's giving me the elbow.

TOM: (*Eagerly*) Let me show you to the door.

MICHAEL: (*To ALISON*) They're both glad to see the back of me.

LESLEY: It's all right – I'll go.

TOM: (*Insisting*) No no – I'll do it.

MICHAEL: (*To ALISON*) They're each hoping to have a private word.

He looks at each of them with a smile. They are standing either side of him.

MICHAEL: Right then. I'm off. (*He goes.*)

TOM and LESLEY give each other a rather strained smile. TOM follows MICHAEL. LESLEY stays but tries to listen from the doorway.

MICHAEL: (*Off*) He kept me at the door for a while making chit chat about this and that. It was pretty obvious he wanted to ask me if I'd mentioned you in any way, but he just couldn't come out with it. I couldn't bear to see him suffer any longer so I put him out of his misery and told him he had nothing to worry about on that score. Relieved as he undoubtedly was to hear it, I had the distinct impression he didn't absolutely believe me.

LESLEY dials a number.

MICHAEL comes in from the kitchen (minus the coat), carrying a plate of scampi.

MICHAEL: It's a fact of life though, isn't it? You tell someone something you know they want to hear, and the minute you tell them they suspect it.

ALISON: Scampi all right?

MICHAEL: I think so, yes.

ALISON and MICHAEL both go off into the kitchen.

The telephone rings in Michael's flat. ANDREW comes out to answer it.

ANDREW: (*Into the phone*) Yes.

LESLEY: I can't stay long, Tom's only gone to the door.

ANDREW: Oh... right... well... I've just arranged a week off. (*Pause*) Are you still there?

LESLEY: Yes.

ANDREW: Oh good. As from today I've got a week off.

LESLEY: (*After a slight pause*) Yes. (*Slight pause*) You're going to have to hurry, Tom will be back any minute.

ANDREW: I've bought two tickets – airplane tickets. I've bought two seats on a night flight to Spain. Flying ten o'clock tonight. Coming?

LESLEY: You're not serious?

ANDREW: Don't you fancy it?

LESLEY: (*Raising her voice*) How the hell can I go to Spain in my situation?

ANDREW: Don't shout – Tom, remember? Look, it's because of your situation I think we should go.

LESLEY: Andrew, I haven't the faintest idea what's going to happen to me. I still don't know what I'm going to do – but I know one thing: as much as I'd love to hop on a plane and fly off with you somewhere, I just can't do it with the way things are.

ANDREW: Don't you understand? There'll never be a better time to go than now.

LESLEY: If I go away with you tonight, what will happen this time next week when the holiday is over? What will I have to come back to?

ANDREW: Your situation won't be any worse than it is now.

LESLEY: At least for the time being I've still got a roof over my head.

ANDREW: Yeah but for how long? A week away will give you time to think.

LESLEY: It'll give me a lot more time than I want.

ANDREW: Look at it this way – it's only a matter of time before the shit hits the fan. The only choice you've got is the way in which it hits it.

LESLEY: What happened to the weekend away seeing a friend?

ANDREW: Sounded good in theory but I don't think you'll be able to pull it off.

LESLEY: (*After a slight pause*) Are you suggesting I keep the baby?

ANDREW: No, no, I'm not suggesting anything... well I am. I'm suggesting you leave everything for a week. Put it on ice. If you're going to face the music anyway, give yourself time to decide how you want to dance – know what I mean? The way I see it is like this: you can either confront Tom with it now and face the consequences, or you can have a wonderful week away with me and face him when you come back. Now putting myself in your position I know what I'd choose. Better to have something out of it. What do you say?

LESLEY: (*After a slight pause*) I think you're a bastard – that's what I say.

ANDREW: What?

LESLEY: There are men in your position who would be offering someone like me a hell of a lot more than a week in Spain.

ANDREW: But I can't go for a fortnight.

LESLEY: Look, I think I'd better stay and sort out my problem, because that's what it is – my problem.

ANDREW: I've bought two tickets.

LESLEY: Take your flat-mate.

ANDREW: (*After a slight pause*) Who?

LESLEY: The one who shares with you.

ANDREW: How do you know about Michael?

LESLEY: Ask him when you see him.

ANDREW: You've made up your mind then?

She doesn't answer.

ANDREW: You're sure you won't come?

Slight pause.

LESLEY (*Quietly*) Positive.

Slight pause.

ANDREW: Right, well I'll see you when I get back then.

LESLEY: No, no I don't think so.

ANDREW: Oh come on, don't be like that.

LESLEY: You're incredible, you know that? (*She hangs up.*)

ANDREW goes off into Michael's bedroom.

LESLEY moves into the middle of the kitchen. She looks pensive. TOM comes to the kitchen doorway looking the same way. They suddenly become aware of each other. A pause. Tom's mother calls from another room. TOM leaves immediately. LESLEY sits at the table with her head in her hands.

MICHAEL and ALISON come out of the kitchen and go into the bedroom area.

MICHAEL: Well, did that little tit-bit make you feel any better?

ALISON: It doesn't really change anything.

MICHAEL: Of course it does – at least you know his wife is messing about as well. That could change a lot.

ALISON: The fact that I know isn't going to change anything. It's if and when Tom knows that's when things might alter.

MICHAEL: Tom doesn't know. It was obvious from his reaction. (*He has an idea*) Hey, maybe I should tell him. I bet if he knew he'd be back here like a shot. (*He makes up his mind*) Yes, I'm going to tell him.

ALISON: Oh no you're not.

MICHAEL: What's the matter with you – it's what you want, isn't it?

ALISON: It may be what I want, but I don't want him just because he doesn't want his wife. I want him because he wants me. Promise you won't do anything to interfere – you won't ring him without me knowing or tell him anything, will you?

MICHAEL: What does it matter why he wants you as long as he does?

ALISON: It matters to me. Promise?

MICHAEL: It's the old pride again, isn't it? Rearing its ugly head.

ALISON: I want him, more than I want anything – but on my terms.

MICHAEL: Compromise.

ALISON: I've been compromising for years.

MICHAEL: So what's one more time?

She shakes her head.

MICHAEL: So you mean to tell me if Tom walked in here now and told you he wanted to make it up to you because he found out that his wife was having an affair, you'd show him the door?

ALISON: Yes.

MICHAEL: What more would you want from him?

ALISON: If he came here today I'd want him to tell me that he'd made a terrible mistake last night and that he'd changed his mind, not because of his wife's affair but because he wanted to live the rest of his life with me. Don't you see? It's important to me that the reason be the right one. You do see, don' t you?

MICHAEL: (*After a slight pause*) Of course I do. It's just that if I were in your shoes, I'd rather have him for the wrong reason than not have him at all.

ALISON: If he doesn't come back – and I don't think he will – it means he's been having me for the wrong reason.

MICHAEL: No it doesn't. But if that's true then it shouldn't hurt,

ALISON: It doesn't. It just stings a bit.

MICHAEL: That's what having a relationship with an attached person is all about, stings and knocks. I've told you what to do about those. If I were you I'd go out. Don't stay in licking your wounds – see a movie.

ALISON: What if he came while I was out?

MICHAEL: Then he'll call again. Better for you if you were out. You don't want to let him think you're sitting here waiting for him.

ALISON: Come with me then. I haven't been to the cinema for years.

MICHAEL: Really? They're talking now, did you know?

They both laugh.

ALISON: Oh very funny.

MICHAEL: Yeah, of course I'll come.

ALISON smiles. Slight pause.

ALISON: You'd better go up and see Andrew. Maybe he'd like you to see a film tonight.

MICHAEL: I wish. I'll see you later – about sevenish.

MICHAEL goes to his flat. ALISON goes into the bathroom. As MICHAEL goes into his flat, ANDREW comes out of the bedroom carrying a small suitcase, some clothes and a pair of trainers. He is extremely happy. As he flings the open case down on the sofa he sings rather forcefully, 'We're all going on a summer holiday...'

MICHAEL: What's going on?

ANDREW: I've been looking for you – where have you been?

MICHAEL: I had to go out. What's with the suitcase?

ANDREW: It's all right, I'm not leaving. Well, not for good, anyway.

MICHAEL: Where are you going?

ANDREW: (*Stopping packing to recite*) 'Where the sea is as clear as a crystal spring – and the sun is as...' I've forgotten the rest. I'm off to Spain for a week.

MICHAEL: Spain?

ANDREW: Eight days and seven glorious nights. It was a spur of the moment thing. There I was at work handing out plane tickets for every conceivable destination and I suddenly thought: I've had enough of this, when is it going to be my turn? Now, I thought. Now is my turn. I got on the blower and booked two night flights.

MICHAEL: Two?

ANDREW: A holiday's no fun on your own. Got a passport?

MICHAEL: What?

ANDREW: A passport?

MICHAEL: (*After a slight pause*) Er – yes.

ANDREW: Up to date?

MICHAEL: I think so.

ANDREW: Fancy coming then?

MICHAEL: Are you serious? I mean it's not some kind of a joke, is it?

ANDREW: (*Pointing*) Tickets are over there. Fly ten o'clock tonight.

MICHAEL goes and picks the tickets up.

ANDREW: They're only a hundred and twenty quid apiece, flight only. No problem with accommodation – I'll sort something out when we get there.

MICHAEL: (*Smiling*) I don't believe it.

ANDREW: Well, what do you say – yes or no?

MICHAEL: Why me?

ANDREW: You're my flat-mate, aren't you? You're the one who's been dropping hints right, left and centre about a holiday.

MICHAEL: Wouldn't you prefer to take Lesley?

ANDREW: (*After a slight pause*) Ah yes. I meant to ask you about her.

MICHAEL: I found the keys, didn't I. Curiosity got the better of me and I took them back to her. Why are you asking me and not her? Or have you asked her?

ANDREW: Look – things are a bit... (*he shakes his hand*) with Lesley at the moment. I need to get away. Need some distance between us. It's a bit messy up here right now. (*He touches his head*) All sixes and sevens, you know? (*Slight pause*) So, what's it to be?

MICHAEL: So you bought the tickets for me and you?

ANDREW: Of course I did. (*Slight pause*) You don't think I'd put out that kind of money if I wasn't pretty sure you'd be interested. Hey, listen – if the money's a problem –

MICHAEL: No. no – there's no problem. I've got the money, I've got a cheque. (*He goes to get his cheque book*) A hundred and twenty pounds you said?

ANDREW: You don't have to give it to me now.

MICHAEL: Yes, I want to. (*He writes a cheque.*)

ALISON comes out of bathroom wearing a dressing-gown. She sits in the bedroom and begins to put on make-up.

ANDREW: I'm not going to take all these. Just a couple of shorts and a few tops should be all right. How are you off for tops? There's one or two here if you want them.

MICHAEL: We're travelling light then, are we?

ANDREW: I'm not even going to take a suitcase – just throw a couple of things in my bag. (*He quickly puts the suitcase just inside the bedroom door.*)

MICHAEL: Currency?

ANDREW: Exchange at the airport.

MICHAEL: How much are you taking?

ANDREW: (*Packing some things into his sports bag*) Two hundred should be enough. Have you got that?

MICHAEL: Yeah, I've got that. (*He hands ANDREW a cheque*) I don't believe this. One minute I'm going to the cinema with Alison and the next I'm off to Spain with you.

ANDREW: And who said life sucks, eh?

MICHAEL: I didn't.

ANDREW: Your passport – better get it – make sure it's in order.

MICHAEL: I can't remember when I saw it last.

MICHAEL goes into the bedroom. ANDREW goes into the bathroom.

TOM comes into his kitchen. He stands near the table where LESLEY is sitting. There is a pause.

TOM: Les?

LESLEY looks up.

LESLEY: I thought you'd gone out.

TOM: What is it? What's wrong.

LESLEY: Just leave me alone. I'll talk when I'm ready.

TOM: So there is something. (*Slight pause*) It's me, isn't it?

LESLEY: I don't blame you any more than I blame myself.

TOM: We can fix anything if we both want to.

LESLEY: I don't know that I want to.

TOM: Is it that serious?

She doesn't answer.

TOM: Talk to me. I'm sure we can sort this out.

LESLEY: Not this time, Tom, It's a mess, it's all a mess. (*She quietly begins to cry.*)

He touches her.

LESLEY: No don't....

TOM: Look, whatever it is we can get through it. We can get through anything... you and me.

LESLEY: Even when there's someone else involved.

There is a pause.

TOM: (*thinking she means his affair*) Look –

LESLEY: Don't say anything. Just sit down.

He does.

LESLEY: Are you happy, Tom? I don't mean reasonably content – I mean happy.

TOM: I thought I was.

LESLEY: I don't think you've been happy for a long time.

TOM: What is happy, anyway? It's a mood. Something you experience every now and then if you're lucky. It doesn't last – it's not meant to. Happy is something you might be for short periods of time. (*Slight pause*) And there have been times, haven't there?

LESLEY: But not for a long time.

MICHAEL comes out of his bedroom and begins to look for his passport in a cupboard.

MICHAEL: I thought it might have been in my bedside cabinet.

LESLEY: Look, Tom – this isn't easy for me.

TOM: I don't want to lose you.

LESLEY: There's someone else!

TOM: All right but –

LESLEY: I've been seeing someone else.

TOM looks at her in total disbelief. He almost slumps down into a chair.

LESLEY: (*Finally*) Aren't you going to say something? Who is he? Is it serious? How long has it been going on?

A pause.

LESLEY: (*Exploding*) Ask something, for Christ sake!

Another pause.

LESLEY: He's younger than me – he's twenty-nine. (*Slight pause*) His name's Andrew – I've been seeing him for three months. (*Slight pause*) He's asked me to go away with him.

TOM still doesn't say anything.

LESLEY: Did you hear what I said? (*Slight pause*) He wants me to go away with him.

TOM: (*After a slight pause*) Do you (*trying to find the right word*) care for him? I mean – do you, love him?

LESLEY: I don't know. (*Slight pause; correcting herself*) Yes. Yes, I do.

TOM looks wrecked.

LESLEY: Tom, I know I'm hurting you but I'm hurting too.

TOM: (*A very large sigh*) Oh Jesus.

LESLEY: And I'm pregnant.

MICHAEL finds his passport.

MICHAEL: (*shouting*) Got it!

TOM: (*Screaming*) You what?

TOM raises his arm and hits LESLEY in the face very forcefully. LESLEY is pushed towards the kitchen worktops. TOM goes after her and takes her by the arm and shakes her – this is followed by another blow across the face. LESLEY loses her balance and falls to the floor, dragging him with her. This whole scene is done in slow motion and the slaps are obviously mimed. There should be some sort of sound and lighting effect here too – anything to help create the dramatic effect of the scene. The sound effect stops and immediately both LESLEY and TOM freeze, They keep their position for some time.

MICHAEL: (*Examining his passport*) Shit! What's the date today?

ANDREW comes out of the bathroom.

ANDREW: The thirtieth.

MICHAEL: When do we get back?

ANDREW: The sixth.

MICHAEL: That's when it's up. The sixth of June.

ANDREW: Well you're all right then.

MICHAEL: Are you sure? They will allow me back on the expiry date? Knowing my luck they'll detain me or something.

ANDREW: It is not out of date until the seventh.

MICHAEL: What if there are delays? What if there's a twelve hour delay and we're not back until the seventh?

ANDREW: Then it's their fault not yours.

MICHAEL: I wouldn't like to explain that to the Spaniards.

ANDREW: If it bothers you that much go and get another one. You'll just catch the Post Office. Mind you, it'll cost you over a tenner.

MICHAEL: (*After a slight pause*) I don't know what to do. What do you think?

ANDREW: I think – I know it's all right.

MICHAEL: I won't then. If you think it's all right then I won't bother.

ANDREW: You don't have to take my word for it.

MICHAEL: What resort are we going to?

ANDREW: I haven't booked accommodation remember? We can stay anywhere we like.

MICHAEL: Fancy a trip to Barcelona?

ANDREW: I don't know that I'll have time for trips. I want to spend most of the time on the beach working on a really good tan. Not easy in seven days. Now pack.

They look at each other and share something. They are both smiling. MICHAEL goes off into his bedroom. ANDREW sits on the sofa and browses through the holiday brochure.

TOM and LESLEY have kept the same position. Pause.

TOM: What do you want?

LESLEY To be left alone.

TOM: (*Screaming*) It can't be my baby, can it?

LESLEY: (*Screaming*) No! (*Slight pause. Quieter*) What do you want me to do?

TOM: I don't think I want you to leave.

LESLEY: You don't think?

TOM: (*Raising his voice*) I'm mixed up too. (*Slight pause*) It's time we need. All right, not together – alone, and not with him.

LESLEY: (*Shouting*) You've never hit me before. Is that why you did it? Because I was stupid enough to get pregnant?

He doesn't answer her.

TOM: (*Trying to calm her*) You said you loved him. Does he feel the same? Yes, of course he does or he wouldn't be wanting to take you away.

LESLEY: (*Turning away; crying*) You're wrong... you're wrong. Oh he wants me to go away with him, yes... (*She laughs ironically*) But only for a week! He's not offering me a future.

TOM: (*Stunned*) And you are considering this?

LESLEY: You've forgotten what it's like, haven't you?

TOM: What?

LESLEY: At the beginning. There were times when there was nothing we wouldn't give up just to sleep together.

TOM: (*Shouting*) I offered you everything.

LESLEY: If I wasn't pregnant would you have offered to marry me?

TOM: Probably. Oh not when we did perhaps but the following year maybe. (*Raising his voice*) The fact of the matter is when did you get pregnant, I offered you a damn sight more than seven days away somewhere.

LESLEY: (*Shouting*) Would you be more sympathetic if he offered to take me on a three week cruise?

There is a slight pause. Mother calls from another room. They stare at each other. TOM leaves the kitchen. After he has gone she grimaces. There is another sound effect similar to the one heard earlier. She puts her hand down to her lower stomach. She gives the impression she is more uncomfortable than she is in pain. She realizes something and hurriedly leaves the kitchen. Immediately she disappears the sound stops.

MICHAEL comes out of the bedroom.

MICHAEL: What time are we leaving?

ANDREW: We've got a while yet. Say we leave here about eight. That'll give us time to get the bus to the airport.

MICHAEL: I'm going down to tell Alison.

He taps her radiator. She doesn't hear it, she is still in her bedroom.

MICHAEL: I promised I'd go to the cinema.

ANDREW: Oh well if you'd rather...

MICHAEL: You've got to be joking.

ANDREW: Take a key. I'm going to shower.

MICHAEL leaves the flat to go to Alison's. ANDREW goes off into the bathroom.

MICHAEL: Oh good – you haven't got ready yet.

ALISON: No but –

MICHAEL: Look, Al... I'm going to have to let you down. But when I tell you why you won't mind. I'm off to Spain. With Andrew.

ALISON: That's wonderful.

MICHAEL: When he said he wanted me and it was urgent he wasn't kidding. We're flying at ten o'clock tonight. Can you believe it?

ALISON: (*After a slight pause*) I don't want to put ice on the fire, but are you sure you've got it right? I'm thinking about last night and the meal and everything.

MICHAEL: I've paid for my ticket. I've almost finished packing.

ALISON: I just don't want you to get hurt.

MICHAEL: It's all arranged. We're going to have a terrific time. (*Slight pause*) I know it's a rotten time for you but I'd like you to be pleased for me.

ALISON: I am.

MICHAEL: What will you do – will you go anyway? To the cinema?

ALISON: No, I'm not going to bother. I think I'll stay in and commit suicide.

He looks at her.

ALISON: Don't worry, I was only kidding.

MICHAEL: I should think so. He's not worth it. Nobody is.

ALISON: Not even Andrew?

MICHAEL: Certainly not Andrew. (*Slight pause*) You haven't heard from Tom then? He hasn't rung or anything?

She shakes her head.

MICHAEL: Do you want to make a bet with me?

She doesn't answer.

MICHAEL: I'll bet you lunch a week tomorrow – that's the day we get back – that Tom will be here talking to you before Monday.

ALISON: (*Smiling*) I think you're going to owe me. Stay here. (*She goes into the kitchen.*)

MICHAEL sits on the bed.

LESLEY comes into her kitchen wearing a bathrobe.

LESLEY: (*To the audience*) When Tom left I thought he went in to see his mother, but he went out. He'll be back, of course. I don't know when but he'll be back. He's got to, hasn't he? (*Slight pause*) With me it's different. I could walk out of the door now and never come back. (*A pause as she looks at the audience. Then she goes to the telephone and dials.*)

The phone in Michael's flat rings. ANDREW comes out of the bathroom to answer it. He is wearing a bathrobe.

ANDREW: Hallo?

LESLEY: It's me.

ANDREW: Hi. Everything all right?

LESLEY: No. Well, yes. (*Pause*) I mean, the balloon's gone up here.

ANDREW: You've told him then.

LESLEY: Yes.

ANDREW: How did it go?

LESLEY: Not as l expected. It's a bit of a mess – but that's not why I called. I was just calling to let you know that everything is all right with me. I mean... I mean I'm not pregnant.

ANDREW: You're not? That's wonderful. (*Slight pause*) Isn't it wonderful?

LESLEY: Yes, it's wonderful. It's tremendous.

ANDREW: What happened?

LESLEY: Well I had my period, that's what happened.

ANDREW: What – just like that?

LESLEY: No, not just like that. Tom got violent and threw me around a bit. It must have done something.

ANDREW: Well it's good news anyway, eh?

Pause.

LESLEY: I've been thinking. Things are obviously different now – a different situation to a couple of hours ago...

ALISON comes out of the kitchen with a bottle of wine and two glasses.

ALISON: (*entering; overlapping LESLEY*) I bought this for after dinner last night but he didn't stay long enough to drink it. Open it.

LESLEY and ANDREW continue their conversation in mime.

MICHAEL: Why don't you keep it? He will be back.

ALISON: Open it. (*A thought strikes her*) Hey, you haven't been doing anything, have you?

He doesn't understand.

ALISON: You sound so sure about Tom. You promised you wouldn't interfere.

MICHAEL: I haven't. I swear I haven't.

She believes him.

ALISON: I just know he won't leave it as it is.

He opens the wine and pours it. She hands him a glass.

ALISON: (*Toasting*) To you and Andy.

MICHAEL raises his glass and they drink.

LESLEY and ANDREW finish their conversation and hang up. Beaming with success, ANDREW shakes his fists and rushes off back into the bathroom.

ALISON: Where are you staying?

MICHAEL: He's going to arrange accommodation when we get there. Maybe for the first night we'll bunk down on the beach somewhere.

ALISON: Romantic.

MICHAEL smiles wickedly.

ALISON: Tom and I never once went away.

MICHAEL: Did he used to go away with Lesley?

ALISON: Nowhere really far. She wouldn't fly and couldn't go by coach because of her ankles.

He looks at her.

ALISON: They swell apparently.

They both laugh. Slight pause.

MICHAEL: Has there been anyone else besides Tom?

ALISON: I had a fling before I met him but nothing serious. I've never really seen myself without him.

TOM enters, left. He walks straight into Alison's flat. ALISON continues talking. Both she and MICHAEL are unaware for a moment that he has entered the room.

ALISON: That's going to be the difficult part. Work is the answer – it usually is.

MICHAEL sees TOM over ALISON's shoulder. He lets her continue.

ALISON: Of course it would have to happen now when I've got a bloody week off. (*Looking at MICHAEL*) What's the matter?

MICHAEL: I think you owe me lunch.

She doesn't understand. MICHAEL nods for her to turn around. She does and sees TOM.

TOM: Celebrating?

ALISON:
MICHAEL: } (*together*) { Yes, actually.
Not really.

ALISON: I didn't hear you come in.

TOM: Obviously.

There is an awkward pause.

MICHAEL: Well, I'm off.

ALISON: You don't have to go.

MICHAEL: Yes I do. I've still got a couple of things to pack.

TOM: Off somewhere?

MICHAEL nods and smiles.

MICHAEL: (*To ALISON*) I won't call in before I leave.

ALISON: Have a great time.

They give each other a peck.

ALISON: Take the bottle with you. Finish it upstairs.

MICHAEL takes the bottle and leaves.

Slight pause.

TOM: (*Indicating her make-up*) Going out?

ALISON: Yes. (*Slight pause*) Actually. (*She takes her wine and goes into the bedroom to finish her make-up and to dress.*)

Left alone, TOM looks rather uncomfortable. After a moment he sits.

Michael enters his flat.

MICHAEL: (*At the bathroom door, calling*) Are you going to be long in there?

ALISON: (*Replying to TOM*) As long as it takes.

TOM: I've got to talk to you.

MICHAEL: What about?

ANDREW comes out of the bathroom.

ANDREW: Something's come up.

MICHAEL: What is it? (*Slight pause*) It's still on, is it?

ANDREW: No, it isn't.

MICHAEL: You're joking. You've got to he joking.

ANDREW: Sorry.

MICHAEL: Has the flight been cancelled or what?

ANDREW: No, no it's still on – but not for us. Well not for you. (*Slight pause*) Change of plan. You've got to understand.

MICHAEL: I've got a feeling I'm not going to.

224

ANDREW: I can't go with you.

MICHAEL: Oh, so you're not going either?

ANDREW: Yes – I am – but not with you.

MICHAEL: Look, what's going on? One minute I'm going to Spain with you – I nip downstairs for a quarter of an hour – and when I get back it's all off.

ANDREW: I've had a phone call. I can't go into it – it's personal.

MICHAEL: (*Shouting*) Personal? I don't care how personal it is – you owe me an explanation.

ANDREW: Things have happened.

MICHAEL: Is it Lesley? (*Slight pause*) It is, isn't it?

ANDREW: I wish it didn't have to happen.

MICHAEL: What do you think I am?

ANDREW: Don't get all worked up.

MICHAEL: You really piss me off, you know that? I mean apart from anything else, you didn't even ask. No decent explanation – no apology, just 'something's come up and it's off'. Without any conscience – nothing.

ANDREW: (*Sitting on the sofa*) I do feel terrible about it.

MICHAEL: You don't feel terrible about anything – you never have.

ANDREW: It's only a holiday.

MICHAEL: It might only have been a holiday to you, but it was going to mean a hell of a lot more to me.

ANDREW: Well it wouldn't have been. Better to be disappointed here than there.

MICHAEL: You can cut that crap with me. I haven't got you wrong.

ANDREW: I'm not what you think. I'm straight, Michael.

MICHAEL: How can you say that?

ANDREW: I know what I am.

MICHAEL: You said earlier you needed to get away from Lesley. Needed distance between you. You said you were all confused – or words to that effect.

ANDREW: I was – I still am about my feelings towards her. But I know exactly where I am with you.

MICHAEL: Why are you doing this? OK, so you'd rather go to Spain with Lesley than with me – but that doesn't make you straight.

ANDREW: Going with you doesn't make me gay.

MICHAEL: You slept with me. You've –

ANDREW: One toss doesn't make a salad, pal.

MICHAEL: No, and it doesn't make a lot of sense, either. You can't have done the things we've done and be straight.

ANDREW: You think I did those things for me?

MICHAEL: You're not trying to say it was all one-sided?

ANDREW: I got nothing out of it.

MICHAEL: You bastard.

ANDREW: I knew what you were when I came here.

MICHAEL: Too right you did. You knew exactly what I was and you used it.

ANDREW: Yeah, I won't deny that.

MICHAEL: That's big of you.

ANDREW: That night we spent together, it should never have happened.

MICHAEL: But it did. And I'll tell you something else. You knew it would happen at some point.

ANDREW: I did it for you.

MICHAEL: Why didn't it seem like that at the time?

ANDREW: What would be the point of doing it if I let you suspect it wasn't mutual?

MICHAEL: What would be the point of doing it and let me think it was? Friends don't do it, Andrew. And room-mates don't either.

ANDREW: It doesn't matter what you say.

MICHAEL: Are you running away? Because if you are you're not going to hide in Spain. You're not running away from me – you're running away from yourself – don't you see that? I don't want to corrupt you – God forbid – but I've never forced you to do anything – and straight people don't do what we did voluntarily.

ANDREW: I know why I did it.

MICHAEL: Then tell me. OK – let's assume that what I've just said is wrong. Do you really think that much of me as a friend?

ANDREW: (*After a slight pause*) Yes.

MICHAEL: Then why do you treat me like shit?

ANDREW: I don't. You only think I do because of how you feel about me.

MICHAEL: Oh, so you are aware of how I feel?

He doesn't answer.

MICHAEL: Answer me this. If you know how I feel about you, how can you bring someone to my flat? How can you ask me to go to Spain and then tell me you want my ticket for someone else? (*Slight pause*) I know what I feel for you isn't mutual – but I can live with that. (*Slight pause*) I don't know why you slept with me that night – but I suspect deep down you do. (*Slight pause*) I might not be that special person for you, Andrew, but at some point, somewhere, you're going to meet him – and when you do – Pow! And it won't matter if you're with Lesley or any other female. You see I think we've all got this... door – inside somewhere. We all have one. Male and female. We don't know where it is but we guard it with our lives, because through that door is the secret to everything. Happiness, misery – (*Slight pause*) It's all very personal and we're very careful as to who we let in. For me – it's you. Now you might not want to go through this door, but it doesn't matter. The fact that I've given you the key gives you great power and makes you stronger than me. And because you're stronger and because you want it... I know I'm going to end up giving you my ticket.

ANDREW: I have to go with Lesley.

MICHAEL: Won't you even mind about what I've said?

ANDREW: A lot of what you say makes sense – but you don't understand me. Sometimes I don't understand myself. I don't want to be gay.

MICHAEL: Do you think I did?

ANDREW: I only ever did it the once.

MICHAEL: Maybe, but I bet you've thought about it more than that.

ANDREW: I think more about women.

MICHAEL: Then why did it happen with us?

ANDREW: Because I knew you wanted it to.

MICHAEL: And?

ANDREW: And I probably wanted to find out what it was like.

MICHAEL: And what was it like?

ANDREW: I don't want to talk about it.

MICHAEL: Can't handle it?

ANDREW: I can handle anything. (*Slight pause*) For me it was a sort of experiment, that's all. It didn't mean anything. I can't help it if it did to you.

MICHAEL: Oh please, don't spare my feelings.

ANDREW: What?

MICHAEL: No, go on.

ANDREW: Nothing more to say. End of story.

MICHAEL: You haven't told me what it was like for you.

ANDREW doesn't answer him.

MICHAEL: Shall I tell you what I think? I think it was great for you – wonderful for you. I think it was so bloody tremendous it frightened the shit out of you.

ANDREW: (*Shouting*) No!

MICHAEL: Then be honest and tell me differently.

ANDREW: You're pushing me and I don't want you to.

MICHAEL: I only want you to look at yourself.

ANDREW: You're confusing me.

MICHAEL: No, I'm trying to sort you out.

ANDREW: Just leave me alone, will you? I curse the day I came here.

MICHAEL: Why? Because I helped you find yourself?

ANDREW: You haven't helped me find fuck all.

MICHAEL: I've made you ask yourself a lot of questions though, haven't I? You shouldn't blame me if you don't like the answers.

ANDREW: (*Angrily*) You're talking shit! You can say what you like but you're talking shit!

MICHAEL: Then what's the problem? If I am why are you so sensitive about it?

ANDREW: (*snapping*) OK, OK. So you're saying I'm bisexual. I did it once and you're saying I'm bisexual. I can still have a preference.

MICHAEL: Of course you can. But can you always stick by it?

ANDREW: Why shouldn't I?

MICHAEL: Why didn't you? (*Slight pause*) Look, I'm not the baddie here. I'm not trying to turn you into something you're not. I'm trying to help you.

ANDREW: And get your seat back to Spain.

MICHAEL: I haven't given it to you yet to want it back.

ANDREW: But you will – you said you would.

MICHAEL: Do you have any idea what you're asking me to do?

ANDREW: It's nothing to what you're asking me.

MICHAEL: I only want you to be yourself.

ANDREW: You want me to be the same as you and I can't – I can't. I hate gays.

MICHAEL: You don't hate me.

ANDREW (*Shouting*) I think you're disgusting.

MICHAEL: Don't say that.

ANDREW: You're no better than vermin.

MICHAEL: Andrew!

ANDREW: Scum of the earth. I'd hate to be like you. I hate everything about you.

They are both shouting now.

MICHAEL: Everything?

ANDREW: You want to know what I felt that night? Sick. I felt sick!

MICHAEL: Then why didn't I see any? Why did you go through with it? Why did you carry on right to the end?

ANDREW: (*After a pause*) You're repulsive – you know that?

He spits in MICHAEL's face. A pause. MICHAEL turns and runs out of the flat. He goes downstairs and races out of the building. ANDREW, after a slight pause, sits on the sofa. His position should match exactly that as at the beginning of the play. He stays there, motionless.

A slight pause.

ALISON: Are you still there, Tom?

TOM: Yes, I'm still here.

ALISON: (*Coming out from the bedroom fastening her earrings*) Twice in two days – what have I done to deserve it?

TOM: I didn't want to leave things the way they were.

ALISON: You've more to say?

TOM: Well, we didn't really say much last night.

ALISON: You said enough.

TOM: (*After a slight pause*) I'm not sure why I'm here.

ALISON: Oh that's great.

TOM: (*After a slight pause*) We've known each other a long time, Al. I think we both deserve better than we gave each other last night.

ALISON: So that's why you've come – to wrap it all up properly.

TOM: Last night I didn't want to wrap it up at all.

ALISON: And today?

Slight pause.

TOM: Lesley's pregnant.

Slight pause.

ALISON: Suddenly everything falls into place.

TOM: It's not mine.

ALISON: Now I'm confused again.

TOM: It's pretty straightforward: she's having a baby by someone else.

ALISON: Tom. Tom, last night... last night I was wrong. I went about things the wrong way. I know I said I didn't want part of you, and on that score nothing has changed... but I said those things because I wanted all of you. I still do.

TOM: Things aren't the same anymore.

ALISON: Of course they're not – and if we're sensible we can turn them to our own advantage.

TOM: There's still no future for us, Al.

ALISON: Don't say that. (*Slight pause*) You're hurt and upset. Let's leave it for now. I don't want to do that but maybe it's what's best for you. We don't have to make any decisions at the moment.

TOM: I do.

ALISON: Yes of course you do as far as Lesley is concerned, but I was talking about us. I understand she's hurt you, Tom, but I'm still here for you. You can't blame me but I'm glad she's done this to you.

TOM: She hasn't done anything to me I wouldn't have done to her in a similar situation. If men carried kids I've no doubt I'd have been pregnant the first three months you and I were together.

ALISON: (*Annoyed*) It was the same for me. Why didn't it happen to me? I'll tell you why – because I didn't want to be pregnant.

TOM: You're telling me Lesley did?

ALISON: No woman need get pregnant today, Tom. If she's having a baby nine times out of ten it's because he wants it – and if she wants it she obviously doesn't want you – and if she says she does you can stake your life it's because the other guy doesn't want her.

TOM: No – that's not it at all. She's confused.

ALISON: Aren't we all.

TOM: She doesn't know what she wants at the moment and neither do I.

ALISON: Let's have a cooling-off period.

TOM: We've been cool for a long time.

ALISON: (*Shouting*) No!

TOM: It's true last night in bed –

ALISON: That was nothing. I didn't mean what I said. I wasn't being honest with you. I lied. (*Getting upset*) Don't leave, Tom.

Pause.

ALISON: Please. (*Quietly*) Don't leave me?

TOM: It would have been easier if this had happened... I don't know... five, six years ago. Everything was different then. (*Slight pause*) You're right – it's not the same anymore. We're not the same.

ALISON: (*Shouting*) I haven't changed.

TOM: (*Shouting*) All right I have.

ALISON: You can't still want her?

TOM: I don't know what I want... only what I don't want.

ALISON: (*After a slight pause*) Me.

TOM: I can't turn to you because Lesley doesn't want me. That wouldn't be fair.

ALISON: Oh we're talking fair now, are we?

TOM: I couldn't do that to you.

ALISON: What you're doing to me is worse. If I'm prepared to take you on those terms then that's my decision. And I will, Tom. I'll take it anyway you want to dish it out only don't go.

TOM: (*Upset*) It's dead, Al – and if now's the time to be completely honest with each other we both know it and have known it for a long time. It's dead.

ALISON: (*Shouting*) No!

TOM: We just haven't got round to burying it, that's all.

ALISON: (*Dragging him into the bedroom*) Come to bed.

TOM: Don't do this.

ALISON: Come on – it'll be much better than the last time, I promise. (*She tries to undress him.*)

TOM: What are you doing?

ALISON: I want you.

TOM: You're making a fool of yourself.

ALISON: It's not for the first time – anyway it doesn't matter anymore.

TOM: (*Struggling with her*) I don't want you to do this.

ALISON: (*Trying to pull him down on to the bed*) Oh but you do, Tom. It's going to be wonderful. You're going to be wonderful.

They freeze. Their position too should now match that of the start of the play.

To complete the picture, LESLEY comes into her kitchen with her suitcase and the note she is about to leave on the door of the fridge. Immediately she is in position, MICHAEL comes on, left. He enters to the same music that is used in the opening scene. He takes up his position, centre.

MICHAEL: (*To the audience*) Well... this is it. The point at which you all came in. (*Pause*) I wish I knew yesterday what I know today. (*He smiles almost to himself.*) How many of us have said that in our time? (*Slight pause*) It's easy, isn't it – to be wise after the event – though some people never learn. Would I have done anything differently? I doubt it. I've always been a sucker for a pretty face. And there's a hell of a lot of us out there. (*Slight pause*) Anyway – I need to know – not just if I'm going to Spain – but how I'm going to come out of all this. (*Slight pause*) Time to find out.

MICHAEL goes up to his flat.

ANDREW comes out of the bedroom carrying a suitcase.

MICHAEL: I was afraid you'd gone.

ANDREW: Just going.

238

LESLEY puts the message on the door of the fridge and leaves her kitchen.

MICHAEL: I thought you weren't taking a suitcase.

ANDREW: I'm not. I'm dropping it off somewhere.

MICHAEL: What do you mean?

ANDREW: Well, I can't come back here, can I?

MICHAEL Of course you can.

ANDREW: I'm going away with Lesley.

MICHAEL: I don't care. Well I do care, of course I care, but it doesn't matter. (*Slight pause*) Look, let's forget about it. It didn't happen, OK? Nothing ever happened between us – it's gone – forgotten.

ANDREW: (*After a slight pause*) No. I want out.

Pause.

MICHAEL: Where will you go?

ANDREW: I don't know.

MICHAEL: Stay until you do then.

ANDREW: You'll never let me go.

MICHAEL: Stay until you've sorted yourself out.

ANDREW: (*Shaking his head*) No.

MICHAEL: What do you want from me? My airticket? You've got it. You want me to accept you're going away with Lesley – I accept. If you want me to be here when you get back, I'll be here.

ANDREW: It's useless, you've got to see that.

MICHAEL: I'll beg. I beg you please, don't do this to me.

ANDREW: (*Turning on him*) Hey, listen pal, I'm not doing anything. You're doing all this yourself.

MICHAEL: Jesus Christ, can't anyone reach you?

ANDREW: At last you've got the message.

MICHAEL: All right, don't stay until you've sorted yourself out – stay until I've sorted myself out. (*Backing away and sitting in the armchair*) Do something for me – do something for someone else for a change.

ANDREW: Coming back here isn't going to help either of us.

MICHAEL: It'll give me something to hang on to.

ANDREW: Exactly.

MICHAEL: Only long enough to get on top of all this. Please–I honestly don't know what I might end up doing.

ANDREW: (*Raising his voice*) Don't you threaten me.

MICHAEL: I'm not.

ANDREW: (*Shouting*) You're trying to tell me that you might do something stupid.

MICHAEL: All right then, yes I might.

ANDREW: Do it then! You want to stick your head in the oven – there's fifty pence for the gas. (*He throws him a coin.*)

MICHAEL: (*Getting up*) You flatter yourself. You think I'd top myself for you? Nobody would do that. You're a bastard – and once a bastard always a bastard.

ANDREW: Time to go.

MICHAEL: Yeah, go on, piss off!

ANDREW gets his sports bag and suitcase.

ANDREW: Just one piece of advice before I go –

MICHAEL: I don't want it.

ANDREW: Next time you advertise for someone to share – don't choose anyone so good looking. (*He throws the key down on the coffee table*) Well, that's it. I hope I'm not leaving anything behind.

MICHAEL: Only me. Bastard!

TOM frees himself from ALISON's grip and goes into the living area.

MICHAEL: (*Taking the suitcase from ANDREW and throwing it down the stairs*) I hope there's a ten hour delay! (*He does the same with the sports bag*) I hope it pisses down the entire week!

TOM lakes his key out of his pocket and leaves it on Alison's table.

ANDREW leaves.

MICHAEL: (*Calling after him*) I hope your balls fester and drop off!

Suddenly ANDREW trips and falls down three or four steps.

MICHAEL goes into his flat. He is obviously very upset. He stands in the centre of his living-room with his back to the audience.

TOM comes out of Alison's flat as ANDREW falls down the stairs. TOM goes to him and helps him to his feet.

TOM: Are you all right?

ANDREW: (*In extreme pain*) He fucking wished this on me.

TOM: (*Picking up Andrew's luggage*) Can you get up?

ANDREW: I've twisted my ankle.

TOM: Try walking.

ANDREW gets up.

TOM: Here, wait a minute.

He takes ANDREW's arm and puts it around his neck.

TOM: That's right, put your weight on me, I'll give you a hand to the door. Are you going far? Can give you a lift?

ANDREW: The airport.

TOM: (*After a slight pause*) Well, come on – I've got nothing better to do.

TOM and ANDREW freeze at the end of the corridor.

Music begins to play: Freddie Mercury and Monserrat Caballe singing Barcelona.

ALISON remains motionless on the bed but MICHAEL is upset and begins to move: in a small area at first but the more frustrated he becomes the larger the area he covers. His emotion and frustration build to a peak and eventually they break out and he starts to throw the cushions off the sofa and across the room. When he has done that he tips the sofa over on to its front. Then he starts in another part of the room slowly but surely wrecking it. He sweeps everything off the top of the unit and does it with such force he ends up on the floor in a heap of rubbish. He is still upset and is crying but very subtly his sobs turn, to laughter – the laughter goes on until he's quite hysterical. He is holding something in his hand. He rolls over on to his back and thrusts his hand into the air in time to Freddie Mercury singing Barcelona. *He has the plane tickets. He carries on laughing as –*

– the curtain falls.

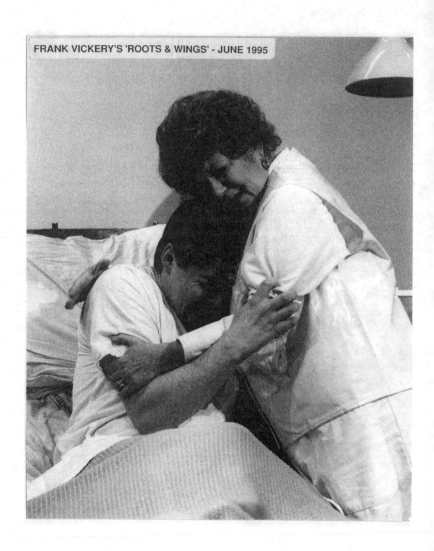

FRANK VICKERY'S 'ROOTS & WINGS' - JUNE 1995

Roots and Wings

First performed at the Sherman Theatre, Cardiff
18th May 1995.

Cast:

Ruby	–	Menna Trussler
Griff	–	Hubert Rees
Nurse	–	Lorraine Cole
Nigel	–	Greg Ashton
Vernon	–	Dafydd Hywel
Rita	–	Sue Roderick

Creative Team:

Director	–	Phil Clark
Designer	–	Jonathan Fensom
Lighting Designer	–	Keith Hemming

NOTE

Act One Scene One
can be performed separately, as a one-act play entitled
The Drag Factor.

"A great night-out... Frank Vickery is one of the few
playwrights to write such effective dramatic comedy for the
stage."

South Wales Evening Post

Act One

Scene One

A hospital corridor. 9.45am.

We are facing across the corridor, centre of the back wall is a set of red double doors with windows in them. There are two chairs set against the wall, left. Two chairs similarly and a coffee machine, right.

Traffic noise is heard as the audience are entering the auditorium.

The house lights fade to Black-out. As they do so, one almighty crash – the sound of a car crash – is heard.

The stage lights come up to reveal RUBY sitting in a chair, left of the double doors. She is a woman in her mid-fifties. She is wearing the uniform – including hat – of a lollipop lady and has a shopping bag on her lap. She has a large, white, man's handkerchief in her hand and is wiping her nose with it. After a moment, she gets up and peers through the door windows into the room beyond.

NURSE: (*Female; off*) I'll be back in a minute.

RUBY steps back to let the NURSE through.

The NURSE comes out of the room carrying a tray covered by a white cloth. She has a stethoscope around her neck.

RUBY: Is that it? Can I go in now, nurse?

NURSE: (*Shaking her head*) Not quite finished with him yet. Shouldn't be long though.

RUBY: How is he this morning?

247

NURSE: A definite improvement on yesterday, I'd say. (*She pauses slightly before making to leave, left.*)

RUBY: I heard somebody laughing just now. Was it him?

NURSE: No, it was me. He's a real live wire once he starts, isn't he?

RUBY: He's a hell of a boy, mind. He's never happy unless he's making people laugh. (*She laughs.*)

NURSE: (*Making to leave; smiling*) Ten minutes and he'll be ready for his audience.

RUBY puts her hand on the NURSE's arm, stopping her.

RUBY: Good God, he's told you as well, has he?

NURSE: (*After a slight pause*) Sorry?

RUBY: Still, that's the best way to be, I suppose. I keep telling Griff – that's my husband – 'Things will be much better now it's all out in the open,' I said. Griff's only just recently found out. I've known for a while. It's not so bad when you've had time to get used to the idea, see, is it?

NURSE: (*Suddenly realizing what RUBY is on about; smiling*) I won't be long. (*She exits.*)

RUBY sits in the chair again, but after a second or two she gets up and looks into the room. She can't really see anything so she sits back down. She takes a box of Roses chocolates out of her bag, opens it and eats one. She then takes off her hat and puts it in her bag along with the chocolates. There is a pause as she eats the chocolate.

GRIFF enters, right. He's about the same age as RUBY. He is carrying his tucker-bag and is wearing his British Rail guard's uniform complete with hat.

RUBY looks up and sees GRIFF.

RUBY: (*Going to him*) Oh, Griff. You came after all.

GRIFF: Let's get this straight now before we start, right? I'm not here for him – it's you I've come for.

RUBY: You can't say that, he's our son.

GRIFF: He might be your son, Ruby, but I told him Saturday night, if he was going to carry on with all that nonsense he'd be no son of mine. I meant it then and, accident or no, I mean it now.

RUBY takes GRIFF by the arm and walks him downstage, centre.

RUBY: Don't talk like that – he might never come out of here!

GRIFF: (*Moving away, right, and putting his bag down on the chair next to the coffee machine*) He's got a couple of bruises, a few cracked ribs and a knock on the head. He's not going to die, Ruby. He'll be out of this place by Thursday – you take it from me.

RUBY: (*Following GRIFF*) Look here, he didn't come round hardly at all yesterday and he talked a heap of nonsense for a solid hour last night.

GRIFF: He's been talking nonsense since last Saturday if you ask me.

RUBY: Well, I'm not asking you and I told you this morning, you've got to forget last Saturday.

GRIFF: I can't.

RUBY: Well, you're going to have to. (*She moves back to her seat and sits*) For the moment, anyway.

GRIFF: (*Sitting on the chair next to his tucker-bag*) It's like a bloody nightmare. It keeps playing over and over in my head.

RUBY: (*After a slight pause*) There's no way he'll be out of here this weekend. He's in no fit state. (*She has a thought*) They're hiding something from me, I'm sure they are.

GRIFF: Don't talk rubbish.

RUBY: They are, I can tell.

GRIFF: They've said he's all right.

RUBY: Yes, but they're not going to tell me everything, are they? And you must be concerned as well if the truth be known, because nothing could shift you to come here with me this morning. (*She has an idea and stands*) They haven't sent for you, have they?

GRIFF: No.

RUBY: You're sure now, they haven't rung to tell you to come here?

GRIFF: Would I be dressed for the afternoon shift if there was anything wrong?

RUBY: Tell me why you changed your mind, then?

GRIFF: For you. I changed it for you. I didn't want you to be on your own.

There is a slight pause. RUBY sits back down on her usual chair. GRIFF takes a pack of sandwiches out of his bag.

RUBY: There was a policeman here earlier on confirming there was no other car involved.

GRIFF: So what do they think happened then?

RUBY: They know what happened. He fell asleep at the wheel.

GRIFF: Well, I'm not surprised – should never be doing two jobs. I don't know anyone who can survive on three or four hours' sleep.

RUBY: Yes, he has been overdoing it lately.

GRIFF: Sandwich?

RUBY: Good God no, I can't eat now.

There is a pause. RUBY takes another chocolate out of the box and eats it.

GRIFF: (*Eating*) When he gets out of here later this week, perhaps you'd better suggest him giving up that 'club' lark.

RUBY: I'm not suggesting anything of the sort.

GRIFF: Well, he's hardly going to listen to me, is he?

RUBY: You still don't get it, do you. Griff? (*She moves to him*) If Nigel decides, for whatever reason, to give up one of his jobs, it'll be his day job in Cardiff. It's not going to be the clubs, you can bet your bottom dollar on that.

GRIFF: Let's be honest, you wouldn't talk him out of doing it anyway, even if he would listen to you.

RUBY: No, you're right, I wouldn't.

GRIFF: God, you must be as proud as he is.

RUBY: (*Moving down, left*) I am. He's damned good at what he does and you thought so too till you realized who he was.

GRIFF: (*Looking at RUBY*) Yes, and I'll never forgive him for that – or you either.

RUBY: How else was the boy supposed to tell you?

GRIFF: Like any other normal person.

RUBY: Griff, if he was normal, there'd be nothing to tell.

GRIFF: Am I that bad a father that I couldn't be told in the privacy of my own house?

RUBY: In a word, yes. (*She moves to him again*) You know what you were like when he wouldn't take that job with you on the railway.

GRIFF: That was a damned good job, that was.

RUBY: (*Moving away again*) Yes, I know it was – but he didn't want it, did he?

GRIFF: No, he'd rather go and dress windows in Cardiff. The writing was on the wall then. (*A slight pause*) Well, that's it as far as the club is concerned, you know that, don't you?

RUBY: What do you mean?

GRIFF: We're home every Saturday night from now on because there's no way I can show my face in that place again.

RUBY: Oh, for goodness' sake, what's the matter with you? Anyone would think he robbed a bank or committed murder or something.

GRIFF: I think I could cope better with it if he had.

RUBY: (*Firmly*) Look, it's not easy for me either, mind.

GRIFF: I was the butt of all the jokes in work yesterday.

RUBY: Well, that's just great that is, isn't it? There they all were in the club Saturday night –

GRIFF: Exactly –

RUBY: All your work mates having a marvellous time, and today? Today they mock him for it.

GRIFF: It's not Nigel they were mocking, it was me.

RUBY: You think you're by yourself in that? I get it too, mind. I get in supermarkets, in bus queues, I get it when I stop the cars to let the children cross the road. It happened last week. The car window was down and I heard this woman say, (*she turns and faces down left*) 'See her by there? Her son dresses up in women's clothes.' I waited till the last child was across the road and I stood right in front of her car. 'My son is a female impersonator,' I said. 'He does it for a living. I heard your husband does it for kicks!' With that, the car revved up and if I hadn't jumped to one side... (*she jumps left*) I swear to God, she'd have run me over.

There is a pause. RUBY sits back down on her chair.

GRIFF: It sounds like everyone knew except me.

RUBY: He tried to tell you.

GRIFF: So when did you find out?

GRIFF stares at RUBY during the following.

RUBY: Well, I was in his bedroom one day, dusting – and he'd left the wardrobe door open. (*A small smile spreads across her face as she remembers – then she becomes aware of GRIFF's gaze and the smile is quickly removed*) When I asked him about it, he told me.

GRIFF: He'd have told you eventually, anyway. You've always been close and that's half the trouble.

RUBY looks at GRIFF.

GRIFF: Don't look like that, it's true. Me and him... we've never had anything going for us. He's embarrassed me all his life.

RUBY: (*Returning to her chair*) The trouble with you is you've got a short memory. You want to think back to last Saturday in the club.

GRIFF: I don't have to think back to it – I can't get the bloody thing out of my brain.

RUBY: You were having a marvellous time.

GRIFF: And that's what hurts the most.

RUBY: (*After a slight pause*) Tell me why you like the drag acts, Griff?

GRIFF: I don't know... they're a bit of fun, I suppose.

RUBY: Exactly. You thought The Dolly Sisters were the best act the club had booked in months. You were killing yourself laughing. I know because I watched you. You laughed so much I thought you weren't going to stop.

GRIFF: (*Standing and moving down right*) And the fact is I haven't laughed once since.

RUBY: They were marvellous, Nigel and his friend – everybody loved them, they were so professional. All right, maybe it was a bit cruel to call you up on the stage with them, but you were glad to go at the time. You were having a ball – till Nigel took his wig off.

GRIFF: I wanted to die.

RUBY: I swear to God, I didn't know he was going to do that. And in fairness, I don't think he'd planned it either. I think he just seized the moment when he could.

GRIFF: (*Quietly*) I just wanted to crawl in a corner and die.

RUBY: You hid your feelings pretty well then.

GRIFF: No, I didn't. (*After a slight pause*) When I wiped my eyes everyone thought, including you, it was because I was laughing so much and it was – until I realized it was my boy up there. (*A slight pause. He sits back down*) You can't imagine how I felt.

RUBY: Of course I can.

GRIFF: No, you can't. It's different for a father.

RUBY: (*Moving to him*) In what way?

GRIFF: I can't explain it.

RUBY: Try.

GRIFF: I felt so...

RUBY: Disappointed?

GRIFF: (*Trying to find the words*) Cheated.

RUBY: Even after all the laughter?

GRIFF: Because of all the laughter.

RUBY: You're saying you'd have taken it better if they didn't like him so much?

GRIFF: It would have been a lot less embarrassing for me, yes.

RUBY: So you'd have rather he had died up on that stage then, would you?

GRIFF: Yes.

RUBY: (*Shouting*) Is that what you're saying?

GRIFF: (*Shouting*) Yes!

RUBY: (*After a slight pause during which she moves down left*) Nigel hasn't done anything that you haven't done in the past.

GRIFF: What are you talking about?

RUBY: You've dressed up as a woman before now.

GRIFF: I have not!

RUBY: What about the Blackpool trip then? I can still remember you now, prancing up and down the aisle of that bus wearing my green lurex dress and Mary Morgan's false hairpiece. I'm sure Nigel can remember you as well. There's a photo of you too, somewhere.

GRIFF: That was only a bit of fun.

RUBY: And last Saturday night wasn't?

GRIFF: That's a different thing altogether.

RUBY: No, it's not. The only difference is that you entertained forty people on a bus and he entertained four hundred down the club.

GRIFF: No, no – you can say what you like, there's a lot more to it than that.

RUBY: Tell me why you did it then, Griff?

GRIFF: (*After a slight pause*) I don't know – I was probably drunk.

RUBY: Come on – you can do better than that.

GRIFF: I can't remember.

RUBY: Well I can.

GRIFF: Then why the hell do you want me to tell you?

RUBY: I want to hear you say it. (*A slight pause*) OK, I'll help you out. You always saw yourself as a bit of a lad, didn't you? Hard to imagine looking at you now, but you like attention, Griff. Nigel follows you for that. That's why you were quite happy to join the drag act up on the stage. You like making people laugh. The trouble is you think that last Saturday the joke was on you.

GRIFF: It was.

RUBY: Then it was on me, too.

GRIFF: No, it wasn't. You knew who you were looking at. You knew why you were laughing.

RUBY: (*Sitting next to GRIFF*) I wasn't laughing at you. Griff, and neither was anyone else.

GRIFF: They might not have laughed at me at the time but they've laughed at me enough since. I'm the talk of the place. We all are. (*A slight pause*) I shouldn't have found out the way I did.

RUBY: No, I know, love, I know. (*She puts her hand on his leg*) Only last week I said to him, 'You'd better tell your father quick,' I said. 'You take that booking at the club and he's bound to find out sooner or later.' (*A slight pause*) I think the plan was to tell you after his spot, or later on when we got home, but you were enjoying yourself so much at the time...

GRIFF: Do you think he's... (*A slight pause*) He is, isn't he?

RUBY: What?

GRIFF: You know what I mean.

They look at each other for a brief moment.

RUBY: Well... they say it doesn't go hand in hand, you know, but... yes, he is. (*A slight pause, during which she stands and moves down left*) Do you know what hurts me the most? Oh, not that he'll never get married... but that I'll never show a little grandchild of mine across the road and into school. (*A slight pause*) And then I thought, well there's nothing I can do about it, you can't have the penny and the bun, can you? I'm going to have to settle for the fact that my son is a cabaret artist... and a very good one at that.

GRIFF: I wish it was that easy for me.

RUBY: It's not a question of it being easy, Griff. Our hands are tied. We play the game with the cards we're dealt. We either accept him for what he is or we don't. (*A slight pause*) Do you know how he told me?

GRIFF shakes his head.

RUBY: Do you want to know?

He nods.

RUBY: I suppose it was about two years ago now. (*She returns to her chair*) It was a Saturday morning and you were in work. I knew there was something up, he was hanging around my feet, you know generally getting in the way. In the end I said, 'Come on, what is it? If you've got something on your mind, spit it out.' He was at the table and he told me to sit down, so I did. The whole atmosphere changed. The sparkle went from his eyes and he came over all serious. I didn't like it at all. 'Hey, what is it?' I said. 'You're frightening me now.' He held his arms out across the table and grabbed me by the hands so tight I could see the whites of his knuckles. He looked me straight in the eye. 'I've got a brain tumour,' he said, 'and I've only got three months to live.' Oh my God, I could feel myself floating off. Then he yanked my hands and it suddenly brought me back. 'No, I haven't,' he said. 'It's all right, I'm not going to die. I'm only gay.' I could have bloody killed him... it's a funny old world though, isn't it, 'cause I kissed him instead.

There is a pause.

The NURSE returns.

NURSE: (*Seeing GRIFF*) Oh, Mr Gregory. Nigel asked me if you were here. I'll tell him.

GRIFF: (*Getting up*) Er, no... I'm not staying.

NURSE: Oh, can't you pop your head round, I'm not going to be much longer.

GRIFF: I've got to get to work.

NURSE: All right – go on, nip in now, then, if you want to.

GRIFF: (*Shouting*) No, I said! You bloody deaf or what?

The NURSE looks at RUBY then exits through the double doors into the room. There is a pause. GRIFF turns to leave.

RUBY: (*Shouting after him*) You're going to be a lonely old man, Griff.

GRIFF: (*Turning immediately*) You never tried, not once, not once when he was growing up, to interest him in –

RUBY: (*Moving to GRIFF*) Hey, you can't blame me. Now it's not my fault. That's the first thing Nigel said to me. He said, 'Now look, Mam,' he said, 'you mustn't blame yourself,' and I don't. How he's turned out has got nothing to do with me at all.

GRIFF: You saying it's my fault?

RUBY: You're the one who dressed up and entertained them on the bus. Who's to say what put the idea into his head?

GRIFF: (*After a slight pause*) You don't think it was that, do you?

260

RUBY: No, Griff. You didn't make him what he is and neither did I.

GRIFF: Well, we must have done something.

RUBY: All I've done is to accept him for what he is because he's my son and I love him.

GRIFF: I can't think like that.

RUBY: You still love him, don't you?

GRIFF doesn't answer.

RUBY: (*Moving away, down left*) If you don't feel the same as me then I feel sorry because you're going to miss out on something very special.

GRIFF: Special?

RUBY: Yes, special. (*She turns to face GRIFF*) You're a hypocrite, Griff Gregory, and not a very nice one at that.

GRIFF: Is there any other kind?

RUBY: (*A thought strikes her*) It's Monday. Did you remember to put the rubbish out?

GRIFF: Have I ever forgot?

RUBY: (*After a slight pause*) Everything will be all right in the end.

GRIFF looks at RUBY.

RUBY: (*Moving to GRIFF*) We've still got him – that's all that matters. We could have lost him in that crash. How would you have felt then?

GRIFF: A lot like I do now, I suppose.

RUBY: Look, when you go in there and you see him –

GRIFF: I'm not going in there. I told you when I came here it was only for you.

RUBY: I'm sure he'd like to see you.

GRIFF: Well, we can't all have what we like.

RUBY: Refusing to see him isn't going to make it better.

GRIFF: And going in there is?

RUBY: It's not going to make it any worse.

GRIFF: I can't go in there. I can't look him in the face.

RUBY: Why, it's the same face you looked at last week.

GRIFF: It's the same face I looked at last Saturday – minus the make-up.

RUBY: And the wig. Don't forget the wig. (*She laughs.*)

GRIFF: It's not funny.

RUBY: Of course it is; it's bloody hysterical. We'll all be laughing about now in a couple of months.

GRIFF: I should have put my foot down. I knew the way things were going right from early on. (*A slight pause*) And then when he went off to London, well, that was good enough. I saw it coming. I should have done something – took him to football matches and –

RUBY: Oh, for goodness' sake, Griff, what's the matter with you? You don't honestly think that watching twenty-two men kick a ball around would have made any difference? You don't live in the real world, you don't. Buying him an Indian outfit for Christmas when he was small instead of a Post Office set wouldn't have changed anything. Good God, even I know that. (*A slight pause*) Look, you're doing what I first did, you're blaming yourself and you shouldn't. You're looking for a reason and there isn't one.

GRIFF: There's got to be.

RUBY: (*Returning to her seat*) Well, there's not.

GRIFF: What went wrong then? Tell me, I need to know because something somewhere went wrong. (*He follows her*) There must have been a time when he realized he was what he was. I mean, you don't just wake up one day and choose to be something like that, and if it's got nothing to do with you or me and the way he was brought up, then what has it got to do with? Where's the reason for it? I don't believe it when you say there isn't one. (*He turns away slightly*) Why didn't he tell us about it at the time, maybe he could have had help, we could have taken him to see somebody who could have talked to him, somebody who could have listened to him and then all this could have been avoided. (*A thought hits him*) Maybe it's not too late. He could go private. We can pay. I bet it would only take a few sessions with someone who knew what they were doing, someone recommended who could get to the heart of his trouble straight away. I don't think it's as big a problem as it first looks, it's only a question of preference, isn't it? So it shouldn't be difficult to find someone who could straighten him out. Get him to see it's only a matter of choice and once all that's sorted, I'm sure the other thing, the dressing-up thing will right itself. What do you think?

RUBY: (*After a slight pause*) I don't know much about it, Griff. I suppose there are books you can get on it but I'm sure as hell not going into the library to find out. All I know are the few bits and pieces Nigel has told me. From what I can gather it's not a life-threatening disease, well apart from this AIDS thing. And I know it's not something you can go and have 'straightened out' either. It's not like having a tooth pulled and then there you are, that's it, everything's back to normal. (*A slight pause*) If it's only a matter of preference, like you say, is it really that big a deal that he prefers something else? I know it's disappointing and I know it's not what we want, but we don't have a choice, and although you'll find this hard to believe, I don't think Nigel got much say in it either. You don't choose to be different, do you? You just are.

There is a slight pause. GRIFF sits, up right.

GRIFF: I can't understand how it's all so 'matter of fact' with you.

RUBY: Oh, don't think it didn't break my heart because it did. I've lost count of how many nights I cried myself to sleep. And what made it harder for me was I couldn't show him or you. (*She moves to him*) I had to cry on my own and carry on as if nothing had happened when all my world was collapsing around me. (*A slight pause*) 'I'm glad I told you,' he said. 'It's like taking a big weight off my chest.' Trouble was he took it off his chest and put it on mine. I'm not complaining, you know – that's what mothers are for. (*A slight pause*) Do you know what did help me, though?

He doesn't answer.

RUBY: I picked up my magazine one week and some mother had written in that her son was going through the same sort of thing and do you know what the advice was?

264

He still doesn't answer.

RUBY: (*Moving down left*) I can't remember it word for word but it went something like: 'There are two things parents should give their children. Roots and wings.' Roots and wings, Griff. Our Nigel knows there's always a room for him at home and –

GRIFF: (*Getting up and joining her*) Does that mean he's coming to us when he gets out of here?

RUBY: I don't know, I haven't talked to him about it yet but I hope so. (*A slight pause*) Whatever he wants to do, Griff, or wherever he wants to fly – it's OK with me. I'm behind him all the way. All I want is for him to be happy and there's nothing I wouldn't do to make sure he is.

GRIFF: What if I said he can't come home?

RUBY: What if I said you can bugger off?

GRIFF: He's left home, it's not fair to encourage him back.

RUBY: What's fair got to do with it? He'll need to recuperate. Kevin won't be able to do it now that's for sure.

GRIFF: Who the hell is Kevin?

RUBY: (*After a slight pause*) Er... Nigel's friend. The other half of the act.

GRIFF: (*After a slight pause*) Wait a minute. You're not going to tell me that they live together, are you?

RUBY: Well, I was going to, but it's a bit pointless now, isn't it?

GRIFF: I don't believe this.

RUBY: You're going to have to learn to be more tolerant, Griff. Shouldn't be difficult, you've always said, 'Live and let live'.

GRIFF: Yes, but not when it's your own flesh and blood.

RUBY: It should apply even more then.

GRIFF: (*After a slight pause*) So – my son lives with another man. Is there anything else I should know?

RUBY: (*Moving away slightly, left*) No. I think that's everything.

GRIFF: You sure now? You're not keeping anything back to prevent me having a heart attack?

RUBY: Well, there is the little one they're expecting in June, but apart from that there's nothing.

GRIFF: I wish I could joke about it.

RUBY: Who says I'm joking?

GRIFF: (*Looking at RUBY incredulously*) You're not serious? You are serious, aren't you?

RUBY: Look, Kevin used to be married, right? Wife not up to much from what I can gather. I don't know what her job is. I think it's to do with the military though because I heard Kevin say something about her being (*she pronounces the spelling*) RAF.

GRIFF: Where's all this leading?

RUBY: Well, they had a little girl together. Now the wife has picked up with somebody else and he hasn't taken to the girl, poor little thing. There's a lot of talk of her coming to live with Kevin.

266

GRIFF: In Nigel's house?

RUBY: Well, where else?

GRIFF: (*After a slight pause*) If I don't take in all that's happening, you'll have to appreciate it's because things are moving a bit too fast for me.

RUBY: Too fast?

GRIFF: Last week I thought I had an average twenty-five year old son who lived alone and had a mortgage. (*He moves down left*) Today he's a drag queen who shares a house and bed with a man who's already been married and whose daughter is about to move in. I mean there's only so much a guard with British Rail can grasp.

RUBY: Oh, I don't know, I think you've grasped it all pretty well, Griff.

GRIFF: (*Shouting*) Will you tell me what the hell's happening to us?

RUBY: (*Shouting back*) Will you keep your voice down? You're in a hospital, remember?

GRIFF: I don't care where I am! Up till last Saturday our family was quite... (*he searches for the word*) orthodox.

RUBY: Orthodox? Good God, Griff, you can call us a lot of things but we've hardly been that.

GRIFF: On the surface we were. Now all of a sudden everything's a mess. A mess.

RUBY: No, it's not.

GRIFF: (*Shouting*) If people make fun of our son, it's a mess! If you get talked about by women in cars, it's a mess! If my workmates take the piss, believe me, it's a bloody mess!

RUBY: You shouldn't care what people say.

GRIFF: But I do! It matters when they crack a joke and I can't laugh because we're the butt of it.

RUBY: I don't suppose we get a half of the flak that Nigel does. If he can take the slings and arrows, why can't we? If we stick together as a family, Griff, no one can hurt us.

GRIFF: You don't know what it's like for me. What it was like for me on Saturday night.

RUBY: All right, I'll admit it, finding out the way you did that Nigel was a drag artist perhaps came as a bit of a shock to you – but you've got to come to terms with it like I did.

GRIFF: It's not as easy for me.

RUBY: I wish you wouldn't keep saying it's not easy for you.

GRIFF: (*Insisting*) Well, it's not!

RUBY: Well it should be.

GRIFF: Why?

RUBY: Well... you're normal enough now.

GRIFF: What do you mean?

RUBY: There was a time when we were courting when I used to wonder which side of the fence *you* were going to fall.

GRIFF: You're all right, are you?

RUBY: I mean, everybody has a mate, you know, I understand that – but you couldn't move without that Ritchie Thomas. Talk about Tweedledum and Tweedledee. He was like your shadow till I put my foot down.

GRIFF: There was nothing funny about me and Ritchie. We were like brothers, we were.

RUBY: You don't take your brother on honeymoon with you.

GRIFF: (*Shouting*) I didn't take him on honeymoon.

RUBY: (*Shouting back*) It's a hell of a coincidence that he ended up in the caravan next to us then, don't you think?

GRIFF: It's not fair to throw Ritchie up. Specially now he's not here to defend himself.

RUBY: I'd have said exactly the same if he was alive.

GRIFF: You're a dangerous woman, you are, Ruby.

RUBY: I put it all behind me and didn't think much more about it, but after the fool you made of yourself at his funeral it brought it all back.

GRIFF: How many times have I got to tell you, there was never anything like that between us.

RUBY: (*Quietly*) Funny how he never got married, then.

GRIFF: You want to know why he never got married?

RUBY: Go on, surprise me.

GRIFF: I will. He loved somebody who was already married and it wasn't me – it was you. (*A slight pause*) Well... what do you say to that?

RUBY: I knew. (*A slight pause*) Now what do you say?

GRIFF is speechless. There is a slight pause. The NURSE enters from Nigel's room.

NURSE: There we are then, he's all done and sitting up in bed waiting for you. (*She makes to go.*)

GRIFF: Er... nurse...

The NURSE turns round.

GRIFF: Just now... um.... (*He finds it hard to apologize*) What it was... um...

NURSE: It's all right, forget it.

RUBY: No! It's not all right, is it, Griff?

GRIFF: I shouldn't have... you know, shouted – er – like that. You all do a good job... deserve better...

RUBY: He's apologizing but as you see it doesn't come easy.

GRIFF: Does he know I'm here? Nigel?

NURSE: I would think the whole ward knows.

RUBY: I told you to keep your voice down.

NURSE: (*Nodding towards Nigel's room*) It's no big deal, you know. You can change your mind and go in if you want to. (*A slight pause*) Anyway, I've got to go. (*She smiles. Exits.*)

RUBY: (*After a slight pause*) Ritchie Thomas came to see me in a hell of a state one day.

GRIFF looks at her.

RUBY: He told me how he felt about me... I told him how he felt about you and the poor bugger went home in a worst state than when he came in... (*A slight pause*) I don't believe for a minute you ever got involved, but – you can't deny you didn't know how he felt about you.

GRIFF: We grew up together.

RUBY: All right, so as far as you were concerned you were close. But he had feelings for you –

GRIFF: And you –

RUBY: That he shouldn't have had and you knew it. You accepted it. Why can't you do the same for your son?

GRIFF: It's different when it's your own. And anyway, Ritchie never dressed up in women's clothes, or wanted to as far as I know.

RUBY: Good God, Griff, that's only a bit of fun – you've said that yourself.

GRIFF: I can take a joke and have a laugh as good as the next man, but you've got to admit what our Nigel's into goes a hell of a lot deeper than that.

RUBY: All right, so he does take it a bit more serious. He's got to. It's his job. There's nothing more to it than that. At the end of the day all the dresses get put away in a wardrobe.

GRIFF: Who said?

RUBY: Hell's delight, do you think he walks round the house in a dress, do you?

GRIFF: It's possible. Who's to say he isn't sitting in there now waiting for us dressed up in a sister's uniform?

RUBY: (*Laughing*) Good, you're making a joke of it. I'm glad.

GRIFF: I'm dead bloody serious.

RUBY: Would it be so awful if he was?

GRIFF doesn't answer.

RUBY: It shouldn't matter to us if he wanted to go around naked with a frying pan on his head.

GRIFF: You can say what you like, I can't like him for what he does.

RUBY: All right, don't – you can still love him for what he is.

GRIFF: You mean in spite of what he is.

RUBY: Whatever. Nobody really cares what he does behind his own front door, Griff, and if they do, why should it matter to us?

GRIFF: (*After a slight pause*) You're very good at all this, aren't you? Much better than me.

RUBY: I've had more time, love. It'll get easier, I promise.

GRIFF: But it'll never go away.

RUBY: No, Griff – it'll never go away. (*A slight pause*) Can I ask you something?

GRIFF looks at RUBY.

RUBY: Which is the worst for you? The humiliation of Saturday night or the knowledge that your only son is gay?

GRIFF: (*Shouting*) It's not fair!

RUBY: Of course it's not, but life never is. I want to know what the hardest thing is for you. See, if it's the fact that he's gay, well there's nothing anybody, including Nigel, can do about that. If, on the other hand, it's the drag thing, well... asking him to give up the dresses isn't going to change him either.

A pause.

GRIFF: Do you know what I've gone and done?

RUBY: Surprise me.

GRIFF: You know you brought Nigel's suitcases home with you after the accident? The suitcases with all the costumes. (*A slight pause*) I've emptied them. I emptied them into two big plastic bags and put them out with the rubbish this morning.

RUBY: Oh my God, and you thought that would solve everything, I suppose?

GRIFF: I don't know what I thought. (*A slight pause*) After Saturday maybe I just wanted to get my own back.

RUBY: There was over two thousand pounds worth of frocks in those cases. Not to mention the make-up and wigs.

GRIFF: What can I say?

RUBY: Well, nothing to me. I'd start thinking about how you're going to tell Nigel if I were you.

GRIFF: I don't know if I can apologize to him.

RUBY: And you won't know unless you try. Anyway, seems to me there's apologies due all round. Go in and see him, go on.

GRIFF: You don't know what you're asking.

RUBY: I'm not asking any more of you than I've asked of myself. (*A slight pause*) And you still haven't answered my question.

GRIFF: (*After a slight pause; crossing in front of RUBY*) Going round the clubs like he does – it's like having a tattoo on his forehead.

RUBY: So it's not the fact that he's gay then, it's the drag factor?

GRIFF: Why has everyone got to know?

RUBY: You'd feel better if he tried to hide it?

GRIFF: I'd feel better if he didn't flaunt it.

RUBY: That's what he gets paid for. (*A slight pause*) So it is the drag factor.

GRIFF: I'm never going to be able to accept it like you.

RUBY: There's only one way to accept it, Griff, and that's a little bit at a time. The first thing to do is to walk in through that door, the second is to smile, and if he smiles

274

back, which he will... everything will be plain sailing after that.

GRIFF: How can I smile when all I want to do is knock seven different shades of shit out of him?

RUBY: Oh, you'll smile, Griff. We both will because the chips are down and we can't do anything else. (*A slight pause*) Do you know, when he was a little boy, all I wished was for him to be happy – and he is. Trouble was, I forgot to wish for me to be happy too.

GRIFF: (*Moving to RUBY*) We can walk away, let him get on with it.

RUBY: I can't do that, he's my son, he needs me.

GRIFF: (*Stopping*) Oh well, there you are then: as long as he's got you.

RUBY: And I need him. And although it's not easy for you to admit, you need him too.

GRIFF: (*After a pause: quietly*) Does he need me, do you think?

RUBY: The answer is staring you in the face, Griff. It wasn't me he asked the nurse about, it was you.

GRIFF: He only wants me to condone what he's doing.

RUBY: He's not after your blessing. He needs you to accept him for what he is. that's not the same thing.

GRIFF: What about what I need?

RUBY: Shouldn't come into it. Roots and wings, Griff – remember, roots and wings. (*A slight pause*) You can walk away now if you want to but it's not going to solve anything. Whether you like it or not, you're going to be his father for a long time to come. (*A slight pause*) Closing your eyes isn't going to make him disappear. (*A slight pause*) I'm going in – I bet he's wondering what the hell's going on. (*She heads for the doors.*)

GRIFF: Do you want me to come with you?

RUBY: (*Stopping short of them*) Of course I do: but there's no way I'm going to let you. (*She turns to him*) Not with me. You go in there, you go in on your own, (*A slight pause*) Well what's it to be, Griff? Is it time to take your head out of the sand or what? (*A slight pause. She walks towards GRIFF*) Come on, it can't be as bad as all that. One small step for Griff, one giant leap for Nigel. (*A slight pause*) If it makes you feel any better you'll be killing two birds with one stone.

GRIFF looks at RUBY.

RUBY: You remember that weight we talked about? You know, the one Nigel took off his chest and put on mine? You can't take it away, I know that, but I'd sleep a hell of a lot easier if you took half. Isn't that what husbands are for?

GRIFF: And sons?

RUBY: (*After a slight pause*) Kids. They're all the same: armache when they're small – heartache when grown.

They share a moment. They are almost close.

RUBY: Oh, Griff!

RUBY turns and goes into Nigel's room as if she has given up on GRIFF.

RUBY: (*Off*) There you are! Oooh you're looking much better today. How are you feeling, all right?

GRIFF stands motionless for a moment. Slowly he turns to look towards Nigel's room. After he has stared for a moment or two the lights fade to Black-out.

Shirley Bassey is heard singing, As Long As He Needs Me.

Scene Two

Inside Nigel's hospital room. 9.45am.

The double doors from the corridor are blue on this side.

There is one hospital bed in the room, surrounded by the usual hospital paraphernalia, including a bedside cabinet, and a chair, right. There is a window to one side.

The music fades and the lights come up.

NIGEL is in bed, having his blood pressure taken by the NURSE. He has a dressing on his forehead. VERNON is standing with his back towards the others, looking out of the room window.

NIGEL: ...so there I was sitting in my dressing-room quietly putting on my make-up when this bloody big butch committee man stomped in and said, 'Hey, are you bent?' 'Why,' I said, 'have you got a crooked arse?'

NURSE: (*Laughing*) Don't you ever stop?

NIGEL is about to say something again but before he has the chance, the NURSE pops a thermometer into his mouth. She continues to check his blood pressure. VERNON looks over his shoulder at the others before returning to the window.

277

NURSE: It's coming down nicely.

NIGEL: (*Taking the thermometer out of his mouth*) Said the actress to the –

NURSE: (*Snatching the thermometer out of NIGEL's hand*) You're incorrigible, you know that.

The NURSE smiles and pokes the thermometer back through NIGEL's lips.

NIGEL: (*With the thermometer still in his mouth*) Don't you like my jokes?

NURSE: I love them, but first thing in the morning?

NIGEL: It's very nice first thing in the morning.

NURSE: (*Covering a smile*) What is?

NIGEL: Laughing of course, what else?

There is a pause.

NIGEL: Is my father out there?

NURSE: Oh... I thought.... (*She looks over at VERNON.*)

NIGEL: No, that's Vernon. My father-in-law.

VERNON looks and half smiles at the NURSE.

NURSE: Are you married?

NIGEL: Depends on how you want to look at it, love. He's not there then, is he? My dad?

NURSE: He wasn't ten minutes ago. Your mother is though and has been for quarter of an hour. (*She takes out the thermometer, checks it and returns it to its holder on the wall*) Well, at least that's back to normal.

NIGEL: (*over-acting*) My God! I'm normal! What am I going to do? I'll never work again!

The NURSE laughs as she enters the details on to Nigel's chart.

RUBY's face appears in the window the other side of the room door. She stretches here and there but can't see very much.

NURSE: Behave yourself. Oh, by the way; what religion are you?

NIGEL: Church of England, love. What else would a queen be?

NURSE: Are you gay, Nigel?

NIGEL: Is the Pope Catholic?

NURSE: Are you a practising homosexual?

NIGEL: No, love, I'm perfect at it.

NURSE: Be serious. I hope you take precautions.

NIGEL puts his hand on his chest as if to enquire what the NURSE means.

NURSE: Condoms.

NIGEL: Oh, God, no, love. I can't get on with them. I use cling-film. I roll my own.

NURSE: (*To VERNON, laughing*) How do you put up with him?

VERNON doesn't answer but he tries to smile.

NIGEL: Have you finished with my body?

NURSE: Not quite. I'm going to get you a clean dressing for your head. (*She turns to go.*)

RUBY sees the NURSE walking towards her and quickly disappears.

NIGEL: Have you got time to do my nails as well?

NURSE: (*Laughing again*) This is a hospital not a beauty salon.

NIGEL: Never! I thought I was in the wrong place!

NURSE: (*Laughing*) You're mad.

NIGEL: Did I tell you about the fat man and the girl with the wooden eye?

NURSE: I'll be back in a minute. (*She exits.*)

RUBY: (*Off*) Is that it, nurse? Can I go in now?

NIGEL: It's a hell of a waste, isn't it?

VERNON: What?

NIGEL: (*Giving his nails a quick look over*) The way I have with women. Kev isn't half as good at it.

VERNON: Does that surprise you?

NIGEL: Well, yes, it does, yes – under the circumstances.

VERNON: How do you mean?

NIGEL: Well, he doesn't look much like you. I would have thought he'd have inherited at least one of your – what would you call them – virtues? (*He smiles and stares at VERNON.*)

VERNON stares back at NIGEL for a moment, then looks away.

NIGEL: Where is he anyway? He hasn't come in to see me yet.

VERNON: Why did you introduce me as your father-in-law?

NIGEL: Because that's how I see you. Anyway, you told me to call you it once.

VERNON: (*Turning to him*) When?

NIGEL: One night when you were pissed out of your brain.

VERNON: You mean the night we had a couple of lagers together?

GRIFF: (*Off, shouting*) I meant it then, and accident or no I mean it now.

NIGEL: The old man's here then. God, now the shit will hit the fan.

RUBY: (*Off, raising her voice*) Don't talk like that. He might never come out of there.

NIGEL: Listen to her. She's dramatic beyond.

During the following VERNON turns away to look out of the door.

GRIFF: (*Off, shouting*) He's got a couple of bruises, a few cracked ribs and a knock on the head. He's not going to die, Ruby. He'll be out of this place by Thursday – you take it from me.

NIGEL: I hope he's right – I got a dress-fitting Friday, eleven o'clock. (*He gives a small laugh, then realizes that VERNON is turned away from him. A slight pause.*) I'm sorry, I embarrassed you in front of the nurse, didn't I?

VERNON: I just feel there's a time and place for everything.

NIGEL: Yes, you're right... and I'm sorry. I don't know what's the matter with me. I just can't seem to stop myself going one step over the mark. I do it all the time. I did it on Saturday. I wasn't happy to get my old man up on stage and give him a good time, if you know what I mean. No. I had to go and reveal myself to him, didn't I, in front of all those people.

VERNON: It must have been awful for him.

NIGEL: It wasn't wonderful for me, love.

VERNON: (*Turning towards NIGEL*) Then why did you do it?

NIGEL: I don't know. I never know. There I am living my life with everything going all right, and then all of a sudden for no reason at all I say or do something that's completely over the top. I just get carried away and I don't know why. It's frightening, isn't it?

VERNON: Perhaps you should learn to exercise a bit more control.

NIGEL: (*Agreeing whole-heartedly*) Yes – doesn't sound half as much fun though, does it? (*He laughs*) Where the hell has

Kevin got to, do you think? I want him to bring a weekend case in. I can't see them keeping me in much longer, can you?

VERNON: You've had an accident, Nigel. The car's a write- off, have they told you?

NIGEL: They haven't told me anything, love. It's like the frigging secret service in this place. You come in with concussion and they treat you like you've got three months to live. They're keeping something from me, though, I know they are.

VERNON: You were quite poorly yesterday.

NIGEL: Yes, but today I've made a brilliant recovery. All right, I'm bruised all over, but it only hurts when I laugh. Bed rest, that's all I need, and I can have that in the house.

VERNON: I think you're here for a couple of days yet.

NIGEL: How do you know? Have they said something?

VERNON: They're hardly going to say anything to me.

NIGEL: That's what I mean. It's easier to get information out of the DHSS.

VERNON: I think you'd do best to rest up and not worry about anything.

NIGEL: I suppose you're right. (*A slight pause*) How come you're here?

VERNON: What?

NIGEL: And so early. Even before the old girl and that's saying something.

VERNON doesn't answer, just shakes his head.

A pause.

VERNON: (*Crossing to chair, right of the bed*) What happened? Do you remember?

NIGEL: With the car?

VERNON nods.

NIGEL: We weren't drunk or anything... neither of us. We don't drink when we're working, though I felt like it on Saturday.

VERNON: You veered off the road for no apparent reason. The car's wrecked and you've made one hell of a mess of a thirty-foot oak.

NIGEL: You've seen it then?

VERNON: The car?

NIGEL: The tree. You've been there. Seen the damage.

VERNON: Er... no. (*He walks to the left, around the bed.*)

NIGEL waits for an explanation.

VERNON: That policeman said. Earlier on. (*A slight pause*) You don't remember?

NIGEL shakes his head.

VERNON: Maybe that knock on the head has done more damage than you think.

NIGEL: I remember everything, but don't remember him saying anything about a thirty-foot oak.

VERNON: Perhaps it was a birch, then. (*He shrugs it off. A slight pause*) When you say you remember everything...

NIGEL: I mean, I remember everything.

They look at each other. A pause.

VERNON: You told the policeman you fell asleep at the wheel.

NIGEL: I'd have told him anything to get rid of him. Ohh, he had terrible bad breath, did you notice? If he hasn't got halitosis, love, I'm not one of the Dolly Sisters.

VERNON: That's not what happened then? You didn't fall asleep at the wheel?

NIGEL: It was good enough for him.

VERNON: Meaning it's good enough for me?

NIGEL: I didn't say that.

VERNON: Tell me what happened.

NIGEL: What do you want to know?

VERNON: The truth.

NIGEL: (*After a slight pause*) I'll make a deal with you. I'll be honest with you if you'll be honest with me.

There is a pause; VERNON comes to sit at the bottom of the bed facing the audience.

VERNON: You saw me, didn't you?

NIGEL: When?

VERNON: Saturday night. At the pull-in. Half-way through Coedcae Lane – the picnic area. (*He stands and rambles on*) It didn't mean anything, and I've never done it before. I don't want to hurt Rita. It was just one of those things, you know, a one-off...

NIGEL appears to be hearing all of this for the first time.

VERNON: (*Turning to look at NIGEL and realizing he's put his foot in it*) You didn't see me, did you?

NIGEL: No.

VERNON: Shit!

NIGEL: But you saw me obviously.

VERNON: (*Moving around the bed to centre*) I was convinced you –

NIGEL: I saw a car parked there but I didn't recognize it.

VERNON: I thought you'd followed me. I thought Kevin had smelled a rat and you'd followed me.

NIGEL: We were coming back from our gig, Vern. I stopped for a pee, that's all.

A pause.

VERNON: What happens now?

NIGEL: Meaning am I going to tell Kevin?

VERNON: Meaning are you going to tell his mother?

NIGEL: I wouldn't do that.

VERNON: Good, that's a weight off my mind.

NIGEL: Well, not to Rita anyway. Kevin, now – that's a different story.

VERNON: Can't you keep it to yourself? I mean it's not as if it's going to happen again.

NIGEL: We don't have any secrets between us. We're painfully honest with each other. Ask him if you don't believe me.

VERNON: Perhaps you won't tell Rita but Kevin might. (*He turns to look at NIGEL*) It's not all that long ago we – well, you know...

NIGEL: What?

VERNON: We're really close now. I don't want anything to upset it all.

NIGEL: No doubt that slipped your mind when you pulled into Coedcae Lane, popped into the back seat with whoever she was and got down to it. You surprise me, Vernon, I didn't think you were one to put it around.

VERNON: I'm not! I've told you – it's never happened before. (*He looks out of the window.*)

NIGEL: You only ever did it once and you got caught. Christ, Vern, you really were shit out of luck.

VERNON: Suddenly it was on a plate and I took it.

NIGEL: Aaaah, an opportunist shagger.

VERNON: Rita... well, the last eighteen months she hasn't been... know what I mean? She hasn't been interested in me at all. Not in that way.

NIGEL: You'll have me feeling sorry for you in a minute.

VERNON: It's not natural for a man to go that long.

NIGEL: It's not natural for a man of your age to be in that position in the back of a car in Coedcae Lane.

VERNON: So you did see me then?

NIGEL: I saw a load of arms and legs. I tried to get a better look and peed over my foot. Ruined a fabulous pair of shoes.

VERNON: Can I trust you not to say anything?

NIGEL: (*After a slight pause*) That's why you're here, isn't it? You thought I saw you and you wanted to gag me. And there's me thinking you were in here because you were worried about me; well thank you very much, Vern.

VERNON: I am worried about you – I'm just worried about Rita finding out as well. She mustn't, Nigel. (*A slight pause*) We've been married twenty-five years next month.

NIGEL: Happy anniversary.

VERNON: She's planning a big do.

NIGEL: I know, I'm the cabaret.

VERNON: If Rita found out she'd kill me.

NIGEL: Have you made a will then, Vern? I should if I were you.

VERNON: Don't joke about it.

NIGEL: Who's joking?

VERNON: You're going to give me away, then?

NIGEL doesn't answer.

VERNON: One mistake and ffittt. Gone. I lose everything.

NIGEL: You're not going to lose nothing. I reckon we're all allowed to make one mistake, don't you? Look at me on Saturday.

RUBY: (*Off, shouting*) So you'd have rather he had died up there on that stage then, would you?

GRIFF: (*Off, shouting*) Yes.

RUBY: (*Off, shouting*) Is that what you're saying?

GRIFF: (*Off, shouting*) Yes!

NIGEL: Poor sod.

VERNON: It's not easy for him. I know, I've been there.

NIGEL: He's pathetic.

VERNON: He's your father.

NIGEL: That only makes it worse. (*A slight pause*) I said I didn't know why I did it but the truth is I did. (*A slight pause*) I looked down at him from the stage and there he was gripping his pint, looking so butch and laughing from arsehole to breakfast. (*A slight pause*) God knows why but suddenly I remembered the time when he came home from work and saw me knitting. He went apeshit – and now here he is I thought having the laugh of his life and I was giving it to him. It was cruel, I know, but he had it coming – for years he had it coming. I'm sorry now of course.

VERNON: That's something at least. (*He sits in the chair next to the bed.*)

NIGEL: Not that I'd tell him. He doesn't deserve it so don't you say anything either. (*A slight pause*) You and I are not all that different when you stop and think about it, are we?

VERNON: How do you work that out?

NIGEL: We didn't mind putting our hands in the fire at the time – but today? Today we don't want to have our fingers burnt.

VERNON: Hang on, I thought you weren't going to say anything.

NIGEL: I'm not. Your secret is safe with me, don't worry.

VERNON: What will you tell Kevin?

NIGEL: Nothing. What he doesn't know won't harm him, I suppose.

VERNON nods and smiles; there is a slight pause.

VERNON: You still haven't told me what happened on Saturday. (*He gets up and moves down right*) All I know is that you weren't drunk and you didn't fall asleep at the wheel.

NIGEL: What has Kevin told you?

VERNON: (*After a slight pause*) Nothing yet.

NIGEL: And he won't. Not until he's spoken to me first. Where did you say he was? He is here you said, isn't he?

VERNON: He's just down the corridor.

NIGEL: Fetch him for me then, Vern, please? Tell him I'm waiting to see him.

VERNON: He was in the car too, you know.

NIGEL: I know that. Look, I might have had a knock on the head but I haven't forgotten who was with... (*He suddenly realizes the implication of what VERNON has said*) What are you trying to say? What's going on? Is he a patient here? Is he hurt?

VERNON: You got off lucky.

NIGEL: He is, isn't he? What's happened? Is he all right? (*He raises his voice*) Tell me what's going on!

VERNON: (*Shouting back*) You should never have been in those lanes.

NIGEL: That's great coming from you! What's the situation?

VERNON: (*After a slight pause*) He's got some head injuries.

NIGEL: (*After a slight pause*) Oh, that's all right then. (*A slight pause*) It is all right, isn't it? Is it an injury like mine or what?

VERNON: We'll know more later.

NIGEL: I want to see him. (*He struggles to help himself out of bed.*)

VERNON: What are you doing?

NIGEL: What's his room number?

VERNON: You can't go to him.

NIGEL: Try and stop me.

VERNON: There's only one allowed in at a time.

NIGEL: So?

VERNON: Rita's in there.

NIGEL: (*After a slight pause*) It's serious, isn' t it? It must be for you both to be here.

VERNON: Both your parents are here and you might be home by the weekend.

NIGEL: So it's not serious. Is that what you're saying?

VERNON doesn't answer.

NIGEL: (*Shouting*) What are you saying! Tell me what's going on!

GRIFF: (*Off, shouting*) No, I said! You bloody deaf or what?

There is a slight pause.

The NURSE enters the room carrying a tray with bandages, scissors and plaster, et cetera. She stops just inside the room and looks from NIGEL to VERNON. She senses something is wrong.

NURSE: What's up? (*To NIGEL*) And no wisecracks.

NIGEL: I want to know what you're keeping from me.

NURSE: What makes you think we're keeping anything.

NIGEL: I'm not stupid. I know something's going on.

NURSE: Oh, that. (*She indicates that she means GRIFF shouting in the corridor*) Your father's arrived but he's not staying. He's going on to work. I asked him if he –

NIGEL: I'm not on about him. I don't give a shit about him.

NURSE: (*Moving to the bed and preparing to renew NIGEL's head dressing*) Well, that's not very nice.

NIGEL: (*Raising his voice*) What's happened to Kevin?

NURSE: Kevin who?

NIGEL: If somebody doesn't start giving me some answers, I'm going to scream!

NURSE: Now this isn't going to hurt. (*She starts to take the old dressing from NIGEL's forehead.*)

All of a sudden NIGEL screams.

NURSE: I've hardly touched you.

NIGEL clenches his fists and makes the most frustrating noise possible.

VERNON: Tell him, go on. (*A slight pause*) Kevin Edwards. Room four. Tell him.

There is a slight pause. During the following, the NURSE continues to change the dressing.

NURSE: Well – it's early days yet. We'll know more in the next forty-eight hours. We've had patients like him in before and they've made a complete recovery so I wouldn't get too alarmed at this stage.

NIGEL: I don't believe you! (*He raises his voice*) You should be a politician not a nurse. You just made me a speech and told me sod all!

NURSE: (*Raising her voice*) Keep still.

VERNON: (*Shouting*) He's unconscious! (*A slight pause; quieter now*) He hasn't come round since the accident.

Nothing is said for a while. After a time the NURSE removes NIGEL's dirty dressing with metal tweezers.

NURSE: There you are, how's that? (*She disposes of the dressing in a paper bag and continues to re-dress the wound.*)

NIGEL: I want to see him.

NURSE: You've got no chance, sunshine. You can't get out of bed.

NIGEL: If I could, would you take me?

NURSE: No.

NIGEL: Why?

NURSE: It's family only.

NIGEL: You've got to be joking. (*To VERNON*) Did you hear what she said? (*To the NURSE*) I am family. (*To VERNON*) Tell her who I am.

VERNON doesn't answer.

NIGEL: (*Shouting at VERNON*) Tell her!

NURSE: I have grasped the situation.

NIGEL: And?

NURSE: Rules are rules.

NIGEL: I've got to see him, don't you understand? And he'd want to see me anyway.

VERNON: Would he?

NIGEL: Of course he would. Come on, Vern, how can you say that?

VERNON: I'm still in the dark. Something's up. If I knew what really happened on Saturday...

NIGEL: (*To the NURSE*) Please. Fix it for me?

NURSE: Andrea my name is, not Jimmy Savile.

NIGEL: I'll do all the jokes if you don't mind. What do you say? Can you sort it out for me?

NURSE: I'd have to get permission.

NIGEL: From who, the staff?

NURSE: And the family.

NIGEL: Well, that part's easy. Vern, tell her it's OK.

VERNON doesn't answer.

NIGEL: Vernon?

VERNON: It's not me... it's Rita.

NIGEL: What?

VERNON: She's upset... and she doesn't want...

NIGEL: What?

VERNON: (*After a slight pause*) She doesn't want anyone to see him.

NIGEL: Even me?

VERNON: Especially you.

NIGEL: Why?

VERNON: Work it out for yourself.

NIGEL: (*After a slight pause*) I want to see him, Vern, so you'd better fix it.

VERNON: I don't think I can.

NIGEL: Try.

VERNON: She's very upset.

NIGEL: She's not half as upset as she'd be if I had a word with her. Do you follow me? Do you understand what I'm saying here, Vern?

VERNON: Give her a day or two – she'll calm down.

NURSE: I'd give her longer than that. (*She opens a clean dressing.*)

NIGEL: I want to see him now.

VERNON: Why rock the boat?

NIGEL: Rock it? I'll sink it if I have to.

NURSE: I think you'd better try and get yourself better before you start to worry about anyone else.

NIGEL: Oh, piss off!

NURSE: (*Outraged*) I beg your pardon!

NIGEL: Look, are you married? Of course you are, you've got a little girl.

NURSE: I'm divorced. Why?

NIGEL: Nothing. It doesn't matter. Don't you understand? Don't either of you understand?

VERNON: There's nothing you can do for him. The nurse is right. (*He sits in the chair next to the bed.*) Get yourself well first, then worry about Kevin.

NIGEL: I want to see Rita then.

VERNON: What?

NIGEL: What's the matter, Vern? (*To the NURSE*) The colour's drained right out of his face, look.

The NURSE puts a clean dressing on NIGEL's forehead.

VERNON: (*Getting up and moving down right*) The way things are at the moment, the further I keep you two apart the better.

NIGEL: Would that be for my sake or yours?

VERNON doesn't answer.

NIGEL: I just want to talk to her that's all. Nothing to do with you and Saturday night. You don't honestly think I'm going to tell her that I saw your lily white bum bobbing up and down in the moonlight? (*To the NURSE*) I did.

VERNON buries his head in his hands.

NIGEL: She blames me, doesn't she?

VERNON: She always said you drove too fast. (*To the NURSE*) There's no truth in what he said nurse, he just did it to embarrass me.

NIGEL: It wasn't my fault – not really.

VERNON: You saying it's Kevin's fault then?

NIGEL: We were... there was...

NURSE: You were having a domestic, that's what happened, wasn't it?

There is a slight pause.

VERNON: Was it?

NIGEL: (*To the NURSE*) How did you know?

NURSE: Been there, darling, and done it. (*A slight pause*) I'm divorced, aren't I? I recognize the signs. It doesn't take a genius.

VERNON: Is that what happened? You and Kevin had a row?

NIGEL: (*After a slight pause*) Yeah. That's about the long and short of it, yeah.

VERNON: Serious?

NIGEL: We crashed the fucking car, didn't we? (*A pause*) I've been saying for weeks that there's something up but he kept denying it. Why he chose to tell me there and then in the car God only knows.

VERNON: Tell you what?

NURSE: They're splitting up.

NIGEL: Do you mind! (*A slight pause*) He's chucking it all in, Vern. Me, him, the act, the lot. I kept screaming at him to think about what he was giving up, but you know Kevin, when he's got something in his head... Four years together and a promising career all down the Swanee.

VERNON: (*After a slight pause*) I'm sure he didn't mean it. People say a lot of things when they're arguing.

NIGEL: (*Shouting*) That's why we were arguing, you silly bloody... (*He pulls himself together*) All right, I said, you think we're all washed up – but you can't go back.

NURSE: Back?

VERNON: Back?

NIGEL: Yes. It's a big mistake to think you can go back, I said.

VERNON: To where?

NIGEL: To who.

VERNON: To who then?

NIGEL: To who do you think? His cowing wife, that's who.

NURSE: You're kidding.

VERNON: Are you sure?

NIGEL: No, I'm making it up because I enjoy being this hysterical. (*A slight pause*) He's been seeing her for the past couple of weeks.

NURSE: I'd better carry on.

During the following, the NURSE fills in NIGEL's chart at the bottom of the bed.

NIGEL: Yes, why not, every bugger else is.

GRIFF: (*Off; shouting*) Will you tell me what the hell's happening to us?

RUBY: (*Off; shouting*) Will you keep your voice down? You're in a hospital, remember.

GRIFF: (*Off; shouting*) I don't care where I am. Up till last Saturday our family was quite – orthodox.

NIGEL: Orthodox?

RUBY: (*Off; shouting*) Orthodox? Good God, Griff, you can call us a lot of things but we've hardly been that.

GRIFF: (*Off; shouting*) On the surface we were. Now all of a sudden everything's a mess.

NIGEL: You can say that again.

GRIFF: (*Off; shouting*) A mess!

NIGEL: (*To the NURSE*) I thought he'd have gone home by now.

VERNON: When is all this supposed to be happening with you and Kevin?

NIGEL: (*After a slight pause*) 'You're making a big mistake,' I said. 'You can't change your whole lifestyle just like that' – but he was having none of it. 'What about me?' I said. 'What's going to happen to me? I love you. Where do I stand in all this?' Next week apparently, Vernon. He's moving out next week. I knew we had problems but I didn't think it was anything on that scale.

NURSE: My fella went and I didn't even know he'd gone till I had a phone call.

NIGEL: So I'm supposed to be grateful now, am I?

NURSE: Didn't even say 'So long' to his daughter.

NIGEL: I'm not going to be able to say 'Hallo' to mine.

VERNON: (*Firmly*) Kate isn't your daughter, Nigel.

NIGEL: She was going to be. When there was a problem and that cow of a mother didn't want her, what did I say? I said, 'It's all right, Kev. We'll have her come to us.' How many others would have said that? I was going to give up my day job to look after her. It was all planned. I mean we've told people.

VERNON: (*Moving towards the bed*) Kate was going to live with you?

NIGEL: You'd have seen more of her then, I could have promised you that.

VERNON: You and Kevin couldn't have brought Kate up, Nigel.

NIGEL: Why not?

VERNON: It wouldn't have been right. She needs a mother and a father. All kids do.

NIGEL: Oh, wake up, Vern. Even I'd have made a damned sight better mother than the one that doesn't love her now.

VERNON: Why has he made the decision to go back? I can't work it out.

NURSE: (*To VERNON*) He probably told him why in the car. That's what the row was about.

NIGEL: I thought we were happy. I think I could have accepted it more if it was another man... but his wife.

VERNON: It doesn't make sense. I can't understand why he would run back to her?

NURSE: He's not running *to* her, he's running *from* him.

NIGEL looks rather incredulously at the NURSE.

NURSE: Well, that's how I see it anyway.

NIGEL: No, you're wrong. He's running from himself. 'I want to be normal,' he said. Christ – don't we all?

VERNON: Wait till Rita finds out.

NIGEL: It'll be just up her street.

VERNON: You've got to be joking. You might not be her favourite person at the moment, but she likes you. She's hated Erica from day one.

GRIFF: (*Off, shouting*) There was nothing funny about me and Ritchie. We were like brothers, we were.

RUBY: (*Off, shouting*) You don't take your brother on honeymoon with you.

GRIFF: (*Off, shouting*) I didn't take him on honeymoon.

RUBY: (*Off, shouting*) It's a hell of a coincidence that he ended up in the caravan next to us then, don't you think?

NURSE: (*To NIGEL*) And you thought you had trouble.

VERNON: He took a mate on honeymoon? What sort of family are you?

NIGEL: I don't think you're in a position to criticize, do you? (*A slight pause*) I didn't know about that though... (*He indicates that he means his father and his friend*) And who the hell is Ritchie, anyway?

NURSE: There you are. Let me help you up.

The NURSE helps NIGEL sit up.

NURSE: All right? Ready for your visitors then?

NIGEL: I wish they'd all go home. (*To VERNON*) You included.

NURSE: You don't mean that. I'll send them in, shall I?

NIGEL: Why not. It's like a cowing three-ringed circus in here anyway.

NURSE: I can send them all away if that's what you want. You don't have to see anyone.

303

NIGEL doesn't reply.

NURSE: Nigel?

NIGEL: Do what you like.

The NURSE covers a smile. She makes to turn away with her tray of things.

VERNON: (*Stopping the NURSE*) You didn't believe him, did you, nurse?

The NURSE doesn't understand.

VERNON: You know... the bum... the moonlight. It's a load of rubbish.

The NURSE takes a breath, not really knowing how to react. She shakes her head and her eyes widen. She exhales through her nose and smiles, turns and exits.

A pause.

VERNON: I think I pulled that off. (*A pause*) Perhaps I'd better go too, then.

NIGEL: Yes, go on, go. Talk about rats and the sinking ship.

VERNON: You wanted me to leave a minute ago.

NIGEL: You've had what you came for so you can bugger off now if you want to.

VERNON: That's not fair. I'll stay as long as you want me to. (*Pause*) Of course I was hoping to have a word with you about... well, you know... but I do care about you. We both do, Rita and myself.

A slight pause.

NIGEL: When we met – I mean when *we* met – (*he indicates himself and VERNON*) when Kevin brought me to your house, you were both marvellous about it. I wasn't sure if you were on my side, but at least you weren't against me...

VERNON: Yes...

NIGEL: I'm just wondering where you stand now. Do you approve of his plans or not?

VERNON: Do you want the truth?

NIGEL: And nothing but.

VERNON: I don't know. Up until a quarter of an hour ago I didn't know anything about them.

NIGEL: You must have had a gut reaction when I told you. What are you feeling, Vern? I can't work it out.

VERNON: (*Shaking his head and thinking about it*) I want what he wants I suppose.

NIGEL: What if he doesn't know what he wants? What if he turned to you tomorrow and said, 'Dad, talk to me. I'm all mixed up and I need help.' What would you say then, Vern?

A pause.

VERNON: (*Moving to the bed*) You are one of the better things that happened to Kevin.

NIGEL: Remind him then, will you, because he's forgotten.

VERNON: Well, we haven't. Whatever happens between you, me and Rita will always be grateful for what you did for him.

NIGEL: I can't take all the credit. You made it easy for me.

VERNON: We just wanted what was best for him – at the time there was no doubt about it.

NIGEL: At the time? What about now? What about now, Vern?

VERNON: I don't know. I thought you were happy too.

NIGEL: Hey, listen, I didn't influence him.

VERNON: Of course not.

NIGEL: He was well aware of his preferences before he met me.

VERNON: I know that. (*A slight pause. He sits on the left side of the bed*) We knew how things were with him long before you came along... or at least we thought we knew. Although he never talked about his... preferences, as you say, me and Rita, we assumed. (*A slight pause*) Then one day he surprised us and brought Erica home. Surprised? We were gob-smacked. I was delighted, I encouraged it even though Rita didn't like her. I was so glad to be wrong about him. I kept telling Rita he'd grow out of it and now I thought he'd proved me right. I pushed him into that marriage and it all but destroyed him.

NIGEL: So what are you saying? You saying he should stay with me or what?

VERNON: When he left his wife, Rita thought he might have come home to us. We waited but there was no word, nothing. London was the last place we thought he'd have run to. That was the worst year of our lives. Then one day the phone rang –

NIGEL: I know – I dialled it.

VERNON: We couldn't believe it when he got in touch. We didn't mind even when he wrote and said you were in tow.

NIGEL: Oh, that's very kind of you.

VERNON: No offence meant. (*He stands.*)

NIGEL: Well, plenty taken.

VERNON: Anything he wanted to do was all right by us at the time, we were so glad to have him back. I felt guilty –

NIGEL: And responsible for the mess he'd made of his marriage, yeah, Vern. I've heard of all this before.

VERNON: You know how long it took him to forgive me and to pick up the pieces. I don't want to say anything that might put us back to square one.

NIGEL: There you are, you see? I knew if I pushed you hard enough I'd get you to show your hand.

VERNON: No, you don't understand.

NIGEL: But I do, Vern. I understand perfectly. Kevin can do whatever he likes. He can toss me aside like stinking lettuce if he wants to because the bottom line here is that whatever he wants is all right with you.

VERNON: Look. (*A slight pause*) When you lose someone – well, it's awful.

NIGEL: Tell me about it!

VERNON: If you're lucky enough to get them back – you put up with a lot just to hang on to them.

NIGEL: I'll bear that in mind.

VERNON: I know you're hurting. And you're probably upset because you think I've let you down...

NIGEL: Good God no, Vern, what makes you think that! (*A slight pause*) You're unbelievable. (*A slight pause*) Do you know what I think? Vern? Everything's falling into place now. I think it was all an act with you. Oh, not this here now today, I meant you and me from day one. You remember that day, Vern? It was the day Kevin introduced me and you put your arm on my shoulder and said 'Welcome to the family' – but you didn't approve of me at all. It was all an act, wasn't it? I was 'put up' with for Kevin's sake. I was all right just as long as I was what he wanted, but the minute you think he wants something else, you see your chance and you dump on me – and you've dumped on me from a great height.

VERNON: I understand how you feel.

NIGEL: Do you?

VERNON: Of course.

NIGEL: Tell me then. (*A slight pause; raising his voice*) Go on, tell me how I feel.

VERNON doesn't answer.

NIGEL: (*Quieter*) You haven't a clue. You couldn't even comprehend it. I feel less than nothing. Less than that piece of dandruff on your shoulder there. Even a piece of dandruff is a piece of dandruff. Me? I'm just a freak; it doesn't matter that I'm a very good freak, that I'm a talented freak. In your eyes and the eyes of my old man out there, I'm just a piece of shit. The only difference between you is that you want to flush me away, and him? I'm the accident in his pants – he can't get rid of me that easily. He thinks I'm the big embarrassment people won't let him forget but the truth is – the truth is he won't let himself forget. (*A slight pause*) No, Vern, believe me, you couldn't possibly know how I feel.

RUBY: (*Off*) Roots and wings, Griff – remember roots and wings.

NIGEL: Fathers – they make me sick. (*A slight pause*) I'd make a better parent than either of you put together.

VERNON: (*After a pause*) If there's anything I can do.

NIGEL: Don't make me laugh. You know I wish people wouldn't say that, they rarely mean it.

VERNON: Will you be all right?

NIGEL: Oh, don't worry about me yet, Vern. There's a lot more talking to be done yet.

VERNON: But you said it was over.

NIGEL: No, not quite. It's not over till the fat lady sings.

VERNON: What?

NIGEL shakes his head and gestures for VERNON to forget it.

NIGEL: How can you do it to him?

VERNON: What?

NIGEL: You said yourself that living with a woman all but destroyed him.

VERNON: I'm just going to be there for him, that's all.

NIGEL: You're walking on very thin ice, Vern. Be warned, when it's that thin you're bound to get yourself wet.

VERNON: I'm not going to make the same mistake twice if that's what you're worried about.

NIGEL: You bet your arse you're not, because if I've got anything to do with it you're not going to have the opportunity.

VERNON: What do you mean?

NIGEL: I've put too much into this relationship to throw it away.

VERNON: What are you going to do?

NIGEL: The only thing I know how. I'm going to fight! I love him too much to give him up without a scrap. I'll take on you, him, Rita and that tart of a wife if I have to.

VERNON: (*Almost afraid to ask*) What have you got in mind? You're not going to start throwing mud, are you?

NIGEL: Mud? I'm going to throw everything I can get my hands on, love.

VERNON: (*Very worried*) When you say everything...

NIGEL: I mean – everything! I wouldn't be at all surprised if Rita doesn't end up cancelling that silver wedding do.

VERNON: You wouldn't.

NIGEL: All's fair in love and war, Vern. I' d get very worried and start panicking if I were you.

RUBY enters.

RUBY: There you are! Oooh, you're much better today. How are you feeling, all right?

NIGEL: A hundred per cent. One hundred per cent. Sit down, Ma, 'cos it's... showtime!

The introduction to Shirley Bassey's I Am What I Am *begins.*

RUBY stands and looks agog. She does not see VERNON standing a yard on behind her.

The lights snap off leaving the stage in darkness.

Just as Bassey begins to sing –

– the curtain falls.

Act Two

The stage is divided in two, with half the room and half the corridor visible; one of the double doors is now red, representing the door inside the room, and the other blue to represent the corridor outside.

The music played at the end of Act One starts at exactly the same place. After Shirley Bassey has sung the first line, the sound cross-fades from this to her singing the last two lines or so of the final verse. As this cross-fade takes place, the lights come up.

The action is continuous. RUBY and VERNON are holding the same positions as when we last saw them. NIGEL is singing along with Shirley Bassey, his hands held up in the air.

The singing and music finish. There is a slight pause.

RUBY: What the hell was all that about?

NIGEL: Mam, this is Vernon.

RUBY: What? (*She turns round and sees VERNON for the first time*) Oooh. (*She laughs nervously in an attempt to save her embarrassment*) Hallo Doctor. I'm Nigel's mother.

NIGEL: He's not the doctor.

RUBY: You'll have to excuse my son. (*Almost mouthing the words*) He's in show business. (*She suddenly realizes what NIGEL has just said and turns to him*) What?

NIGEL: This is Kevin's father.

RUBY: (*Looking immediately at VERNON; after a slight pause*) Of course you are. You're a spit of him, has anyone ever told you? (*A thought strikes her*) Wait a minute. (*She moves to the*

312

other side of the bed, standing to the left of NIGEL) What's he doing in here before me?

NIGEL: Would you like to answer that one, Vern?

GRIFF sheepishly opens the door to the room and steps inside.

RUBY: (*Pleased with herself*) Oh, look, Nigel – your father's come in to see you.

NIGEL: (*Singing the theme song from the TV show*) 'Mr and Mrs, da da da da da da, love one another.'

GRIFF: What's going on?

NIGEL: (*Launching into a mock game-show*) Right, here we go then folks. Ready for your first three questions? This is for your mother, OK? If you caught my father having sex in the back of a car, would you (a) change your address, (b) change your car, or (c) change your husband?

RUBY: (*To VERNON*) How long has he been like this?

VERNON: Ever since I've known him.

NIGEL: Wrong. (*He makes a noise like a buzzer*) Next. Your turn, Vern. If you took a mate with you on honeymoon, what would your wife say? Would she say, (a) I don't care how close you are he's not putting his boots under my bed, (b) is that bed going to be big enough for all of us, or, (c) we can't all sleep together. I wouldn't know which way to turn?

GRIFF: (*To RUBY*) Did you hear that? That's all your fault, that is.

RUBY: Mine?

NIGEL: Wrong! (*He makes another buzzing noise*) You're next, Griff. If your only son turned out to be gay, would you (a) find him a girlfriend, (b) find him a boyfriend, or (c) find him a shrink to straighten him out?

RUBY: (*Shouting to GRIFF*) I told you to keep your voice down.

GRIFF: (*Shouting*) I don't shout!

RUBY: You're shouting now. And look at your colour. (*To VERNON, smiling*) Least little thing and he's red as a beetroot. He can't help it, he suffers with hypertension.

GRIFF: I don't know why I bothered coming in here.

RUBY: Of course you do.

GRIFF: (*Shouting*) And there's nothing wrong with my blood pressure!

RUBY: You know there is. One day you'll start telling yourself the truth.

NIGEL: Seems to me we all live in 'Secret City', don't you agree, Vern? Dad?

RITA comes in from left. She is a woman in her early forties. She looks wrecked as she's been at the hospital for just over twenty-four hours. She is extremely uptight and is very anxious about the condition of her son; she also has a few other things on her mind. She makes for the coffee machine and looks for change in her purse.

GRIFF: I should never have listened to you. So much for that smile you said I'd get.

RUBY: Nigel, smile for your father.

314

VERNON: I'd better go.

NIGEL: (*To VERNON*) Don't even think about it.

RUBY: Nigel.

The NURSE enters the hallway from right.

NURSE: (*Seeing RITA*) Oh... hiya.

VERNON: You don't want me here, it's a family thing.

NURSE: All right?

NIGEL: You are family – for a bit longer, anyway.

NURSE: How's Kevin doing?

GRIFF: I'd better go.

RITA: (*Searching her purse*) The same.

RUBY: (*To GRIFF*) You just dare, Nigel!

NIGEL: What?

RUBY: (*After a slight pause*) I've forgotten what I wanted you for now.

NURSE: No change?

RITA: Yes – I just need a bigger purse I suppose.

RUBY: (*Remembering*) Oh, I know. Haven't you got anything to say to your father?

NURSE: You sure you're all right?

RITA nods. She's not really all right.

NIGEL: Yeah, good night Saturday, wasn't it?

GRIFF: Right, that's it. (*He makes to go.*)

NURSE: See you then.

RUBY: Griff!

GRIFF: You heard that, didn't you?

The NURSE exits looking slightly concerned about RITA.

During the following, RITA gets a cup of coffee from the machine.

VERNON: I'm not very comfortable here.

NIGEL: So, squirm.

RUBY: Nigel!

RITA: (*Calling after her*) Nurse!

RUBY: There was no need to say that to your father.

GRIFF: I should never have come in here.

The NURSE appears in the corridor.

GRIFF: I don't know why I let you talk me into it.

NURSE: (*To RITA*) Yes?

RUBY: Nigel, do your mother a favour and give your father a smile.

NIGEL gives GRIFF a very quick, false smile putting both thumbs under his chin as he cocks his head to one side.

GRIFF: (*Infuriatedly*) It's like a mad house here...

RITA: (*Shaking her head*) Nothing... it's all right.

The NURSE leaves.

GRIFF: (*Turning to go*) I'm going to work.

RUBY: Griff?

GRIFF: (*With his back to RUBY*) You can say what you like – me and him are finished. (*He heads for the door.*)

NIGEL: Did we ever start?

RUBY: No, don't say that. (*To GRIFF*) He didn't mean what he said. He's all mixed up – he's probably delirious.

GRIFF exits through the blue door and immediately enters through the red door which leads him into the corridor. He literally bumps into RITA who has a cup of coffee in her hand; some coffee spills on to the floor.

RUBY: (*To NIGEL*) Well... you've done it now.

NIGEL: No, I haven't done it now. I did it last Saturday.

GRIFF: Oh, I'm sorry.

NIGEL: And I'm not sorry.

RUBY: (*Getting upset*) I can't take much more of this. I've had a gutsful between the pair of you.

VERNON: (*To RUBY*) Are you all right?

RITA: (*To GRIFF, very impatiently*) I'm fine, I'm fine.

GRIFF and VERNON get out their handkerchiefs to offer them to RITA and RUBY respectively.

GRIFF: Here.

VERNON: Have a hanky.

RUBY: It's all right, I've got one. (*She takes one out of her pocket.*)

RITA takes GRIFF's hanky and begins to use it to dry herself.

GRIFF: Sit down, come on.

RUBY: (*Snappily*) No, I'm all right.

VERNON: Tea?

RITA: No.

GRIFF: Are you sure?

RUBY: Yes.

VERNON: Coffee?

RITA: All right.

GRIFF: I'll bring it over.

RITA sits down. GRIFF gets two cups of coffee from the machine during the following.

RUBY dries her nose. As she is doing so, VERNON mouths to NIGEL to 'Let me go'. NIGEL smiles and shakes his head. RUBY sees this however and is suspicious.

RUBY: There's nothing going on here, is there?

VERNON: Like what?

RUBY: I don't know.

NIGEL: She's very quick, my mother.

RUBY: So I'm right then, am I?

VERNON: (*Quickly*) No.

NIGEL: You answered that a bit too sharply then, Vern. You'll never convince her now.

RUBY: You are who you say you are, are you?

VERNON: What do you mean?

NIGEL: She's inferring you might be some sort of extra-marital affair. Am I right, Mother?

RUBY: Well...

VERNON: You're barking up the wrong tree there.

NIGEL: Good God, yes. Vernon loves women, don't you, Vern? Oh, and by the way, I don't want either of you to mention trees for the rest of the day, is that understood?

RUBY: Trees?

VERNON: It's what they collided into.

GRIFF goes over to RITA and hands her a coffee before sitting down next to her.

RITA: Thanks.

GRIFF: You're still a bit wet.

RITA: It's nothing – really.

A pause.

RUBY: You've gone and let me down as far as your father's concerned, you know that, don't you?

NIGEL: I've been letting you down as far as he's concerned ever since I was born.

RUBY: Now there's no need for that. (*To VERNON*) Griff thinks the world of him really. (*To NIGEL*) And you love him too if the truth be known.

RITA is more than a little shaky and upset. She runs her hand through her hair in an attempt to pull herself together.

GRIFF: Trouble?

RITA: Sorry?

GRIFF: You look a bit... you know.

RITA: It's been a long night.

GRIFF: It's been a long weekend.

RUBY: (*To VERNON*) You know, I've been rabbiting on here, you must think I'm very rude. I haven't asked you once how Kevin's doing.

VERNON: He's holding his own.

NIGEL: Well it's a change from holding mine. (*He laughs.*)

No one joins him.

NIGEL: I'm sorry. That wasn't funny, was it?

RUBY: That's the trouble with you. You never know how far to go.

GRIFF: Who is it? Father? Husband?

RUBY: If you knew what it took to get your father to come in here.

RITA: Son.

GRIFF: Snap.

NIGEL: It shouldn't have taken anything.

RUBY: It wasn't easy for him. He was offering you an olive branch.

NIGEL: (*Yawning*) Now you know what I said about trees! Oh God – I've come over all tired. I'm going to put my head down for a minute.

GRIFF: Kids.

VERNON: Perhaps if we go outside –

RITA: Is it just one?

NIGEL: No, you're all right where you are.

GRIFF: Oh, yes.

VERNON: It's best if I go.

RITA: Me too.

NIGEL: Just stay where you are...

RUBY: Let him go. I'll stay here with you.

NIGEL: No, he wants to be here. You do, don't you, Vern?

NIGEL and RUBY look at VERNON. He smiles rather uncomfortably.

NIGEL snuggles down into the bed. RUBY straightens the blankets around him then sits next to the bed. During the following she strokes the back of NIGEL's hand. VERNON just looks on.

RITA: Is he going to be all right?

GRIFF: He'll be home by the weekend, but I don't know that he'll ever be right.

VERNON moves to look out of the window in the door.

RITA: Oh, I'm sorry.

GRIFF: Not half as much as I am.

RITA: (*After a slight pause*) My son's in a coma. He was involved in an accident. (*She begins to get upset*) He hasn't come round yet.

RUBY: Him and his father had a bit of a to-do on Saturday.

VERNON: I know. He told me about it.

RUBY: That's just like him – typical of him. He's like an open book.

GRIFF: (*Not really sure what to say or how to handle the situation*) He's going to be all right though, is he? Your boy?

RITA: (*Trying to pull herself together*) I lost him once, I can't lose him again.

VERNON: You know, I'm surprised we haven't met before.

RUBY: I'm not. Nigel keeps that side of his life away from his father. Griff has only just found out. He's still coming to terms with it. How did you take it?

GRIFF: You on your own?

RITA: My husband's here somewhere.

RUBY: I bet you were sympathetic. You look the sympathetic type to me.

VERNON: I was supportive, yes.

GRIFF: When you say you lost him... your boy now, I mean –

RITA: He went away.

RUBY: That's a good word, supportive.

RITA: Disappeared.

RUBY: That sums it up about right, that does. Supportive.

RITA: We didn't hear anything from him for thirteen months.

RUBY: I wish to God our Griff could find it in himself to be that.

GRIFF: How did you get him back?

VERNON: If he's only just found out then you've got to give him time.

RUBY: That's exactly what I said to him out there.

RITA: He just got in touch.

RUBY: You've got to give yourself time, I said. It'll all come right in the end.

RITA: He got himself together and he got in touch.

RUBY: That's what I keep telling myself, anyway, but none of us know what's round the corner see, do we?

VERNON looks at RUBY, but doesn't answer her.

RITA: When he came home he had a whole set of new problems but me and Vernon, that's my husband, we didn't care. He was back and that's all that mattered.

GRIFF: (*After a slight pause in which he gets up and wanders down right*) I didn't want my son to go either. Oh, he didn't just disappear like yours. His year away was all planned. London. (*A slight pause*) Did yours go to...?

RITA: Yes.

GRIFF: They all seem to bugger off there, don't they? (*A slight pause*) We were never close – still not. I played it very cool. 'Go,' I said, 'it'll make a man of you.' I can still see his face now. I didn't really know what his expression meant, not at the time, anyway. I don't know how it would have turned out if he hadn't gone. Either way I suspect things would have stayed the same. (*A slight pause*) He never listened to me, it was all his mother, but I can't help wondering what would have happened if I'd said something. Would it have made any difference if I'd said, 'Stay – I want you to stay.' (*A slight pause*) Would you have stopped your boy if you could?

RITA: I'd have tried.... His circumstances were – different, and difficult though. He really was running away. (*A slight*

324

pause) Still, that's all behind him now. And I do believe what happened then happened for the best. And for the first time in his life, I think he's happy. He has a partner who loves him and a family who cares. What more could he want – could anyone want. I certainly wouldn't wish his past on him again.

RUBY: (*Still stroking NIGEL's hand*) He's fast now. (*A slight pause*) You know, I try not to think about it but can you imagine what might have happened if they hadn't had that call?

VERNON: Who?

RUBY: The police.

GRIFF: (*Not really knowing what to say*) I'm sure he'll be all right – your boy.

RUBY: (*Getting up and going to VERNON*) If that man, that anonymous man, hadn't rung in, God knows how things would have turned out. I tell you, if he was here now, I'd kiss his feet.

VERNON looks very uncomfortable.

RITA: Your son's going home the weekend you said?

GRIFF nods.

RUBY: Do you think he'd come forward if we offered a reward?

VERNON: I've no idea.

RITA: You don't know how lucky you are.

RUBY: We could put a hundred up. Fifty pounds each, what do you think?

VERNON: It'll probably be a waste of time.

RITA: (*Standing and moving down left*) I feel so guilty.

VERNON: And maybe he's got a reason for being discreet.

RUBY: What, he doesn't want to show he was there, you mean?

RITA: I wasn't there, you see.

VERNON: It's possible.

RITA: At home – when the call came.

VERNON: And if that's the case, I doubt that a hundred pounds will flush him out.

RUBY: True.

RITA: (*Insistently*) I should have been there.

RUBY: Shame though.

GRIFF: It's easy to blame yourself.

RUBY: I'd have liked to have shook his hand and thanked him... wouldn't you?

VERNON: (*Awkwardly*) Yes – who knows, you might anyway.

RITA: There was no one at home.

RUBY: Do you think I could ask you a favour?

VERNON looks at RUBY.

RITA: Vernon was out on business.

RUBY: Oh, not now. Griff's gone so it's pointless now, but – well, the truth is, I think you're marvellous.

RITA: And I had a night out... with the girls.

RUBY: You're so – well, I don't know how to put it – in control. (*She flicks her thumb up from a fist of fingers*) Get it? (*She does it again*) You know, the gas advert.

VERNON smiles slightly and nods.

RUBY: God knows I've tried putting things across to him but it's like talking to a brick wall.

VERNON: Nigel?

RUBY: (*Shaking her head*) No, Griff.

RITA: I didn't say who I was with so Vernon couldn't get in touch.

RUBY: And I'm sure we could make some progress if he'd meet him half-way and open up a bit.

VERNON: Griff?

RUBY: No, Nigel!

RITA: The truth is, I'm being punished.

GRIFF: Oh, I don't think so.

RUBY: I can help out there though. I've always been able to get through to him, but Griff... well, I was beginning to think he was a lost cause.

VERNON: Until when?

RUBY: Until you came into it.

RITA: I should have changed my job.

GRIFF: What?

RUBY: Do you think you could have a word with him?

VERNON: Me?

RITA: None of this would have happened if I'd worked somewhere else.

VERNON: I don't even know him.

GRIFF: You've lost me now.

RUBY: I'm sure if he had someone to talk to. Someone in the same boat, so to speak.

RITA: I hate lies and now I'm paying for them.

GRIFF: Lies?

RUBY: A couple of hours with you over a pint and I'm sure something will rub off.

RITA: I suppose I was flattered to begin with.

RUBY: What do you think, could you have a word?

RITA: I had no idea where it would lead to.

VERNON: What would Nigel say?

RUBY: (*Going to him, confidentially*) Oh, I don't think we should tell him.

GRIFF: Are you trying to tell me what I think you're trying to tell me?

RUBY: If he thought for one minute that we were involved it would put the mockers on it good and proper.

RITA: Me and Vernon have our problems it's true –

RUBY: And the same would go for Griff for that matter.

RITA: But we should have worked at the marriage not drifted apart,

RUBY: No. This is our little secret, right? Not a word to no one, that's my advice.

RITA: You think I'm awful, don't you?

RUBY: (*Looking over to NIGEL*) Ahh – he's resting lovely now. If you want to nip out and check on Kevin.

VERNON: Yes, all right. (*He makes to leave.*)

NIGEL stirs.

VERNON: On the other hand, his mother's with him.

RUBY: What are you afraid of?

VERNON: I'm not afraid of anything.

RUBY: What does Nigel know that I don't?

GRIFF: (*Taking RITA's cup*) Have another cup of coffee... I am.

RUBY: You haven't answered me.

RITA: Do you think I should say something?

GRIFF: (*Moving to the coffee machine*) To who?

RUBY: (*Having an idea*) Perhaps someone else knows about it.

RITA: Vernon.

VERNON: Someone else?

GRIFF: Your husband?

VERNON: Like who?

RUBY: Your wife. (*She heads for the door.*)

VERNON: No, look – don't do that.

GRIFF: What would you want to tell him about?

VERNON: (*Moving away down centre*) I've been a bit of a naughty boy.

RITA: (*Moving away down centre*) My affair.

GRIFF: (*After a slight pause*) What would be the point of that?

RUBY: I knew there was something.

RITA: It's not too late to be honest. Maybe if I come clean, Kevin will take a turn for the better.

GRIFF: I don't think it works like that.

VERNON: Nigel found out.

RITA: So you don't think I should say anything then?

GRIFF: I'm a guard with British Rail. I'm not a Marriage Guidance Counsellor.

VERNON: To be honest, I'm not sure what he's going to do about it.

RITA: I just thought you could help. Sometimes it's better talking to a stranger.

RUBY: You think he might say something to your wife?

GRIFF: I don't know what to tell you.

RITA: I feel so guilty, advise me.

VERNON: I think there's every possibility of it.

GRIFF: I don't think I would even if I knew what to say.

RUBY: But why? Why would Nigel want to do that to you?

VERNON: It's a long story.

RITA: If I thought it would do Kevin any good, I would tell Vernon everything.

GRIFF: Everything?

RITA: Yes. You know, who, when, where, how long it's been going on for...

GRIFF: I don't think that would benefit anyone really, do you?

RITA: (*After a slight pause*) Maybe not – except me. Maybe I'm looking to get the whole thing off my chest.

GRIFF: Well, you have in a way – you've told me. (*He holds out a cup of coffee to RITA.*)

RITA: Yes. (*She takes the coffee.*)

GRIFF sits.

RITA: The one good thing about talking to a stranger is that at least there's not going to be any recriminations. (*She sits next to him*) I mean, it's highly unlikely that we'll ever see each other again after today – or after the weekend anyway, once your son... I'm sorry what did you say his name was?

GRIFF: Nigel.

RITA: (*After a slight pause*) Nigel. (*A slight pause*) Nigel?

GRIFF: Nigel.

RITA: Oh my God!

VERNON: You don't know this but Kevin and Nigel are splitting up.

GRIFF: What's the matter?

RUBY: What? No way – I don't believe it.

VERNON: It's true.

RITA: I've just realized who you are.

VERNON: Nigel told me.

GRIFF: Do I know you?

RUBY: He hasn't said a word to me and he tells me everything.

RITA: You have to promise me you won't say anything.

GRIFF: To who?

VERNON: Wake him up and ask him if you don't believe me.

RITA: Nigel.

GRIFF: About what?

RUBY: They've had a row, I expect; it's nothing that won't blow over.

RITA: Me and Peter.

GRIFF: Who the hell is Peter?

RITA: My boss.

VERNON: No, I think there's more to it than that.

During the following, RUBY holds NIGEL's hand and strokes his hair.

GRIFF: You've lost me again now. Why would I tell Nigel about you and your boss?

RITA: You don't know who I am, do you?

GRIFF: Should I?

RITA: I'm Rita. (*A slight pause*) Rita. Vernon's wife.

GRIFF: Vernon?

RITA: Kevin's father.

GRIFF: That might help if I knew who Kevin was.

RITA: Kevin. Kevin.

GRIFF: Kevin.

RITA: Nigel and Kevin.

GRIFF: (*After a slight pause*) Oh... (*The penny drops*) Oh hell. (*He gets up and moves away downstage.*)

RUBY: Kevin is everything to Nigel. I hope he's not going to hurt him.

VERNON: I think the best thing is not to get involved.

RUBY: Oh, I couldn't do that. I've stood by him all his life... I couldn't stand aside now. And you shouldn't either if what you say about them is right.

VERNON: It's a bit more complicated than that.

RUBY: No, it's not – it's simple... (*she gets up and moves downstage*) if they have a tiff and turn to us, all we have to do is turn them back to each other. They'll sort it all out. It's like my mother used to say to me, 'You've made your bed now go and lie on it.'

VERNON: But Kevin doesn't want to lie on it. Not that bed anyway. He doesn't want to live that kind of life any more.

RUBY: Well, bully for him.

VERNON: You know he used to be married. You did know, didn't you?

RUBY nods.

VERNON: According to Nigel he wants to give it another shot. I'm not sure why…. There's a child involved. Maybe it's got something to do with her.

RUBY: Well, knowing Nigel, he won't give up – not without a fight.

VERNON: (*Sighing*) Yes. I'd say you know him very well in that case.

RUBY: And I'll be standing there right next to him too.

VERNON: You really should let them get on with it.

RUBY: No, indeed I'm not. I'm going to help him get as much ammunition as I can.

VERNON: That's what I was afraid of.

RUBY: No one hurts my boy and gets away with it.

VERNON: Look, can I make a deal with you?

RITA gets up and joins GRIFF.

GRIFF: What sort of a deal?

RITA: I don't know. I just don't want you to say anything.

RUBY: To who?

VERNON: To Rita.

RITA: To Vernon.

GRIFF: It's none of my business.

RUBY: What's it worth to keep my mouth shut?

RITA: That's very good of you.

VERNON: You're going to have to gag Nigel as well.

GRIFF: No it's not. I just don't want to get involved.

RUBY: It's not going to be easy. What's in it for me?

VERNON: (*Meaning NIGEL*) Well, it's for him really.

RUBY: For him then?

RITA: If there's anything I can do in return.

VERNON: I told Nigel I'd stand by Kevin in his decision to leave...

RUBY: You'd support him you mean?

VERNON: Yes – but if Rita's kept from hearing where I was on Saturday, then I'll stand back and be impartial.

GRIFF: The best thing to do is to forget all about it.

RUBY: Not good enough. To keep your little secret safe I want you to encourage them to stay together.

RITA: I don't know how to thank you.

VERNON: What if it doesn't work?

RUBY: If it doesn't work, it doesn't work. Just promise me you'll do your best.

RITA: I don't know what you must think of me.

GRIFF: It's not for me to judge. To each his own I suppose.

RUBY: (*Offering VERNON her hand*) Is it a deal?

RITA: (*Offering GRIFF her hand*) Thank you.

Both couples shake hands.

The NURSE comes in with a small tray. On it are some pills and a small container filled with water.

NURSE: It's all right for some. I haven't had a coffee since six o'clock this morning.

GRIFF: Join us if you like.

NURSE: I daren't. It's all right anyway. I go to break in half an hour.

RITA: Is Kevin back yet?

NURSE: Due any time. They're not usually very long. Excuse me. (*She goes into Nigel's room.*)

GRIFF: Have they taken him somewhere?

RITA: He's gone for a brain scan.

NURSE: (*Entering the room and seeing NIGEL*) My God, look at Sleeping Beauty.

GRIFF: Tell me, what do you make of it all?

NURSE: Come on, sunshine – time for your medication.

The NURSE gently wakes NIGEL.

GRIFF: You know... with the boys and that.

NIGEL: What did you wake me for? I was having a lovely dream.

NURSE: Was I in it?

NIGEL: A lovely dream I said.

RITA: It's like you said, I suppose – to each his own.

NURSE: Come on – get this down your neck.

NIGEL: Ooooh, you've gone and broken it now.

NURSE: (*Shocked*) I don't believe you.

VERNON: (*Making to leave*) Excuse me.

NIGEL: Where are you going?

VERNON: To the Gents.

VERNON leaves Nigel's room.

RITA: It does get easier.

GRIFF turns to look at RITA.

VERNON approaches RITA.

NIGEL: (*To the NURSE*) I need to go too. Can you get me a bottle?

The NURSE hands NIGEL a bottle from the bedside cabinet. He takes it and places it between his legs under the blankets.

RITA: (*Seeing VERNON*) Vernon. Where have you come from?

VERNON: I've been in with Nigel. How's Kevin?

RITA: There's no change. Vernon, this is – did you tell me your name?

GRIFF: No... it's... er... Griff.

RITA: I'm Rita. Griff is Nigel's father.

VERNON: I know. We were both in there together for a while.

GRIFF: A short while. Is he still performing?

VERNON: He's still Nigel if that's what you mean.

RITA: Have a cup of coffee – you look like you need one. (*She moves to the machine*)

VERNON: No, I'm all right... it's the Gents I need. (*He exits right.*)

RITA: He hasn't taken it very well. (*She looks off right, after VERNON*) He and Kevin were really close lately. They never used to get on but they've been really close lately.

NIGEL: It's no good. I can't do anything with you two in here.

NURSE: Well, I'm not leaving. I'm going to take your blood pressure.

NIGEL: Again?

RUBY: I'll pop out then. About five minutes is it, Nurse?

NURSE: Fine.

RUBY leaves the room and enters the corridor.

The NURSE takes NIGEL's blood pressure during the following.

NIGEL: I've always been the same. I've never been able to pee in front of anyone. And I can't do it in here. (*Meaning the bed*) It feels all wrong. Perhaps if I could sit in a chair?

NURSE: I know what you're up to and you can forget it.

RUBY: (*Seeing GRIFF*) Griff? I thought you'd gone ages ago.

GRIFF: Have a guess who this is.

RUBY: Kevin's mother.

GRIFF: How did you know!

RUBY: I didn't. I just put two and two together. (*She moves to RITA*) How is he, all right?

RITA half smiles and shrugs.

RUBY: Don't worry, I'm sure he'll be fine. (*She puts her hand on RITA's arm.*)

RITA looks at RUBY's hand.

GRIFF: They've sent him down for a brain scan.

RUBY: Let's hope you'll never have to have one of them then.

GRIFF: Now don't start.

RUBY: I'm only making light of it. God knows it's depressing enough here as it is. (*To RITA*) Still hasn't come round yet I take it?

RITA shakes her head.

RUBY: I'm Ruby by the way.

RITA: Rita.

RUBY: You're a spit of Kevin, has anyone ever told you?

NIGEL: (*Holding out the empty bottle to the NURSE*) You may as well have this back – it's hopeless.

The NURSE takes the bottle and places it back on the cabinet; she then leans back over NIGEL to continue.

GRIFF: Do you want a cup of coffee or something?

RUBY: Yes, all right, go on then.

GRIFF: Rita?

RITA: Please.

GRIFF obliges. RUBY stares at RITA and smiles sympathetically.

NIGEL: If it's still normal can I sit up in a chair?

NURSE: Shut up, I'm counting.

RUBY: I don't like hospitals but it's a good job we got 'em, innit?

GRIFF is obviously having trouble with the coffee machine. He taps it a few times.

NIGEL: You'd better say yes – you're in a very vulnerable position.

NURSE: Not half as vulnerable as you are, sunshine. I've smothered many a man with these before now. (*Meaning her breasts.*)

NIGEL: I bet you have.

GRIFF begins to hit hell out of the coffee machine.

RUBY: Don't do that.

GRIFF: But it's not working.

RUBY: You'd have enough to say if some teenager started doing that to one of your trains.

GRIFF: There's only a load of steam coming out.

RUBY: A bit like you that is then, innit? There's another machine down the corridor. Go and get it from there.

RITA: (*Sitting back down in one of the chairs*) Don't bother for me, I've had two already.

RUBY: Nonsense. It's no bother for him. Go ahead – go on.

GRIFF looks at RUBY. She gestures for him to leave. GRIFF exits.

There is a pause. RUBY sits next to RITA. There is another pause.

RUBY: You don't have to talk if you don't want to. I understand. Sometimes it's nice just to sit and be quiet, innit? (*Another pause*) I find that hard, I do, though. The minute someone stops talking I always feel I got to chip in, you know. (*Another pause*) You like a bit of quiet, though, I can see. (*A slight pause*) Nothing wrong in that. (*A slight pause*) If that's what you're in to.

RITA: You're a road-crossing patrol officer I see.

RUBY: A lollipop lady, yes. It's only a couple of hours a day but it keeps me off the street. (*She laughs*) Get it? I always say that – but no one ever laughs, only me. What do you do?

RITA: I'm a PA.

RUBY: (*Quickly trying to work this out*) Oh... right. Have you worked for the Borough Council long?

RITA: I'm a personal assistant.

RUBY: (*Laughing*) Good God and there's me thinking you were a park attendant. So you're a secretary then?

RITA: A personal assistant, yes.

RUBY: 'Take a letter Miss Jones', that sort of thing.

RITA doesn't answer.

RUBY: The only lap I ever sat on was Father Christmas's. And then he frightened me so much I wet him soaking.

RITA: Embarrassing.

RUBY: Oh, it was – I was thirty-six at the time. (*She laughs*) I'm not normally this chirpy you know, I'm only doing it to cheer you up.

RITA: I'm sorry but I'm not in the mood.

RUBY: I can see that, that's why I thought I'd try and make you laugh – or smile. (*A slight pause*) I suppose I'd be the same if my son was – well, you know. Still, anything can happen. Last night wasn't very good for Nigel but today he's as right as rain. Have you been in to see him?

RITA shakes her head.

RUBY: No, of course you haven't. We'll go in together now. Soon as the nurse have –

RITA: Er... no!

RUBY: What?

RITA: I don't want to see him.

RUBY is shocked and just stares at RITA.

RITA: Have you ever been in the car with him? Have you seen the way he drives?

RUBY: (*In Nigel's defence*) Hey look, you hang on a minute, by here now. I know you're going through hell, but you want to stop and think about what you're saying.

RITA: I'm surprised there hasn't been some sort of accident before now.

RUBY: Now you've hit the nail on the head by there. *Accidents* are accidents. I know you're in a bit of a state but... you don't think for a minute either of them would choose to be in here, do you?

RITA: (*Reluctantly*) No.

RUBY: No. You know Nigel thinks the world of your Kevin – and to be honest, I do too. (*A slight pause*) You and Kevin – are things good between you?

RITA: (*After a slight pause*) They're all right.

RUBY: All right isn't the same as good – well not in my book, anyway. (*A pause*) There was a time when I used to

wonder what things would be like if they were different –
but if things were different then the boys wouldn't be who
they are, and if they weren't who they are, who's to say we
would have loved them as much?

RITA looks up at RUBY but doesn't say anything.

*During the following, the NURSE enters Nigel's details on to his
chart.*

NIGEL: Kevin is going to be all right, isn't he?

RUBY: You don't look old enough to be Kevin's mother.

NURSE: I've told you all I know.

NIGEL: But what do you think?

NURSE: I think you should stop worrying and rest up.

NIGEL: I can't. Not while Kev's like he is.

RUBY: Had him young did you?

NIGEL: (*After a slight pause*) Perhaps later on... when
everyone's gone home you'll take me in?

The NURSE doesn't answer.

RITA: I was twenty-three.

NIGEL: I've got to see him. I need to.

The NURSE still doesn't commit herself.

RUBY: And what's Kevin now – twenty-four, twenty-five?

NIGEL: I've got to tell him I'm sorry.

RITA: Twenty-four.

NURSE: For causing the accident?

RUBY: (*Doing a quick mental addition*) You're forty-seven then.

NIGEL: It wasn't an accident.

NURSE: (*After a slight pause*) What?

RUBY: I was twenty-nine having Nigel.

NIGEL: I was so upset.

RUBY: I'm fifty- (*she mouths*) five now.

NIGEL: He was saying terrible things.

NURSE: You mean you crashed the car on purpose?

RUBY: It's hard to believe that there's nine years between us, innit?

NIGEL: The last thing I remember thinking was, if I couldn't have him, she wasn't going to.

RUBY: Bit of a career woman, are you?

NURSE: Do you realize what you're saying?

NIGEL: I've got to tell someone or I think I'll go crazy.

RUBY: I've never had any ambition myself.

NIGEL: I didn't think it would turn out like this. I thought we would both die together.

RUBY: I didn't work at all until this little number came along.

NURSE: Look, I didn't hear what you just said, right? If anything went wrong with Kevin you could be in deep shit.

NIGEL: Why do you think I need to know that he's going to be all right?

RUBY: It was my friend's job really. She asked me to cover for her while she went to visit her daughter in Australia and she never came back. I didn't know she had died till they sent her ashes home.

NIGEL: You should see our act.

NURSE: Maybe I will.

NIGEL: Yeah... (*a slight pause*). And maybe you won't.

RUBY: Have you ever been to Australia?

RITA shakes her head.

RUBY: No, or me.

NIGEL: We're very good, you know.

NURSE: I bet you are.

NIGEL: We could get somewhere if we really pushed it. (*A pause*) He still loved me, he said... (*He becomes upset, crying quietly, his head forward.*)

The NURSE puts her arm around NIGEL's shoulders.

There if a slight pause. RUBY looks at RITA and smiles. She might even touch RITA's hand.

RUBY: He's going to be all right, I'm sure he is. And it's like I said... no one's to blame. Believe me love, it's the easiest thing in the world to point a finger.

VERNON enters.

VERNON: Kevin's back.

RITA: What?

VERNON: In his room. He's back.

RITA: (*Standing*) Right.

VERNON: No, don't go, yet. They're still making him comfortable.

RUBY: Now's your chance to pop in and see Nigel.

RITA: Yes.

VERNON: No! Er – on the other hand, they've probably finished with Kevin by now.

RUBY: (*To RITA*) Go in and see Nigel first, go on. Two minutes – you won't be long.

RITA goes into Nigel's room. RUBY makes to follow her but stops briefly to have a quick and quiet word with VERNON.

RUBY: Don't worry. I'll see that nothing's said. (*She enters Nigel's room*) All right, Nurse?

NURSE: (*To NIGEL*) You've got visitors.

RUBY: Look who's come to see you.

NIGEL: (*Seeing RITA*) Rita. (*He quickly hides his tears.*)

RITA: Before you say anything, I did blame you, but I know that's not going to get us anywhere.

VERNON stands outside Nigel's room, pondering. He then goes to the coffee machine and has a drink without any problem whatsoever.

NIGEL: I'm sorry. It should never have happened.

NURSE: It's a perfectly natural reaction after an RTA. I call it the 'if only syndrome'. 'If only I did this' and 'if only I did that'.

RITA: I don't want you blaming yourself. It's like your mother said – it was an accident.

NIGEL: But what if Kevin –

NURSE: Look, I'm not really a religious person, but do you know what we often do on the wards in situations like these? We all hold hands and close our eyes together.

RITA: Pray, you mean?

NURSE: You can call it a prayer if you want to. I just think it helps sometimes to concentrate and think about the person we want to get well. You might even feel better for it yourself.

RUBY: It definitely sounds like a prayer to me. What do you say, Reet?

NURSE: Come on. Shall we do it or what?

RITA: (*After a slight pause*) Why not.

The NURSE holds out both her arms and everyone in the room hesitantly joins hands.

NURSE: Now close your eyes.

They all look at each other then eventually close their eyes.

A pause.

GRIFF enters the corridor from right, carrying two coffees. He stops when he sees VERNON.

GRIFF: We haven't met properly. Vernon, innit? (*He offers his hand but it's holding a coffee. He offers his other hand but that has a coffee in it as well. He places both cups on top of the coffee machine.*)

VERNON: Vernon.

They shake hands.

GRIFF: (*After a slight pause*) Bit of a circus all this, isn't it?

VERNON: (*After a slight pause*) Is it me or has it gone very quiet in there? (*Meaning Nigel's room.*)

GRIFF: I can't handle it myself.

VERNON: What?

GRIFF: You know – Nigel and – er – Kevin. (*A pause*) You cope all right, do you?

VERNON: I don't think too much about it. Especially now with Kevin...

GRIFF: Of course. (*A pause*) Have you known long?

VERNON: About the boys?

GRIFF nods.

VERNON: Right from the start or just about.

GRIFF moves away and nods his head several more times.

VERNON: I know about Saturday.

GRIFF: What?

VERNON: Nigel told me what he did. I know it must have been awful for you but try not to take it out on him. He's hurting. I know you are too, but – don't make the same mistake I did.

GRIFF: The truth is I don't like him very much. What mistake did you make?

VERNON: I tried to change him. Well, I encouraged it which is much the same thing.

GRIFF: Do you blame yourself for how he turned out?

VERNON: I did for a while, then the more I thought about it the more common sense took and explained it. It's no one's fault.

GRIFF: So you don't think anything could, you know – influence them then.

VERNON: No, not in either way. (*A slight pause*) That wasn't always the case, though. I remember in the beginning, when we first found out, I was looking for all kinds of reasons and people to blame. (*A slight pause*) The three of us went on a trip to Blackpool once. Kevin must have only been about eight. There was this dick-head on the bus who dressed up in a wig and a frock and I know I blamed him for a while.

For a moment GRIFF doesn't know where to look.

351

VERNON: Things haven't always been good between Kevin and me. We've both made mistakes but thank God we've been big enough to learn by them.

GRIFF: So you accept him now?

VERNON: You'll be surprised what you'll accept when you view the alternative. It depends on how you feel I suppose – and what you're prepared to let stand in the way.

The NURSE opens her eyes.

NURSE: There you are then.

The others open their eyes.

VERNON: You know, it's definitely gone quiet in there. (*He looks through the door windows.*)

GRIFF looks thoughtful through the following scene.

NURSE: That was all right, wasn't it? Now I'm going to have to go. Duty calls.

RUBY: Thank you. Nurse.

RITA: Yes, thank you.

NIGEL: Let's hope it'll do some good.

NURSE: I feel better for it already.

RUBY: I didn't like to say anything but I feel different too.

VERNON comes to sit down on one of the chairs.

NIGEL: You're all right are you, Mam? The old man's got enough on his plate with me without having you see the light.

RUBY: I just feel – nice. Do you know what I mean, Reet? I can't explain it really... but it's like a big cloud has just passed over and I feel all nice and warm.

GRIFF sits next to VERNON.

NIGEL: (*Meaning Ruby's coat*) I'm not surprised you're hot in that thing.

RUBY: You can make fun if you like.

NURSE: And he will.

RUBY: (*To RITA*) What about you, Reet? Can't you feel it?

RITA: Not really.

NIGEL: I don't think it's God, I think it's the change of life.

RUBY: I've never had a flush like this before.

NIGEL: That sounds like a cue for a song.

NURSE: No, it's my cue to go.

RUBY: You don't have to run, I'm not going to sing.

NURSE: (*Playfully*) There are other patients on this ward besides your son, you know.

The NURSE goes into the corridor.

RUBY: (*Meaning the NURSE*) Smashin' girl.

NURSE: (*Seeing GRIFF and VERNON*) Everything all right?

VERNON: (*Standing*) Yes... what about in there?

NURSE: Fine.

VERNON: (*After a slight pause*) Kevin's back, I'm just going to go and see him. (*He makes to leave.*)

NURSE: Good, I'll come with you.

VERNON leads off and the NURSE follows him. VERNON exits. The NURSE is almost out of sight when she stops, turns and comes back to speak to GRIFF.

NIGEL: There's something I've got to tell you.

NURSE: Still here then. I thought you'd have gone ages ago.

GRIFF: Just going. (*He doesn't move. A pause. He eventually moves to pick up his bag.*)

RITA: I want to know what happened and I want to know why.

During the following, NIGEL tells RITA, in mime, what happened in the car and why.

NURSE: You can tell me to mind my own business if you like –

GRIFF: Mind your own business.

RITA: (*To NIGEL*) How long has he been seeing her?

NURSE: I can see you don't get on, you and Nigel. You remind me of me and my father.

GRIFF: You don't know what you're talking about.

NURSE: He's a very proud man, too.

GRIFF: Leave it there now, will you? I don't want to talk about it.

NURSE: But you should. All right perhaps not to me but you should talk about it.

RITA: (*To NIGEL*) And you knew nothing about it?

NURSE: He chucked me out, my father. I was seventeen. I got myself into trouble and he couldn't cope with the shame. (*A slight pause*) I had a little girl. You should see them together now.

GRIFF: It's not the same thing at all.

NURSE: Of course it is.

GRIFF: He's nothing to me. There was never much between us before but it's all gone now.

NURSE: That's pride talking.

GRIFF: I'm telling you. I can't bear to look at him.

NURSE: Because you're hurt.

GRIFF: Because I'm ashamed.

RITA: Why did he tell you in the car?

NURSE: You won't admit it but you're closer than you think.

GRIFF: No.

355

NURSE: You're a proud man, Mr Gregory.

GRIFF: He's broken me.

NURSE: Then pick up the pieces and start again.

GRIFF: I can't.

NURSE: You mean you don't want to.

GRIFF: I mean I can't.

RITA: (*Her attitude changing*) Are you're saying it wasn't an accident?

RUBY: (*Defending Nigel*) Don't take any notice of him, he don't know what he's saying.

NURSE: I know you're ashamed and pride is a terrible thing, but it's only there shielding your hurt. I know it sounds corny, but it's true, you know. You can hurt the ones you love and the ones who love you back.

GRIFF: You think Nigel's hurting.

NURSE: More than you know.

NIGEL is now upset.

RITA: (*Outraged and upset*) Suicide?

RUBY: He's delirious, that's what he is. He's talking a load of nonsense.

NURSE: And if you don't put things right, or meet him half-way, or do something, then you'll never know. (*A slight pause*) Do you know what my little girl asked me last week? She asked me if a caterpillar could love a butterfly – and the answer to that is: why not? (*A slight pause*) Right. That's my little speech over. I'm off now to clean bedpans.

The NURSE exits right. GRIFF is left just standing there.

NIGEL: So you see it's all my fault.

RUBY: No!

NIGEL: If anyone should be in a coma it's me.

RUBY: Don't say that.

RITA: If anything happens to Kevin, I'll never forgive you.

RUBY: Now nothing's going to happen to him, right? (*A slight pause*) I'm going to get something to drink. Anything for you, Reet?

RITA doesn't reply.

RUBY: How about a nice cup of tea... if I can coax one out of the machine. Nigel?

NIGEL: No.

RUBY goes out into the corridor and sees GRIFF still standing there.

RUBY: Well, you're a fine one, you are.

NIGEL: Try and understand how I felt.

RUBY: I send you off for coffee and I don't see you for quarter of an hour.

GRIFF: They're there, look. (*He points to the two coffees on top of the machine.*)

RUBY: We don't want 'em now, we're having tea instead. (*She helps herself at the machine.*)

NIGEL: I panicked and over-reacted.

RUBY: What time do you start work?

GRIFF: I'm just leaving.

NIGEL: I must have been out of my head.

RUBY can't get anything out of the machine and kicks it in frustration. There is a slight pause.

RUBY: He didn't really mean it, you know.

GRIFF: Shut up, I don't want to hear.

NIGEL: I didn't mean to hurt him – you do realize that, don't you?

RUBY: Emotionally, he's all over the shop.

GRIFF: (*Shouting*) Shut up, I said! I'm sick of everyone making excuses for him. I've had a gutsful of people telling me to give him time, to give myself time – I've had enough. Enough, right? I don't want to hear stories about caterpillars and butterflies.

RUBY: Caterpillars and bloody butterflies? Who the hell have you been talking to?

VERNON rushes on suddenly. We shouldn't be able to tell from his initial reaction whether he is anxious or excited.

VERNON: Where's Rita?

RUBY: (*Pointing to Nigel's room*) What is it? What's wrong?

VERNON: It's Kevin.

VERNON rushes into Nigel's room, RUBY and GRIFF follow.

VERNON: (*To RITA*) Come quick, it's Kevin.

RITA: (*Thinking the worst*) Oh, my God!

VERNON: No, it's all right. It's all right, he's opened his eyes. He did. He opened his eyes and spoke to me.

RITA: What did he say?

VERNON: (*After a slight pause*) He said – he said: 'Where's Nige?'

There is a slight pause.

RITA and VERNON rush into the corridor followed quickly by RUBY. The NURSE enters the corridor from the opposite direction and sees all the commotion.

NURSE: What's happening?

RUBY: (*Without stopping*) It's Kevin. He's come round.

RITA, VERNON and RUBY exit; the NURSE rushes off after them. GRIFF is left alone with NIGEL.

There is a pause.

NIGEL is obviously very emotional about Kevin and is drying his face with his hands.

A long pause.

GRIFF: Good news then I suppose.

Another pause.

NIGEL: What are you doing here?

GRIFF: I'm not apologizing.

NIGEL: Neither am I.

GRIFF: That's all right then.

NIGEL: So what are you doing here?

GRIFF: I'm with your mother.

NIGEL: She's in with Kevin.

GRIFF: You want me to go?

NIGEL: You can please yourself.

GRIFF: All right, I'll go then. (*A slight pause*) That's fair enough. (*Another pause*) You're not going to stop me, are you?

NIGEL: No.

A pause. GRIFF turns to leave.

NIGEL: What do you want from me?

GRIFF: Oh, I can't have that.

NIGEL: There's lots of things I can't have either.

GRIFF: Do you have any idea what you did to me Saturday night?

NIGEL: Yes – but that was nothing to what you've done to me all my life.

GRIFF: It hasn't been easy for me.

NIGEL: You think I've had an easy ride? (*A slight pause*) I've been to hell and back to get where I am – but I am what I am and I'm damned if I'm going to apologize for it. (*A slight pause*) Don't tell me how hard it's been for you. Where were you when I didn't know what I was... who I was? Eh? (*He shouts*) I was an only child for Christ's sake! Who could I turn to? You couldn't talk to me about the weather, let alone the facts of life! (*He starts to laugh but the laughter is tinged with tears*) Do you remember me asking you what a wank was?

GRIFF doesn't answer.

NIGEL: 'Ask your mother,' you said. (*Shouting*) 'Ask your mother,' and you wonder why I turned to her...

GRIFF: I haven't been a bad father.

NIGEL: No... you've been a very bad father. (*A slight pause*) 'What's a wank, Mam?' I said. Do you know what she told me? 'It's the opposite to a wink.' (*Shouting*) 'It's the opposite to a wink,' she said, 'now shut up and eat your Weetabix.'

GRIFF: (*After a pause, quietly*) I'm sorry.

NIGEL: What's that, I didn't hear it?

GRIFF: (*Shouting*) I said I'm sorry!

There is a pause.

NIGEL: Yeah... me and you both. I don't know that we'll ever get it right... but for what it's worth, I wish I hadn't done what I did on Saturday. I can't apologize for it but I wish I hadn't done it.

GRIFF: (*After a slight pause*) I suppose there's a lot we both can't apologize for... your costumes for one thing.

NIGEL: You mean my dresses?

GRIFF: I was angry.

NIGEL: What are you saying?

GRIFF: I got rid of them.

NIGEL: (*After a slight pause*) It was some sort of symbolic gesture, no doubt.

GRIFF: I don't know what it was.

NIGEL: Probably deep down in your subconscious you were getting rid of me. (*A slight pause*) Yes, well – we seem to be stuck with each other no matter what, don't we?

GRIFF: I still don't like what you do – what you are.

NIGEL: I still haven't forgiven you for it.

GRIFF: So you blame me.

NIGEL: I blame you for lots of things.

GRIFF: (*After a slight pause*) So where do we go from here?

NIGEL: I don't know.

GRIFF: We must be making some progress. I thought you'd flip when I told you about the dresses.

NIGEL: (*Shaking his head, then smiling*) I've got twenty more in the house. (*A pause*) Who's Ritchie Thomas?

GRIFF: (*On the defensive*) What do you want to know about him for?

NIGEL: I heard you and the old girl talking about him, that's all.

GRIFF: He was a mate... (*he corrects himself*) a friend. (*He moves around to the other side of the bed.*)

NIGEL: Why haven't I heard of him before?

GRIFF: We grew up together. He's been dead for years.

NIGEL: What did he die of?

GRIFF: Why do you want to know?

NIGEL: (*Raising his voice a little*) I just want to know what he died of.

GRIFF: What difference does it make?

NIGEL: (*Shouting*) Tell me what he died of!

GRIFF: Mind your own bloody business!

A pause.

RUBY comes into the corridor followed by the NURSE who is pushing an empty wheelchair. They are on their way to Nigel's room.

RUBY: I wonder if that little prayer or whatever it was had anything to do with it, Nurse?

NURSE: Who's to say? It might have even been that little trip to the scanner and back.

RUBY: I reckon there's a bit more to it than that.

The NURSE and RUBY enter Nigel's room.

NURSE: (*To NIGEL*) Guess where you're going!

NIGEL: Home?

NURSE: Not quite. There's someone in a room down the corridor that's desperate to see you.

NIGEL: (*Smiling*) How is he doing?

NURSE: You'll see for yourself in a minute. You won't be able to stay long though, he's got to be checked over by the house doctors who are probably on their way as we speak, so it's just a quick in and out, all right?

NIGEL: Sometimes they're the best.

NURSE: Naughty.

The NURSE gets NIGEL into the wheelchair and begins to wheel him out.

NIGEL: (*As he goes*) You will be here when I get back. Mam?

RUBY: Yes.

GRIFF: I don't think I will.

NIGEL and GRIFF stare at each other for a moment.

NIGEL: (*to the NURSE*) Come on.

They move into the corridor, heading for the exit.

There is a pause.

GRIFF and RUBY look at each other before she looks away.

GRIFF: What?

RUBY: (*Looking back at GRIFF*) What?

GRIFF: You may as well say it.

RUBY: What?

GRIFF: What you were going to say.

RUBY: I wasn't going to say anything.

GRIFF: You've got something on your mind.

There is a slight pause. RUBY looks away and shakes her head.

NIGEL: (*To the NURSE*) Wait a minute.

NIGEL and the NURSE stop in the corridor.

GRIFF: It's no good.

NIGEL: Will he remember anything?

RUBY: What isn't?

GRIFF: Me and Nigel.

NIGEL: About Saturday. The crash.

GRIFF: Too much water's gone under the bridge.

NURSE: I'm not sure. It's possible.

The NURSE and NIGEL exit.

RUBY: You've talked to him then?

GRIFF: It was a waste of time.

RUBY: I could have told you that.

GRIFF: What?

RUBY: Look, the only way you can make any headway with Nigel is to be honest with him – and how can you do that when you can't even be honest with yourself.

GRIFF: (*After a slight pause*) All this with him... he thinks it's my fault, he told me.

RUBY: Griff, can't you see what he's doing? He's trying to make you feel guilty, responsible, because the minute you start taking some of the blame, he'll start taking it from you.

GRIFF: Don't be ridiculous.

RUBY: (*Sitting on the right edge of the bed*) He will, believe me, he will. Trust me. Work it out together. (*A slight pause*) It's a big job and it's not going to happen overnight. It's going to take time – maybe the rest of your life – but don't give up on him, Griff. It's going to be a long hard slog, but don't give up on him – that would be easy – and if you can't do it for him, perhaps you'll do it for me.

GRIFF looks at RUBY. There is a slight pause. He can't promise anything.

GRIFF: I wish we could go back and do it all over again.

RUBY: What would be the point of that?

GRIFF: I wouldn't make the same mistakes.

RUBY: No, you'd make different ones. Don't be too hard on yourself. You can't go through life without putting one foot wrong.

GRIFF: You don't blame me then?

RUBY: Nobody gets it dead right, Griff. Not me, you or Nigel.

GRIFF stares at RUBY for a moment.

RUBY: Anyway, whatever you decide to do I want you to take it easy on him for a bit. He's going through a bad patch at the moment and he's going to need all the support he can get.

GRIFF: Support?

RUBY: Yes. If you don't know what it means, have a word with Vernon.

GRIFF: You want me to take a leaf out of his book?

RUBY: A paragraph would be nice.

GRIFF: It must be marvellous to get it right.

RUBY: No one ever does – not the first time, anyway. You've got to be prepared to get it wrong.

GRIFF: I'm half-way there then.

RUBY: What I'm saying, Griff, is that it's all right to get it wrong providing you hang on in there and try again. Of course you've got to want to do it – and you've got to do it yourself. And it's got to come from in there. (*She taps him on the chest.*)

RITA and VERNON come on from right.

VERNON: ...it's routine. They want to have a look at him, you know, give him the once over, just to confirm everything's all right.

RITA: Yes... we've got him back, that's the main thing.

VERNON: But will Nigel, that's the question.

RITA: (*After a slight pause*) What do you think about it all?

VERNON: I don't know. You?

RITA: It's difficult, isn't it? The temptation is to charge in and get them to do what you think is best... but we both know that's not the answer, don't we?

VERNON doesn't reply.

RITA: All we can do is be there for both of them.

VERNON: To pat them on the back?

RITA: Or pick up the pieces. We shouldn't get involved, that's what I'm saying.

VERNON: What if they ask us to?

RITA: We're still making our own mistakes... I think we should let them get on with it. The whole thing could blow over and we could be left taking sides.

VERNON: So we leave things as they are, is that what you're saying?

She doesn't answer him.

RITA: (*After a slight pause*) This morning I wanted two things more than anything else in the world. The first was for Kevin to open his eyes...

VERNON: And the second?

RITA: (*After a slight pause*) I want to change my job.

VERNON: What?

RITA: I'm going to change my job.

VERNON: Why now, all of a sudden? Has it got something to do with Kevin?

RITA: It's got nothing to do with Kevin.

VERNON: (*After a slight pause*) Well... if you're sure it's what you want.

RITA: It's what I want, yes.

The NURSE enters wheeling NIGEL in his wheelchair. He is leaning on the arm of the wheelchair holding his head in one hand. The NURSE takes NIGEL into his room, rolling her eyes at VERNON and RITA as she goes. Something is wrong.

RUBY: (*Seeing NIGEL*) Good God, that was quick.

NIGEL: It was long enough.

VERNON and RITA follow the NURSE and NIGEL into the room.

RUBY: What's the matter?

NURSE: Kevin started to get upset so it was better I took him away. (*Meaning NIGEL.*)

RITA: Upset?

NIGEL: He told me to piss off, that's what she means.

NURSE: (*To NIGEL*) I wouldn't pay too much attention. I've told you – he's going to be totally zonked for a day or two.

NIGEL: Zonked my arse. He remembers everything. He hates my guts 'cos he remembers everything.

NURSE: Believe me, things will be different tomorrow. Give him time to calm down and think about things.

The NURSE gets NIGEL back into bed.

RUBY, GRIFF, RITA and VERNON all look at each other awkwardly.

VERNON: (*After a slight pause*) It's difficult to know what to say now, isn't it?

RUBY: I think we should leave them to sort it out themselves.

GRIFF: Sort what out?

RITA: Yes, the last thing they want is any interference from us.

GRIFF: Who?

VERNON: They won't thank us for it in the end.

GRIFF: What are you talking about?

RITA: I've never liked anyone sticking their nose in my business.

RUBY: Or mine.

RITA: So it would be wrong for us to start doing it now.

GRIFF: (*Shouting*) Doing what! Doing what! What the hell is everybody talking about?

RITA: Nigel and Kevin.

GRIFF: What about them?

RUBY: Don't waste your breath now, Reet. I'll fill Griff in with all the details later.

GRIFF: What's all this secrecy? I hate all this secrecy.

NURSE: Well, you're just going to have to learn to live with it.

GRIFF: What?

NURSE: Along with a lot of other things. Am I right, Nige? Secrets are what makes the world go round. I bet all of us in this room knows at least one.

RITA, VERNON, GRIFF and RUBY all look very uncomfortable.

VERNON: (*To RITA*) Do you think we'd better go and have another look at Kevin?

RITA: Yes.

NURSE: They won't let you see him. The doctor will be with him by now.

VERNON: We're going to have to make a move, anyway.

RITA: Yes. Griff And I need to go to work.

371

RITA, VERNON and GRIFF head for the exit.

NIGEL: What about me?

RITA, VERNON and GRIFF stop.

NIGEL: Kevin's going to be all right but where does that leave me?

No one answers.

NIGEL: Do any of you care?

No one answers.

NIGEL: Before you go – before all of you go – I've got a couple of things I want to say.

NURSE: I'll be back in a minute. (*She exits.*)

NIGEL: Rita. Better the devil you know.

RITA: What does that mean?

NIGEL: It means... better the devil you know. Vern? I am your devil. I'm going to be on your shoulder twenty-four hours a day.

VERNON and RITA leave the room; during the following dialogue they head for the right exit.

RITA: (*Out in the corridor*) What did he mean by that?

VERNON: No idea.

RITA: Do you think it was a dig at me?

VERNON: No, I think it was a dig at me.

RITA: Well my conscience is clear.

VERNON: So's mine.

They disappear off right.

GRIFF: (*After a slight pause*) You got anything you want to say to me?

NIGEL: No. I've got a question for you though. (*A slight pause*) How did he die?

GRIFF doesn't answer.

RUBY: Who you talking about?

NIGEL: Ritchie Thomas.

RUBY: How do you know about him?

NIGEL: I might have got a cracked rib but I'm not deaf.

GRIFF points at RUBY as if to blame her.

NIGEL: And who is he? Why haven't I heard of him before?

RUBY: He was a friend of his. (*She points with her thumb to GRIFF.*)

NIGEL: (*To RUBY*) Tell me about him.

RUBY: Griff?

GRIFF shakes his head slightly.

RUBY: I'll tell you again. Now isn't the time.

NIGEL: Was he my father?

GRIFF almost chokes on his own spittle.

RUBY: What?

NIGEL: You heard.

RUBY: What makes you think that?

NIGEL: I don't – but a lot of things would make sense if he was.

RUBY: Well he wasn't. Believe me, Nigel, he wasn't.

NIGEL: Tell me how he died then.

RUBY: He was a very sad man – he was lonely – confused. (*A slight pause*) He committed suicide.

A pause.

GRIFF: It's time to go.

NIGEL: (*To RUBY*) And you?

RUBY nods.

NIGEL: Will I see you later?

RUBY: Yes... of course you will.

NIGEL: (*To GRIFF*) What about you?

GRIFF: I don't know... you might... yes, all right.

GRIFF leaves the room and waits for RUBY outside in the corridor. RUBY stands just inside the door.

A slight pause.

NIGEL: You're sure now?

RUBY: About what?

NIGEL: (*After a slight pause*) My father.

RUBY: (*After staring at him for a moment*) I'll be back about five. (*She turns and leaves the room. She sees GRIFF waiting for her.*)

GRIFF: I thought we'd walk out together.

RUBY nods. A slight pause.

GRIFF: It's possible, isn't it?

RUBY looks at GRIFF.

GRIFF: He could be his father.

RUBY: In a funny kind of way it would be a lot easier for you if he was, wouldn't it?

GRIFF: Oh, I don't know – it would only be swapping one humiliation for another.

RUBY: So it wouldn't be easier?

GRIFF: I didn't say that.

RUBY: If he wasn't your son, that would relieve you of a lot of things. It would be all right for you to feel how you do about him then because he wouldn't be your own flesh and blood.

GRIFF: (*After a slight pause*) It's a funny thing: over the years, through all that's happened, I've always thought of him as mine.

RUBY: Good.

GRIFF: He felt mine.

RUBY: (*Reassuringly*) Then he is yours...

GRIFF: I want the truth.

RUBY: No you don't, you couldn't handle it – not yet.

GRIFF: When then?

RUBY: I don't know, but I will know – and you and Nigel will too, when the time comes.

GRIFF: What's going to happen until then?

RUBY shrugs. There is a slight pause.

RUBY: Well, hopefully, we'll live a bit, probably we'll die a bit, and with a bit of luck we might even come out of this and grow old together. All of us.

RUBY slips her arm under GRIFF's and they walk off.

The NURSE appears from the same side as they have left and enters Nigel's room.

NURSE: Everybody gone?

He doesn't answer. A slight pause.

NURSE: Are you all right?

NIGEL: Oh yeah, I'm the proverbial bouncing bloody ball, me.

NURSE: Are you going to be OK?

NIGEL: Well, I always have been before. And I've got my old girl – she's always been there for me. It can't be easy being parents.

NURSE: (*Sitting in the chair next to the bed*) Tell me about it.

NIGEL: I haven't made it easy for them.

NURSE: It never is easy. If there's anything I can do for you – you know, whatever... you've only got to ask.

NIGEL: Thanks.

The NURSE makes to leave.

NIGEL: I wonder what sort of parent I would have made.

NURSE: That sounds very much like you're never going to find out.

NIGEL: Well, I mean I'm not, am I?

NURSE: You never know what's round the corner.

NIGEL: Dream on, sister.

NURSE: You don't. Anything can happen.

NIGEL: I've missed my chance – I'm losing Kevin and little Kate.

NURSE: So you're giving up?

NIGEL doesn't answer.

NURSE: I thought you had more spunk than that.

NIGEL: Yeah... I thought so too. (*A slight pause*) She spends a lot of time with us. She likes me... It was so easy to think of her as mine.

There is a slight pause; the NURSE stands behind the chair, leaning on it.

NURSE: He's a lovely looking fella – Kevin. I'm buggered if I'd give him up without a fight.

The NURSE looks at NIGEL and smiles, then winks and leaves. NIGEL is left to ponder on the advice. Music plays as –

– the curtain falls.

Plays by Frank Vickery

Night on the Tiles
A Kiss on the Bottom
All's Fair
Breaking the String
Biting the Bullet
Erogenous Zones
Easy Terms
Family Planning*
In Retrospect*
Loose Ends
Love Forty
Matters Arising*
Never Again*
One O'clock From the House
Pullin' the Wool
Roots and Wings
Sleeping with Mickey+
Spanish Lies
Trivial Pursuits
Tonto Evans*
After I'm Gone
A Night Out
All Through the Night
Green Favours
Split Ends
See You Tomorrow
The Drag Factor
Bedside Manner

All Plays listed above are available from Samuel French Limited except those marked with *.
+ Available from Parthian in *One Man, One Voice* edited by David Adams

Amateur and Professional Repertory
Rights are controlled by
Samuel French Ltd.,
52 Fitzroy Street, Fitzrovia,
London W1T 5JR

For all further rights contact
Agents Bill Maclean Personal Management,
23b Deodar Road, Putney,
London SW15 2NP

Copyright

in ANY form or by any means – photocopying, typescript, recording (including video recording), manuscript, electronic, mechanical, or otherwise – or be transmitted or stored in a retrieval system, without prior permission.

Licences for amateur performances are issued subject to the understanding that it shall be made clear in all advertising matter that the audience will witness an amateur performance; that the names of the authors of the plays shall be included on all programmes; and that the integrity of the authors' work will be preserved.

The Royalty Fee is subject to contract and subject to variation at the sole discretion of Samuel French Ltd.

In Theatres or Halls seating four hundred or more the fee will be subject to negotiation.

In Territories Overseas the fee quoted above may not apply. A fee will be quoted on application to our local authorized agent, or if there is no such agent, on application to Samuel French Ltd, London.

VIDEO-RECORDING OF AMATEUR PRODUCTIONS

Please note that the copyright laws governing video recording are extremely complex and that it should not be assumed that any play may be video recorded for whatever purpose without first obtaining the permission of the appropriate agents. The fact that a play is published by Samuel French Ltd does not indicate that video rights are available or that Samuel French Ltd controls such rights.

PARTHIAN

parthianbooks.co.uk

diverse probing

profound urban

epic comic

rural savage

new writing

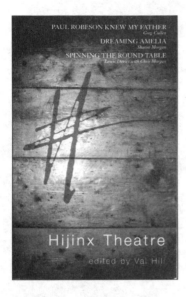

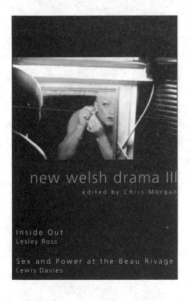
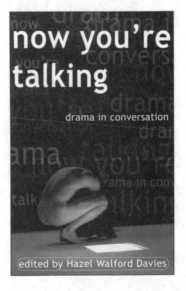